The Adult Rider

The Adult Rider

A Practical Guide for First-Time Equestrians and Adults Getting Back in the Saddle

Sarah Montague

Taylor Trade Publishing
Lanham • New York • Boulder • Toronto • Plymouth, UK

Copyright © 2009 by Sarah Montague

Published by Taylor Trade Publishing
An imprint of The Rowman & Littlefield Publishing Group, Inc.
4501 Forbes Boulevard, Suite 200, Lanham, Maryland 20706
www.rlpgtrade.com

Estover Road, Plymouth PL6 7PY, United Kingdom

Distributed by NATIONAL BOOK NETWORK

Library of Congress Cataloging-in-Publication Data

Montague, Sarah, 1955-
   The adult rider : a practical guide for first-time equestrians and adults getting back in the saddle /
Sarah Montague.
      p. cm.
   Includes index.
   ISBN-13: 978-1-58979-414-6 (pbk. : alk. paper)
   ISBN-10: 1-58979-414-1 (pbk. : alk. paper)
   ISBN-13: 978-1-58979-444-3 (electronic)
   ISBN-10: 1-58979-444-3 (electronic)
   1. Horsemanship. I. Title.
   SF309.M757 2009
   798.2'3--dc22

                                                                              2008052278

Manufactured in the United States of America.

To Emily Fairweather

And to my horses, my teachers

Grey Ghost, Bob, Boston, Winchester, Jonathan Swift, and Ghost

Contents

Part I Choosing a Path: The Disciplines

Part II   Choosing to Learn

Part III   Choosing Safety

Part IV   Choosing a Horse

Part V   Choosing Pleasure

Preface

Suppose . . . and suppose that a wild little Horse of Magic
Came cantering out of the sky;
With bridle of silver and into the saddle I mounted
To fly—and to fly.

—Walter de la Mare, "Suppose"

A Brief History (of Me)

As a young girl, I couldn't wait to get to bed at night, for there I transformed myself into a romantic heroine whose dazzling white stallion with a gold star on his forehead carried me (and I believe there was a doughty sidekick) through numerous adventures. Like many women, whose dreams perhaps overlapped with mine, I had a horse-filled childhood. In England, and later, the United States, horses and ponies, real and imaginary, thronged my days. At school, a dissolute ex-cavalry officer gave me my first formal lessons, and when I escaped the formal confines of the drill team and the indoor ring, it was to swim, riding bareback, with an enormous old mare called Black Cat.

When not actually on a horse, I rode through the pages of books, thrilling to the complex longings of Velvet Brown (forget the Hollywood version with Mickey Rooney and Elizabeth Taylor; Enid Bagnold's classic book is about rite of passage and the circumscribed dreams of women), the simpler pleasures of various teen heroines and their mounts, and a glimpse of pre- and postwar Vienna in the books and memoirs of Alois Podhajsky, who ran the Spanish Riding School during and after World War II. I was oblivious to the romantic complications in Mary Stewart's *Airs Above the Ground*, and its silly spy plot was mere trapping for what I perceived as its principal revelation: the rediscovery of a missing Lipizzaner stallion. This must have had a particular magic for me, for one season I talked myself into one of the Lipizzaner touring companies, befriending a lonely young Austrian and grooming his moon-luminous, gentle mount.

Later, I joined the Pony Club, and tried foxhunting—and both more danger and more discipline entered my riding life. Tales of Misty of Chincoteague and Man O' War gave way to the host of arcane facts the Pony Club requires you to remember. Years later, I can still recall the life cycle of the botfly and the length of the small intestine—not the sort of trivia with which to enliven cocktail parties.

One summer holiday, I took a horsemaster's degree at the Potomac Riding Center in Maryland. (This six-week course resulted in a certificate that, for dilettantes like me, essentially qualified one to teach riding in summer camps. For some, however, it's the first step in a professional teaching career.) I began to compete in horse trials and was chosen for my university riding team. I still hunted during the holidays, hours of frustrating chill relieved by regular infusions of port, England's notorious chipolata sausages, and wild gallops over Salisbury Plain. As of this writing, a heavily protested ban on hunting is in force in England, so these cherished memories are of what may rapidly become a vanishing world.

Adult life has a way of separating a girl from her horse, as implacably and inevitably as it supplants childhood. As Maxine Kumin has written in "Why Is It That Girls Love Horses?" (*Ms.*, April 1983), "Nothing would compensate for that loss of innocence, of the ability to speak the password and walk into a kingdom of virtue and honor." After college I got a job in a big city, then another job in another big city. I had little money and no car, and slowly, after a couple of abortive attempts to ride at the humble excuse for a stable that existed in town, horses and riding receded to an anecdotal dot on my horizon. Occasionally I went to the National Horse Show and watched flawless thirteen-year-olds navigate the Maclay and ASPCA Medal equitation courses on flawless syndicated show hunters. What did it all have to do with me?

And then, life happened. I wound up with a car and a house in the country, and the Chelsea Equestrian Center opened on a revitalized pier in New York City, and suddenly it seemed possible that I might ride again, to learn anew the password. But even then, I thought this would mean genteel circling in the ring. After all, I was middle aged, and my joints were no longer working properly—a conviction amply borne out by my test ride at Chelsea, which left me so stiff that it took me an hour to walk from 11th Avenue to 8th Avenue, and for days I inched down the street like a geriatric crab.

But a decade later I find myself with a horse of my own, back competing at horse trials, hunting, taking lessons regularly from a variety of instructors, and eagerly attending clinics. And if my outer adult relies a little on analgesics, my inner child is alive and well and eager to get over the next fence—"to fly—and to fly." And the point of this book is—you can join me.

Acknowledgments

The following material was used by permission: Nuno Oliveira, *Notes and Reminiscences of a Portuguese Rider* (J. A. Allen, 1976); Waldemar Seunig, *Horsemanship* (J. A. Allen, 2003); Sally O'Connor, *Practical Eventing* (Half Halt Press, 1998); Thomas McGuane, *Some Horses* (Lyons Press, 1999).

A book is always the product of many unseen hands, and one of this type owes much, too, to an amalgam of minds and voices.

I am indebted to Margaret Hutchison, Rusty Lowe, Linda McClaren, and Susan Reichelt for taking the time to speak with me, and for the lessons the three teachers have provided in the ring. Jane Armour, Janet Black, Libby Dowden, Adam Gershberg, Eric Horgan, Helen Isherwood, Michael Page, Sharon Santandra, Bob Smith, and Kristen Smith are other instructors who have shaped my adult riding experience. Friends at CS&W Farm, the Millbrook Hunt, and Netherwood Acres have shown me the many ways mature riders honor their sport and love their animals. Sally Eckhoff contributed spicily to the hunting chapter of this book, and heartfelt thanks go also to my two editors, PJ Dempsey and Dulcie Wilcox, for making my words flesh.

Introduction

Equestrian art . . . is something else which involves complete harmony between horse and rider, and that makes the rider feel that there have been moments of beauty and greatness which make a flight possible from all that is ordinary and mediocre.

—**Nuno Oliveira**, *Notes and Reminiscences of a Portuguese Rider* (**1976**)

Today's Adult Rider

If you read the preface (I won't be offended if you didn't), perhaps my story sounds familiar. You may be one of the many people who gave up riding when you went away to college, or got your first job, or had a baby—when it no longer seemed affordable or practical—when, regrettably, it became not a natural part of life, but a luxury.

Or, more exciting still, you're someone who has always wanted to ride but never had the chance, and it was one of those things that you were going to get to someday, along with traveling by ocean liner, reading *Remembrance of Things Past*, and learning to play the piano. Well, you're not alone. My, are you not alone!

Approximately twelve million people in the United States are involved in some sort of equestrian pursuit (this of course excludes professional race jockeys and harness drivers). And according to the Sporting Goods Manufacturers Association, the percentage of people who have participated in riding in some form grew by 9.3 percent between 2002 and 2003, while the American Horse Council estimates that the industry has a total impact of $102 billion on the country's gross domestic product. So the image of riding as the exclusive province—emotional and empirical—of teenagers, especially teenage girls, is erroneous. Knowing that may help to break down any resistance you have to entering or re-entering the barn. If you imagine yourself as the only lumbering baby boomer in a group of limber teens, you will be unnecessarily intimidated, though it is important, as we'll discuss later, to find an equestrian community into which you fit comfortably.

So abandon those images of yourself relegated to passive dude-ranch riding. Today's rider is every bit as likely to be a woman in her forties whose children are now school age, or one in her fifties finally able to prioritize her professional obligations, or a self-employed man whose business has become successful enough for him to take time off or at last be able to distinguish a weekend from a weekday!

Making Room for Riding in Your Life

"Making room" may be the very thing that's been holding you back. According to the Bureau of Labor Statistics, over 80 percent of employed persons work more than forty hours per week (as of 2006); Americans also work more hours per day and more days than people in many other countries. And according to a number of polls, people perceive their leisure time as dwindling and their work time as increasing. These figures don't even reflect family or social obligations. The sense is that there is no way to fit one more activity (especially one that you're probably secretly defining as selfish) into your over-obligated life. How can you possibly afford to have your day get any fuller and your bank account any emptier?

Certainly, some commitment in time, money, and travel will be involved. And as with any sort of sport, exercise, or new discipline, consistency will yield more rewards. However, once you begin to look into riding schools (something we'll address in chapter 14), you'll discover that, like gyms, many of them are ready and willing to cater to people with nine-to-five jobs and five-to-nine lives. Especially in the warmer, lighter summer months, it's often possible to get a lesson before work or in the evening. And stables are thronged with riding students on weekends, as this naturally tends to be the most oversubscribed time.

But of course it isn't just your work schedule, whatever it may be, that crowds your life. It's your children, or your grandchildren and their activities, or your committees, or your garden, or your spouse or companion. Qualitative time takes up more room than quantitative time. Bear in mind the old axiom that nature abhors a vacuum. The tasks and obligations in our lives, especially the lives of overachieving Americans, tend to expand to fill the available time and space. But the reverse is also true. You may find that once you have decided to make riding a priority, other activities proportionately recede. Couldn't that board meeting take an hour instead of an hour and a half? Or couldn't your report be moved earlier or later? Couldn't you send an e-mail instead of talking for half an hour? Couldn't a friend take your child to soccer practice/the skating rink/the dance class? And might your own lessons parallel your children's afternoon activities?

And on the home front: could your husband/wife walk the dog, make the coffee, water the roses? Could you rely a little more on the microwave and a little less on *Gourmet* magazine?

You get the idea—which is that if it matters, you'll find a way. And more importantly, the people around you will, too. Some obstacles, especially those involving other people, tend to be chimeras—more about the lack of a focus or passion in their lives than a dearth of time. They may resent that fact that you've found a new, energetic pastime. Or they may be totally in awe, but not sure whether the dynamic new you will fit comfortably into your old life (it will).

I once attended a day-long poetry workshop, attended by adult amateurs hoping to write verse. One woman had an astonishing litany of reasons why she couldn't take the time to write regularly. The poet leading the workshop, his patience much tried, finally said, "All you're telling me is that you don't really want to do this. If you did, you'd get up a half hour earlier, and you'd cope."

If this book is in your hands, then you probably already know where your heart is, and you'll find a way to get the rest of your body to follow.

The Changing Equestrian Environment

If you're returning to riding after a long absence, you'll find that there have been some fascinating developments in the past fifteen or twenty years, both in the sport and in such related disciplines as veterinary medicine and psychology. Teaching styles have altered, too, absorbing a wide range of methodologies borrowed from other fields and philosophies. And the field is eager to meet us: as Jennifer Meyer observed in *Horse and Rider* (as early as September 1999), "The generation born in the post–World War II years is turning fifty at the rate of about one every seven seconds, [and] marketers are racing to attract our midlife dollars. The best news for horse lovers is that even equine breed and sport organizations are getting into the act, with brand-new age divisions created to accommodate—and lure—the middle-aged competitor."

If you're new to riding, you may find it more consonant with other lifestyle trends, and other sports, than you imagined, with an emphasis less on obedience and more on communication. As we'll see, what is known loosely as English riding, which has come down to us from the courts, the countryside, and especially the military, was often taught along rather fixed lines. This generalization doesn't apply to the really extraordinary teachers, both prominent and private, who've always helped to shape and distinguish the equestrian arts. But many in the rank and file were content to mouth the rules and platitudes of the various riding manuals without much regard for nuance. In the main, learning was either rough and tumble—picked up in the hunt field or from the sort of maverick itinerant, for example, who had me jumping four-foot fences at school when I had no real skills to speak of—or sound, but unimaginative, with traces of the military environment and expectations still clinging to it. You kept your head up, your heels down, and willed your horse into polite submission. Or, if you were learning in hunter/jumper circles in the 1960s and '70s, you might have been an equitation rider strongly influenced by the rising stars of the U.S. Equestrian Team. William Steinkraus, Mary Chapot, Kathy Kusner, and George Morris were as renowned for their elegance as for their effectiveness. And maybe that particular beauty of form is part of your lost youth, but the important principles are merely dormant, just waiting to be reawakened.

Western riding came to us by way of the Spanish conquistadors and evolved into a practical tool for cattle herding and land maintenance, both here and in similar communities throughout Latin and South America. Because of the (theoretically) more accessible style—saddles have comforting horns to be clutched by the nervous, horses jog and lope instead of trotting and cantering—this form has suffered the most debasement at the amateur level. Many people have experienced at least once the jolting dude ranch–type trail ride, where you're essentially a passive sack atop a willful automaton being led through the woods by a jaded semiprofessional. (Originally, in the 1870s, the term *dude* applied to fancy city folk who went out west on vacation, and has not much departed from this meaning today.) But the confluence of a number of factors and developments has given us a whole new terrain to ride through. Today, Western riding is inviting, challenging, and complex.

Seeing Horses Anew

The increasing monetary value of horses, especially horses used for leisure pursuits instead of racing, and their gradual transition from unpaid agricultural employee (though this is still how they are classed legally) to companion animal has impelled advances in equine medicine and nutrition. At the same time, larger social and cultural trends such as the aging of articulate, affluent baby boomers, the New Age movement, and increasing cultural diversity has affected the way horses are both regarded and trained. Horse psychology, physiology, communication, and, for want of a better word, spirituality have become prominent subjects. Horse whisperers and animal touch/natural horsemanship and healing experts abound—and if there is a certain amount of hype involved, nevertheless the results really have been salutary, encouraging a kinder, gentler environment in which the aim is to communicate with, rather than subdue, your equine partner. This in turn makes the equestrian community one that makes more psychic sense to a newcomer.

Ironically, this is what Xenophon (ca. 430–335 BC), the Greek general generally credited with codifying the first principles of riding, recommended over twenty-five hundred years ago in *The Art of Horsemanship*:

> What a horse does under compulsion he does blindly. . . . The performance
> of horse or man so treated are displays of clumsy gestures rather than of
> grace and beauty. What we need is that the horse should of his own accord
> exhibit his finest airs and paces at set signals.

The Natural Rider

The same types of changes have affected the training of the rider. The advent of sports psychology, kinesthesiology, and studies about learning techniques and the development of the brain, as well as useful and stimulating cross-fertilization among the various sports, has made the teaching of riding more complex and intuitive, relying less on fixed postures and mechanical responses and more on right-brained, kinesthetic memory on the one hand, and a more sophisticated understanding of how both we and our horses think and move on the other.

Finally, advances in sports psychology, medicine, the various physical therapy disciplines, and nutrition have germinated, producing fitness regimes for riders and a greater awareness of how to allow an aging body to take on an age-old sport intelligently and safely.

There have been dramatic changes within the individual disciplines, also. Unquestionably, riding in general has become more expensive, and competition (if you're a rider returning, as I was, to a field in which you once competed) more rigorous, and sometimes seemingly more dangerous. But there have been many positive changes. Safety regulations for many sports have been tightened, and even now, ever-more-vigilant and proactive safety committees are being formed, new breeds and cross-breeds have been introduced or established, and a much wider range of activities has become available and accessible to many adult riders. If, for example, the fences suddenly seem bigger at your "old" level, you will still find a much wider range of shows friendly to the adult amateur, with such classes as "Fossils over Fences" and "Old Enough to Know Better (Still Too Young to Care)" clearly inviting your younger self to come out to play. With luck, you should be able to get the best out of the good old world and the brave new one.

The Western disciplines, too, have closed the gap between sensational rodeo riders and passive dudes, offering a wide range of trail and pleasure classes, excursions, and events.

If you aren't a rider returning to an old love, I hope that the next part of this book will give you some idea of the range of equestrian sports so that you can decide which type appeals to your temperament and your purse. Most disciplines have seen a dramatic increase in participation levels, and while not all related organizations keep separate figures for adult riders (comprehensive surveys are expensive, and most administrative bodies like to put their resources into programs, training, and competition), the figures that are published are an interesting indicator of popularity and geographic distribution.

The magazine *Equus* publishes an annual statistical report on breed registrations and association memberships. According to the most recent report as of this writing ("By the Numbers," January 2008) seven out of ten of the organizations tracked by the magazine experienced double-digit growth in the past decade (and two of those that didn't were pro organizations).

But no one wishes to think of himself or herself as a statistic. Wherever you wind up fitting into the world of riding, the experience will be uniquely your own.

Organization

I hope this book will help to make your equestrian experience coherent. In the forthcoming chapters, I review briefly the major disciplines, summarizing techniques and opportunities for the adult rider. The "Resources" appendix at the end of the book also provides information about key equestrian associations—those representing both the various sports and different horse breeds.

Part I

Choosing a Path The Disciplines

1

The Basics English or Western?

The one thing that we do, as Americans, is divide ourselves into our own departments too easily. How many times have I heard "Well, I'm a hunter" or "I ride Western" or "I am a dressage rider." Well, I think that this is a mistake. We are all horse people. The horses are the same.

—David O'Connor, Olympic equestrian

(*Horse Show*, February 2000)

A Brief History of Horsemanship

You don't need to know the history of riding to choose a riding style, just as you don't need to take a watch apart to find out the time. But if you're new to riding, you might find it pleasurable to realize what a long and glorious history you're entering. If you're a returning rider, you may skip this section (as they say in self-help books). Or possibly you don't remember all those facts absorbed when you were twelve and would like to be reminded of them.

The earliest horse may have evolved right under your feet, or as near to under your feet as plate tectonics would allow. The North American continent is credited with the emergence, in about 55 million BC, of *Hyracotherium* or *Eohippus*, a dainty creature about the size of a corgi (fifteen inches or so high) with four toes and small teeth. As it evolved into the animal we know today, it migrated from North America to Eurasia.

The modern horse, a more massive and complex phenomenon by far than its ancestor, still retains some instincts and characteristics from that early period. It is still a migratory animal, still a vegetarian and grazer, and still haunted by atavistic memories of being on the lunch menu of the nastier, carnivorous predators. (Knowledge and understanding of this plays a crucial role in relating to horses today.)

The earliest history of the domesticated horse is a matter of probabilities rather than certainties. Horses were probably tamed toward the end of the Ice Age and were probably kept for meat before they ever saw service as pack animals.

They were with us still as the Bronze Age saw the emergence of the first carts and chariots, and as an instrument of war, the horse-drawn chariot was a defining presence for the Hittites, Egyptians, and later, the Romans. The humbler cart helped impel the migrations that redrew the maps of Europe and Asia, so almost all nations can claim the horse as an early part of their cultural identity.

Who was the first rider? Like other significant achievements, this honor is disputed. The first material evidence dates from a terra-cotta fragment of the second millennium BC, found in what was then Mesopotamia. This may be a record of the earliest act of riding, but horsemanship, or the *art* of riding, would naturally have evolved a little later.

The Hittites are credited with the creation of the first manual, written by Kikkuli the Mitannian in about 1360 BC, but the most famous of the early equestrian authors is undoubtedly the Greek cavalry officer Xenophon. He memorably articulated the principles of understanding, caring for, and riding the horse in *The Art of Horsemanship*. There was also an early Persian text called the *Avesta*. Issues of war and conquest tended to dominate these early works, but by the Renaissance good riding became synonymous with the conduct of a gentleman, and a number of early published works contributed to the evolving form, including *A General System of Horsemanship in All Its Branches*, by William Cavendish, Duke of Newcastle (1658). Sidesaddles were invented in medieval times, but women didn't actively participate in horse sports until the nineteenth century, after which we made up for lost time!

As with many things we now take for granted, the distinctions among the various riding techniques are relatively recent, given that the history of horsemanship is several thousand years old. And indeed, many of the older forms, both sporting and practical (i.e., related to farming or conveyance), survive in remote regions around the world. This book deals with the options that are likely to be available to you as a recreational rider on the North American continent, although the holiday section will allow you to contemplate at least a visit to more exotic realms.

Narrowing It Down

Somewhere between the images of the residents of Tara galloping over hunt fences and the Marlboro Man surveying a field of cattle lies the actual geography of riding in America. Opportunities to learn both English and Western riding, as these styles are generically known, are available in many areas of the country. But despite what you may have heard, one style isn't really easier than the other, at least not if you plan to ride well. Good Western riding combines balance and a great deal of poise and delicacy. Some of the better practitioners may make it look easy. It isn't. An unschooled body can be maintained more readily in the deep, secure Western saddle, with its convenient, clutchable horn, but the interested rider soon discovers there are a lot more issues to contend with.

So your decision should be based on factors other than ease, and address such issues as your ultimate goals as a rider, the circumstances under which you will ride, geography/locality, the types of horses involved, and two less easily graspable concepts—which equestrian culture you feel suits you, and which style ultimately feels right. One woman of my acquaintance, who started riding in her forties, began learning English on a difficult mare and then found her natural home in Western pleasure as the result of acquiring a seasoned and steady show veteran.

One of the things that attracts us to a sport is akin to what attracts us to clothes or careers: an image of excellence. We are drawn to practitioners who embody the best the sport has to offer; and sometimes we are drawn to an archetype that isn't a person at all, but a general embodiment of the myth or ideal.

Riding offers a number of images of this kind, and if you're to make an intelligent choice, you should know what images you're responding to. If you're returning to riding, your childhood experiences were probably the result of proximity and tradition as much as choice, so here is a chance to re-examine your options.

When you imagine riding, how do you see yourself? Riding bareback along a beach or in a meadow, your own glamorous mane rivaling that of your mount? Or across the plains with cowboys or a Native American guide? Boldly jumping a stone wall, or a clearing a triple in a show-jumping combination? Executing an elaborate haute école ("high school") dressage movement on a Lipizzaner stallion or a handsome bay? Or galloping down a racetrack? Don't be reluctant to embrace the cliché of your choice, because it will lead the way to genuine and viable pleasures.

Of course, you may not picture yourself astride a horse at all, and I will also be discussing the sport of carriage driving, which is gaining in popularity in many regions of the country, and of showing horses from the ground, "in hand."

One way or the other, the picture in your mind's eye can be made to match up with reality (unless you imagine yourself flying with your horse, as I did as a child).

The formal distinctions we perceive between English and Western riding did not exist before the nineteenth century; the two styles have common ancestors. Our codification of them was a function of different cultures' needs and contexts, and were further refined as recreational riding added elements of ritual, regulation, and competition to what had been purely functional forms. In this way, the riding style developed in the courts of Spain could produce Vienna's famed cadre of Lipizzaner stallions, the pinnacle of classical dressage, on the one hand, and the Western rodeo on the other.

Four different traditions and environments influenced what we think of as English riding: the court, the military tradition, the hunt field, and flat racing. What emerged after an evolutionary process that included the modification of older, heavier saddles to lightweight, more balanced ones, the creation by the Italian Federico Caprilli (1868–1907) of the "forward seat," and the maturation of a variety of disciplines, was a position emphasizing lightness, forward motion, and agility.

Western riding evolved in the Americas by way of the Spanish conquistadors and their followers, who settled California and the western states. The conquistadors brought the first horses to inhabit the North American continent since the Ice Age, and the sedanlike, bedizened saddle to the continent. They also established a cattle-centric herding culture that engendered the relaxed, slightly-behind-the-vertical seat needed for everyday work on the range. The competitive versions of cowboys' activities—competitive roping, trail riding, reining, and obstacle courses—require the kind of dynamic virtuosity that seems awe inspiring up close.

Of course, between and around these two schools are myriad related forms, and from them we can map the field of possible disciplines:

From English riding derives such activities as English pleasure, saddle seat equitation, show jumping, and dressage, as well as the multi-tasking marathons known as horse trials. There is also foxhunting (either actual or mock, known as drag hunting), which also has its abstract representations in the show ring, manifested in both equitation and hunter classes that focus more on the horse than the rider.

From Western riding derives Western pleasure, reining, roping, barrel racing, and endurance riding.

And if all you imagine yourself doing is walking through the woods watching the approach of spring or the turning of the leaves, then either choice will work well for you. Horses don't read history books, and the right ones will give generously of themselves in any mode.

Well, you may be thinking, all that is available to me is whatever is up the road. Clearly geography and proximity are going to play some part in where and how you begin, but if you're serious about your potential commitment to riding, I urge you to do some research; you may have more options than you think. Otherwise, you might make the same kind of costly mistake I did—signing up with an expensive riding club in the city before discovering that there were dozens of much less exorbitant, better-run schools near me in the country.

Ultimately, the choice can affect your future with horses. The basics from either tradition, Western or English, taught well, will give you a sense of the mature pleasure to come, but if your first experiences leave you feeling disappointed, or worse, frightened, you may miss a forest of opportunity because of one rotten tree.

All right, then, on to specifics. Mount up and join me. But first, a word about showing.

Showing versus the Real World

At the dawn of the equestrian arts, riding was completely an outdoor activity, or at least enclosed in an amphitheater or arena. Horses were ridden in the open for travel, for war, and for sport.

Men, being men, began playing games on horses almost as soon as they stopped merely eating them and began to see them as a means of locomotion. But as riding developed a more refined component, a parallel universe began to evolve: riding in enclosed spaces, or regulated, designed venues, for training, display, and competition. Today, this parallelism continues in many disciplines, so you might think of the various styles and forms in the show ring as rarified, almost symbolic versions of their real-world counterparts. (Sometimes these counterparts are archaic, as with "park horse" classes and gaited pleasure classes, which replicate nineteenth-century social forms). Hunters, trail and pleasure horses, and driving horses all produce in the show ring the distilled essence of skills they might, theoretically, encounter and need to apply practically. Show jumping, on the other hand, is a purely artificial creation. As in the dog show world, field and breed classes also distinguish practical application from idealized form.

As an adult rider, depending on your age, inclination, and mettle, you may find you prefer the formal and circumscribed versions of the show ring to the less predictable terrain of outdoor riding. Taking a trained show hunter around a tidy course of precisely measured fences is much less harrowing than plunging through the countryside behind a field of riders prepared to take any obstacle that happens to be in their path. And slowly coaxing your horse through the witty and artificial obstacles in a trail class is rather different from meeting up with swollen streams, whipping branches, and the occasional rattlesnake on an actual trail.

Sometimes the show ring is reaching back to a real or mythical past, and if part of what appeals to you about riding is a sense of tradition or a sense of timeless romance, there may well be a class for you. Sidesaddle and formal hunt classes require the rider to dress in a semblance of styles established in the eighteenth and nineteenth centuries, when danger and deportment went hand in hand.

Most dazzling of all, however, are the costume classes at some other shows (notably for Arabian horses), in which competitors wear dazzling outfits reminiscent of *The Thousand and One Nights*, with mysterious veils, dazzling silk pantaloons and tunics threaded in silver and gold, and a sheik's ransom in costume jewelry. It is intoxicatingly beautiful to watch these riders gallop their gleaming horses in the moonlight and feel, for a moment, as if they've stepped out of the pages of a romance or our dreams.

Decisions, Decisions

In order to make your initial decision a little easier, we'll take a look at the basic style and social, cultural, and geographical contexts for each discipline and its related activities. Ultimately, however, you will be using this book as a guide and complement to the empirical. No mere printed words, flat on the page, can equal the sensuously rich, exciting, disconcerting effect of being on a horse—first time and every time.

2

English Pleasure

History and Overview

Depending on your own background and location, English riding may be as familiar as the riding academy down the road or as picturesquely foreign as a scene from *Tom Jones* (the movie, not the crooner). While not as iconic a form as Western riding in American culture, it does convey the promise of elegance and daring. Here we deal with riding done "on the flat." Its jumping, hunting, and hunt seat forms will be addressed separately.

As you can imagine, "pleasure" is not a riding style. As with many other forms, it is a stylized adaptation of reality. At one time, as we've noted, horses were used for transportation, and going from place to place was a necessity, not a pleasure, although riding was a form of social intercourse among the upper classes. With the advent of the automobile and the evolution of recreational riding, working outdoors with horses has become an important training tool and a precious opportunity to see the surrounding world from a unique vantage point.

There are several types of English pleasure—an odd term, when we come to think about it, because of course all riding is theoretically pleasurable. However, the term has come to mean a specific range of activities and an accompanying technique especially executed in particular contexts.

Basic Technique

Basically, English pleasure riding is English riding. The pleasure part refers to expectations about the demeanor of the horse and, in the show ring, exercises to demonstrate that he has that demeanor. (This is also true of Western pleasure, as we'll see.)

At its loosest, pleasure riding is exactly what is sounds like: a stroll, an amble, even a gallop or a chase, taken for no other purpose than itself. In England, and in English riding circles, this is also called hacking. The word dates back to the nineteenth century and derives from the term for a type of light (meaning elegant and light-boned) riding horse and, by extension, what you did on him. Today, organized trails all over the country allow even the most urbanized of us to see the dwindling countryside, while in the show ring pleasure riders are demonstrating that their mounts would be good companions on such excursions.

Pros and Cons

At its best, pleasure riding is the simplest and most quietly enjoyable thing you can do on a horse. The basics of the English (or Western, as we'll see later) technique will teach you balance, control, and confidence at the walk, trot, canter, and gallop. This will allow you the independence and autonomy to make riding outside a regular part of your life.

It is worth taking the time to get yourself to this level because at its worst, trail riding—as it is also called—is the reductive, tiring, boring, and sometimes even dangerous occupation we associate with dude ranches, spas, and resorts in the Poconos. Lest I invite ire, I hasten to add that, when responsibly managed, these are all very good in their way, but they have no more relation to horsemanship than cruise ships have to sailing.

Typically, such rides involve being led by a staff person in a kind of equestrian conga line, usually on horses that are jaded or tired enough to be thought safe for amateurs. School horses are rarely the most thrilling introduction to horsemanship, of course, but at least if you're taking lessons, you know that this stolid character will eventually be succeeded by a more challenging mount, and that you're learning skills that will eventually allow you to develop an independent relationship with the horse.

Commercial trail rides have no such wish for you—essentially you're a horse tourist, never a potential horseman. So, tempting as it might be to try the great outdoors before the circumscribed world of the riding ring, I urge you to try some lessons first, or your trail ride will leave you feeling cramped, disappointed, and exploited.

Leisure and Competitive Opportunities

No matter what branch of riding you ultimately choose to pursue, vigorous outdoor riding can, and in many cases should, continue to be part of your life. However, if you wish to pursue trail and pleasure riding in an orchestrated way, much as you might hiking, there is a parallel structure in place.

In addition to trails attached to such private facilities as resorts and country clubs, trail-riding groups all over the country maintain trails, sometimes through a combination of private and government lands, and for a modest membership fee allow you access to them. In addition, they organize formal trail rides, orienteering, and camping rides and expeditions throughout the year, so your membership gains you entry to a society of like-minded riders. (See appendix B, "Resources.")

As with many aspects of equestrian competition, pleasure classes in the show ring are stylized versions of riding done outside. A horse on the trail should be responsive, comfortable at all gaits (these vary a little by discipline—for English pleasure they would be walk, trot, canter, and hand gallop), well mannered, and nimble. Pleasure classes ask for movements and exercises that are designed to demonstrate in the ring important attributes for the trail or hack. At their simplest, they ask for horses to be shown at three or four gaits in both directions and to halt—perhaps the most important gait of all. More advanced classes include obstacle courses that simulate actual trail conditions. There may be a gate to unlatch, little artificial streams to ford, and potentially disconcerting confrontations with billowing plastic or rubbish bins. The most unflappable horse, with the smoothest gaits, wins.

Other types of pleasure classes include pairs, park—a simulation of nineteenth-century leisure riding, usually with three- or five-gaited horses whose way of going harks back to the first great age of pleasure riding—and those fabulous costume classes.

While breed-specific shows do have pleasure classes, pleasure is also one of the most inclusive forms of competition, as almost any type of horse may be suitable for pleasure riding. These classes are also welcoming to riders who like the idea of a little fanfare and competition but do not imagine themselves in the company of the showier, more aggressive hunter or jumper riders. And shows of all sorts, from big national competition to small local show, offer them.

Riding already seems to many of us to partake of the past as much as the present, but this is deliberately the case in one of the most eye-catching—and increasingly popular—components of pleasure riding: sidesaddle. Originally, of course, the seat was developed because a woman riding astride would have been scandalous. As leisure riding among the upper classes increased in the nineteenth century, these saddles—which have two pommels between which the rider places one of her legs—were carefully crafted to allow women maximum security and independence; it was even possible to hunt on them. Today the classes judge both horsemanship and the riders' lavishly-detailed re-creations of period costumes.

If you think you might be interested in pleasure classes, attend one or two shows (indeed this is true for all competitive fields—spectating gives you a visceral feel for a sport that even the best written description can't match). And be sure to tell your instructor of your interest, once you have found a stable that suits you. (This is discussed in detail in part II.) You will never be offered an opportunity you haven't expressed an interest in. There are also competitive trail rides, but these are addressed in the section on endurance riding.

Opportunities

Pleasure is one of the most hospitable fields for the older rider, in part—let's be candid—because it's less potentially bone jarring than show jumping or horse trials. (This doesn't mean, however, that you can be unfit. If you're really out of shape, you can't ride effectively, safely, or pleasurably. You need to experience only once the rictuslike seizure of limbs that comes after prolonged riding with untoned muscles to realize this.) And perhaps because pleasure is not a class at the international level, training and opportunities seem less skewed to younger riders who are viable national team prospects.

Finally, pleasure riding grew out of—well—pleasure. It offers the prospect of group excursions, rides to see friends and family, and the kind of undemanding outdoor exercise that suits almost all horse and rider combinations. There's no better way to stop and smell the roses, and because of this the ranks have never seemed closed, and entry and re-entry are easier.

Clothing and Equipment

I always feel that the look of pleasure riding has been subverted by advertising. When featured in television commercials, on billboards, or in magazine campaigns, riders are either leathery cowboys or luscious long-haired women wreathed in gauze. (The photographer Robert Vavra is almost singlehandedly responsible for the contemporary soft-focus, feminine image of the horse—the animal always looks like it's been poached from the corner of a romance novel or a greeting card.) Or a jolly pair or group has been magically transported from their backyard barbecues to the saddle, still clad in designer jeans and polos or shorts and halter tops (Ralph Lauren has a lot to answer for, too).

The plain fact is that riding does require some investment in clothing, not for the sake of esthetics, protocol, or pretension (though the former two do come into play in the show ring), but for the sake of comfort. Horsehide and saddles are abrasive and can rub away skin, especially in the novice rider, whose leg may not be steady. Unsecured trouser legs tend to ride up with motion, and unprotected backs, necks, or arms (assuming casual riding outdoors) may be flayed by branches or nipped by insects. Riding in shorts, except bareback (don't try this at home, kids) is excruciating anyway—stirrup leathers will pinch your calves unmercifully. In this age of Lyme disease and other insect-borne ailments, always follow the guidelines of local health authorities and park services when deciding how much to cover up.

Speaking of protection, feet may be the most neglected part of the body—after all, any shoe will fit in a stirrup, right? This blithe assumption does not, however, take into account the punishment riding metes out to unaccustomed arches. At the very least, you need a sturdy shoe with a hard, nonslippery sole and some resistance. This is also much safer on the ground—the foot is vulnerable to barn debris, large hooves, and the one thousand pounds (on average) attached to them. In fact, there is an ankle-length boot known as a paddock boot especially designed for work around the barn.

Eventually, you'll want to invest in a good pair of riding boots—either ankle height (known as jodhpur boots) or knee length (know as dress boots, or field boots if laced). However, if you're just returning to riding, you may be wise to wait a little, tempting as it is to reinforce your resolve with glamorous new clothes. First of all, give yourself time to be sure you're committed—boots are an expensive impulse buy. And if you *are* committed, you may find that the shape of your—newly muscled!—leg changes. Go instead for the quite attractive (and not cheap, either) rubber versions or jodhpur boots. Jodhpur boots can be worn with jodhpurs (naturally) or with breeches, which don't cover the ankle but will do in a pinch. Pinch, by the way, is the operative word in buying legwear for riding. The definitive ways to avoid it without shelling out for tall boots are to wear suede chaps, which give great protection but are devilishly hot in summer, or the new "half-chaps," an abbreviated take on the cowboy garment. Half-chaps are knee-high zip-on sheathes (suede or smooth leather) that give a secure grip and prevent rubbing and wear to clothing. The more expensive examples, paired with jodhpur boots the same make, look very much like dress boots and are considered a respectable alternative at small shows.

Full-length leather dress boots are a significant expense ($700 and upward for custom boots, $500 and more for high-end brands), but if you're planning to ride often (or show—see below), they are probably worth the investment. Low-end stock boots can be had for as little as $140. Or you might find something just right on consignment. Happily, there are also perfectly serviceable inexpensive alternatives in coated rubber.

Coats

Showing requires a more elaborate wardrobe than is needed for casual pleasure riding. After boots, the most important wardrobe fundamental is a jacket. A dress coat in a dark shade or discreet plaid (here, as in cocktail parties, basic black is a sure bet) calls for a white or light-colored shirt. If you need to go formal, as is required in some classes and during regular foxhunting season, you should plan on wearing a black jacket, a white shirt and a stock tie (a cravatlike neck covering) held in place by a simple gold pin. A more run-of-the-mill outing, like a hunter trial or decent-caliber show, can be satisfied with a high-collared shirt and a slender bow tie of the same material—the time-honored ensemble known as a "ratcatcher" or a "choker" (band of contrasting fabric) around the neck of your collarless shirt, again asserted with a simple pin. For most of the occasions you might encounter as a beginning rider, a plain necktie, for women as well as men, is fine.

Preseason foxhunting, phases known as "roading" and "cubbing," calls for that attractive combination of ratcatcher, tweeds, and brown boots. We might infer, though, that comparing a rider to a lonely rodent hunter, or possibly to his Jack Russell, suggests a certain amount of derision. When in doubt, ask.

If you begin to compete in earnest, you should also always check the USEF Rule Book section for your chosen discipline, as it covers all aspects of turnout for each. (Many organizations also issue their own standalone copy of the rules.) And of course, if, like Henry David Thoreau, it is your inclination to "beware of all enterprises that require new clothes," then you don't want to contemplate the competitive side of riding at all!

Training Opportunities

As discussed at the beginning of this chapter, the idea of "training" for pleasure may seem counterintuitive, but even the most casual riding can be improved by skill. If you are looking for a consistent experience with some opportunity for growth, you will want simply to pick a facility that emphasizes responsible indoor or ring riding as a prelude to trail riding.

If you're interested in entering the show ring, of course, your riding becomes more focused and strategic. Again, at the level of local competition your usual instructor will probably be happy to give you tips and encourage you to enter local shows. Beyond that, you may be looking at the realm of the personal trainer and investing in a horse of your own. Some of the resources outlined below will help to guide you in these decisions.

English pleasure has a long-established presence on the American leisure scene, as well as being, as we have seen, one of the default disciplines of many riding schools and resorts, so it will not be difficult to find out specifics about your area.

Kissin' Cousins: Saddle Seat

A related area of pleasure competition revolves around American gaited horses such as the American Saddlebred, the Missouri Foxtrotter, and horses (and mules) bred increasingly for their high action—including the American Shetland pony and the Morgan. These horses' flowing and animated gaits—including, for some, a spirited high step called "the rack"—originated on farms and plantations, where they eased long hours in the saddle and were often good all-around family horses who could ride, drive, and get you to church on Sunday. In the show ring, however, they are dazzling and sometimes rather high-strung performers. (Other breeds, including Arabs and half-Arabs, can also be shown in this discipline.)

Especially popular in the southern and southwestern states, saddle seat riding uses a flatter type of saddle (also derived from the plantation), and the rider's seat is a little more behind the motion than in the basic English posture; the idea is to impel the high action and head carriage of the spirited mount. Show competitors wear a longer and more drapey version of the frock coat—in a variety of dramatic colors—over long trousers, and this is one place where the bowler—lost to the hunt field—is alive and well.

Especially for Grown-ups

The saddle seat community has been particularly proactive about adult riders, with many adult amateur classes available, though of course you will still need lessons in this demanding form. (The actor William Shatner, first commander of *Star Trek's* *USS Enterprise*, now breeds and pilots lively Saddlebreds.)

Sidesaddle

The growing popularity of sidesaddle riding and competition is amusing, given the number of years it took women to be allowed to ride astride, which was, as noted earlier, considered unseemly. Now, of course, the whole world is so unseemly that the elegance and decorum associated with sidesaddle seems to hark back to a more graceful age. And there is the added challenge of eliciting the same response from your mount as you would get if you could put a leg over him. While I have placed this section in the chapter on English pleasure riding, sidesaddle is now a feature of many disciplines, including Western, dressage, and hunt seat, where its advocates believe it to be even safer than riding on conventional saddles. Many of the larger shows have sidesaddle classes, and no special training—except retraining—is needed for the horse, though you will certainly want to take lessons from an experienced practitioner. And for many, the costume element is clearly part of the appeal—classes require appropriate period regalia—long skirts, flowing jackets, and top hats. But the discipline is far from precious or cosmetic—its ranks include top endurance riders, show jumpers, and active riders to hounds. Even in ring classes a group of women surging around at a gallop can look as daring to us as their precursors must have to their eighteenth- and nineteenth-century contemporaries.

3

Hunt Seat

In the minds of many Americans, riding is symbolized either by the lonesome wrangler and his stalwart cowpony or the eager young girl who angles her body perfectly as her horse takes a fence in flawless form.

This latter image, one that lures many a twelve-year-old girl to horsemanship, is the epitome of the hunt-seat tradition as it exists in the show ring. Ironically, it is very far, in both appearance and practical application, from the sport from which it derives its name—hunting.

In fact, show hunters frequently have no field experience and are disconcerted by terrain outdoors, while their riders are sometimes cosmetic in their application of basic principles. At its best, however, the tradition produces confident, attractive riders, able to convey commands to their mounts both explicitly and subtly.

The seat itself is a late development in the history of horsemanship. Up until World War I, the common belief, if it was articulated at all, was that a rider should be behind the vertical when going over a fence, both for safety and to "lift" the horse. This is the form you will see in old hunting prints, and the catalog for the big sale of the contents of the Paris apartments of the Duke and Duchess of Windsor in 1998 reproduces a splendid photograph of the duke winning a steeplechase all but off the horse in his backward inclination. Given what we now know, it's amazing that all— or any—of the parties survived these misguided aerodynamics.

What we now know is the invention of Federico Caprilli, who realized that the body of the rider had to follow the movement of the horse's head and the shift forward of gravity as it travels over a fence. The result was a much safer (for both horse and rider) position for all that seems counterintuitive at first.

If there were a family tree of riding disciplines, as I fancifully suggested above, show jumping would be seen as descending from competition in the military, where up until World War II the greatest concentration of trained riding animals was to be found. Show hunters and hunt seat equitation would have been distilled from field hunting, though inevitably the evolutionary lines have blurred a little.

Show hunter classes, which include work on the flat and over fences, are as American an invention as Hollywood or the Thunderbird, in a practical form that has been inflated into an elaborate fantasy world in which appearance counts for almost as much as performance. The style was codified in the 1960s by the former U.S. Olympic show-jumping team member (now the U.S. team's chef d'équipe and a coach to dozens of champion riders) George Morris. Morris's books on jumping and hunt-seat equitation are the canon of many competitive riders and teachers today. (In England the form evolved a little differently—there is no style called "hunt seat," but the gravitational shift is still reflected.)

Equitation is to riding what étude is to music and dance—an exercise in the flawless execution of the basic forms of such disciplines, with the assumption that the perfect rider will create the perfect horse. (Alas, in the sometimes-pretentious layers of this particular society, the reverse is often assumed.)

In hunter classes, horse and rider represent an idealized form of their real-world counterparts—flawlessly turned-out riders take exquisite mounts around modest courses meant to demonstrate dexterity, even pace, and good manners. Actual hunting is a more rough-and-tumble affair, which is why it has been the subject of so many colorful memoirs and pictures.

Basic Technique

The basic hunt-seat technique assumes that the rider will sit over the horse's center of gravity, with a straight line running from the rider's shoulder through the point of an open hip joint, down through a relaxed, flexed ankle. Some version of this position and technique is what you've probably encountered if you've ever been to a riding school—it is the English seat refined and focused on the idea of jumping. Hunt-seat riders tend to ride a little farther forward than, say, dressage or pleasure riders, as if even flatwork is an anticipation of the elevation over the fence. As one of its most celebrated proponents, George Morris, said in his seminal book *Hunter Seat Equitation*, "Simplicity and economy of movement are the goals of classical technique."

When a jump is taken, the rider allows the horse's momentum and upward thrust to fold his or her body so that the weight follows the shift in the horse's gravity. In hunt-seat riding the aim is to allow this to happen as smoothly and consistently as possible, and it will be no surprise to learn that hunt-seat riding is the heart of competitive classes for juniors riders, who learn form and function simultaneously, much as they might at dance classes or swim meets.

Pros and Cons

It's hard to match the elegance of show hunters and the circles in which they are shown. Also, if you find yourself interested in jumping but know that you'll never be comfortable with the level of boldness required for show jumping or cross-country riding, let alone actual field hunting, then this modified form may be for you.

However, all this elegance comes at a price—sometimes quite a price. Though at local schooling shows modest horse and rider combinations can be seen making their way around a course, the higher levels call for a fairly serious investment in time and money. Good hunters with the form and look judges go for command anywhere from $10,000 to $35,000. Both you and the animal will need to be trained to produce a winning picture. You'll also need to be shipped hither and thither for weeks in order to compete on one of the championship circuits. It's not unusual for people to spend thousands of dollars campaigning for a season. And in this discipline more than most, riding is the nucleus of a social cell involving parties and committees and a general tribal air of exclusiveness. And since hunt seat is the source and basis of the various junior equitation classes and the most coveted prizes for junior riders—the Maclay and ASPCA medals—hunter barns are often abuzz with self-involved teenagers. It's all too easy, if you're not resilient, to feel out to pasture before you have even gotten into the field!

Clothing and Equipment

Because of its ties to formal hunting, competitive hunt-seat riding emphasizes accoutrement more than most disciplines. At the most basic level, if you imagine yourself appearing in a show, you will eventually be investing, as for English pleasure classes, in a good-quality riding jacket, shirt, and dress boots. Many tack shops and Internet sites have good gear on consignment, and there are quite acceptable rubber equivalents available, as I've said.

Arguably, the most important piece of riding equipment you'll ever own is a good helmet, and helmet design has changed drastically since the days of the simple velveteen-covered plastic shell. (See chapter 22 for a full description of safety-approved headgear.) The riding world's investments in sports medicine and structural technologies have made it possible for an ergonomically correct protective helmet to look nearly as sleek as the ineffective but dashing old standard, the hunt cap. In any case, black velvet-covered helmets, buff breeches, and black boots are de rigueur in a hunter class, and in formal, full-dress classes—called "appointments" or "Corinthian" classes—you must appear in full hunting regalia, including a sandwich case, string gloves, black Melton jacket, patent-leather topped boots (for women), and a hunt's particular "colors," providing you've earned the right to wear them. If nineteenth-century prints are what drew you to riding in the first place, this could be the choice for you, as long as you don't attempt to emulate their hair-raising jumping style and their hair-raising hair. All lovely hair must be positively out of sight. This is why heavy hairnets are still made.

Again, at local shows this degree of sartorial propriety may not be necessary. Be guided by your environment and peers.

Participation Opportunities

The hunter world is one of the best established in the American equestrian scene, though perhaps still a little more so on the East Coast and in traditional (read gentrified) communities elsewhere, so opportunities abound for entering this lively scene on and off the horse. It's true that there is some traditional emphasis on junior riders; nevertheless, there are plenty of classes for adults to participate in without embarrassment. Hunter classes are, after all, judged on the horse's performance— "manners and way of going," they call it—rather than the rider's.

However, if you live in an isolated rural community, this may be a more challenging affinity for you.

Leisure and Competitive Opportunities

You can find hunt seat, or what passes for it, at many riding schools where English riding is emphasized, and it's a strong component in learning to jump. Many schools run small shows and encourage their students to participate, so it might be possible, in your area, to get a feel for the hunter world before you take out a second mortgage on your house. All levels of classes are available, for both experienced and novice (or green) horses and riders, some just on the flat, without fences, some over modest (two feet, six inches) obstacles.

Training Opportunities

As with participation levels, training opportunities abound in varying degrees. Hunt seat is a style as well as a technique, so if you imagine yourself eventually in the show ring, you will be working on refining the look that judges expect. A fluency and forward inclination of the body immediately identify this style—and you'll need dedicated drilling and an outside eye to achieve them. If you wind up riding at a hunter barn, this is the technique you will be taught—otherwise, you may eventually wish to import a trainer to your home. Perhaps more than in most disciplines, there can be an abrupt economic angle of incline here.

4

Hunting

*Subsequent disillusioning experience has taught me that but few
horses jump like Sorcerer, so gallantly, so sympathetically, and with
such supreme mastery of the subject; but none the less the enthusiasm
he imparted to me has never been extinguished, and that October
morning ride revealed to me the unsuspected intoxication of foxhunting.*

—E. Œ. (Edith) Somerville,
Some Experiences of an Irish R. M.

Men have been hunting on horses for almost as long as they could sit
on them, but the sport of field hunting as we know it today was codified in
the eighteenth century (stag and boar hunts since medieval times). It traveled from Great Britain and Ireland to North America with the first
colonists, especially those who settled in the South. Southern life, with its
spacious plantations, more closely replicated the world of the English estate
from which hunting comes forth than the weather-constrained and less ex-
travagant North, though there are now hunts all over the country, and the
Masters of Foxhounds Association celebrated its centennial in 2007.

To the uninitiated, *hunt* is both a verb and a noun, though to refer to
a subscription pack as "the hunt" shows you're a hodad. The quarry is

usually a fox, though in Europe, in a holdover from earlier times, deer are still sometimes hunted, and in some regions of the United States, coyote is considered—well—fair game. Hounds running after anything other than the approved prey are said to be "rioting" and will be severely "rated" (punished) by the huntsman. Loosely defined, whatever hunt club you're referring to is the collective entity made up of participants and staff. Hunts are local affairs, with different hunts taking the name of the region or territory they cover, such as Old Chatham or Beaufort. Members pay a fee to belong to the club, which in turn takes care of the upkeep of the land it has been allowed to ride through, the hounds, and the hire of the huntsman, a paid professional. Whips—riders who patrol the perimeters of the area being hunted to help keep the hounds in order—aren't always paid, though many hunts have a paid one. Although hunts are often used in film to symbolize upper-class life, hunts in fact are usually quite democratic, with everyone from the blacksmith to the squire participating. In American terms, this means that people of mixed means and backgrounds meet cheerfully on common turf, and if the idea of hunting appeals to you, you need not feel that you must transform yourself into somebody grand (social climbing is not appreciated; good manners and good horsemanship are). You do, however, have to be invited, first to "cap" (pay as you go for a limited number of days out), and then to join.

Not all hunting is a glamorous chase across the picturesque countryside. If the fox has "gone to ground"—in other words, returned to its burrow—or if the hounds lose the scent, you wait, often with the rain dripping down your neck and the cold creeping up your legs. At such times, there is the immediate consolation of a ready snack or even a quick nip, though you want to be careful when snacking: you don't want to have to take off after hounds three bites into your lunch. The midhunt nip of sherry or port remains a sacred ritual to many, but a properly turned-out lady never rides with one of those hogleg flasks attached to her saddle. Those are for men only. Women may carry a sandwich case where a tiny flask might hide. You may also carry your libation in your jacket, but not in something that hurts if you fall on it. (Pint bottles and baby food jars are definitely out.) Try a tasteful, flat silver flask that's small enough to fit into the palm of your hand, and stash it in your pocket. And it's all well-nigh impossible without the eventual promise of a hot bath. All in all, hunting requires equal parts vigor and patience. And, as I've said, the quarry varies, too, depending on the locale—in my area of upstate New York, coyotes are often more common than foxes.

You also need not rule out hunting if you're squeamish about blood sports or have strong views about animals' rights. In the United States, some hunts are what is known as "drag hunts," so named for the false lure of anise that is dragged through a preplotted course to simulate the path of a running fox. This way, the field can get in a good run without any fatalities and with less time spent standing in relentless drizzle waiting for the fox to break cover—another example of American ingenuity at work!

Because hunts are social events as much as they are sporting ones, your participation may well arise naturally from your growing involvement in the horse community in your area, but there is no reason not to be proactive. Ask your riding instructor about local hunts, or check in your tack shop, where you might see notices for hunt-sponsored events and contact information.

A full listing of all the accredited hunts in the United States may be obtained from the Masters of Foxhounds Association, at www.mfha.com. (See appendix B, "Resources.")

As with many horse-related activities, the hunt secretary is usually a busy volunteer, so be patient if your calls are not immediately returned. With gentle persistence, you may well be able to obtain an introduction—a must—and then be invited to "cap," or ride as a guest. As an outsider, you'll be held to the most rigorous standards of hunting etiquette, and you may find yourself burning quite a lot of midnight oil trying to memorize the rules. But a morning among civil people on gallant horses can convince most of us that the constraints are part of the fun.

And what of the experience itself? It's exhilarating, but it can also be alarming if you're not used to riding in a crowded field. In a sense, you wind up ceding some of your hard-won authority over a horse to more basic and atavistic instincts. He will be in a state of excitement among his fellows, and the herd instinct will take over. Terrain, though usually well maintained and examined ahead of time, is still likely to be uneven. (I once rode straight downhill on Salisbury Plain, a nerve-racking experience compounded by the unexpected arrival of tanks performing military maneuvers.) And jumping, instead of requiring an even pace over a tidy course, is often done at a gallop with several other horses, or in a line of thirty or more horses plunging with eagerness. If you're chasing a real quarry, its path, and the path the hounds take, dictate the terms of the chase, so you need to have steady nerves, a reasonably good seat, and an acceptance of the unexpected. Most of all, you need a fit, serviceable mount that suits your skill level and temperament.

If you can think of the whole process as a ritualized form of nature at work, then there is nothing more thrilling than watching a fox break cover and run cannily across a field, hounds in pursuit. (For the softhearted, this is often quite a bit later, when the pack has picked up the scent, giving "Reynard" plenty of time to get back to his Sunday paper.) As noted on the website of the Masters of Foxhounds Association, "Man is the audience privileged to watch, as hounds and fox or coyote, the actors, unveil the plot with never ever the same act repeated twice."

Pros and Cons

If you like to jump, have come to feel constrained in the ring, and don't mind a good gallop, hunting is enormous fun, not only for the speed and thrills, but for the fascinating hound work—following a line, "working a check" (when they've lost the scent), and crying out in excitement (known as "speaking") when they've picked it up again. But it's not for the fainthearted, although it is possible to follow some hunts as a "hilltopper"; there is usually a group of these riders, often older or less confident, who ride at a slower pace and watch the action from a distance. You also need patience and the ability to take pleasure in just riding in the countryside. When hounds check, the field (all riders behind the Master and huntsman) is often left sitting in a field for half an hour, rain or shine. (Real estate agents do a lot of business this way!)

And it's probably not for you if you are on a fairly tight budget. As an occasional hunter, unless someone is loaning you a mount, you need to be able to pay for the hire and transportation of a horse, and there are hidden hazards here. Hiring out horses is an unregulated profession, and whether the horse is perfectly decent or wildly unsafe—either is possible—it's still going to run you anywhere from one hundred to four hundred dollars to engage it for the day. The "capping fee," or admission charge for guests, is variable—several hundred dollars in coveted areas, and as little as fifty dollars in others—and the horse's transportation may not be included in the rental cost.

If you're sufficiently smitten to want to pursue hunting on a regular basis and have been invited to join a hunt club, there will be a yearly fee, and more significantly, the purchase and maintenance of a horse capable of keeping pace. If you're used to indulging in a modest regime of lessons and an occasional day out with the hounds, joining a subscription pack will definitely escalate your expenses. Yearly subscriptions are hard to average, based as they are on regional and even local distinctions. In my area, one hunt asks for the equivalent of a gym membership, while another costs as much as a term at a pricey boarding school. But if you and your bank account can take it, the game's afoot.

Leisure and Competitive Opportunities

Recognized hunts exist all across the country (171 clubs in 35 states as of this writing), and the schedule varies according to climate. (In the Hudson Valley area of New York State, for instance, the season starts in late summer and runs all the way to Christmas.) This means that many of you do have the opportunity to try the sport (once you are a secure rider, please). To arrange an invitation, you must contact the hunt secretary. Hunting is one of the last strongholds of elegant amateurism. This means that most hunts are organizations with "honorary" management and very few staff members who actually get paid. Some very large hunts may actually be listed in the telephone book, and you can check the MFA listings at the website noted above, but you're also likely to hear of them by word of mouth. Local tack shops or schools often know which hunts—especially those that organize competitions—are in the area. It is worth doing a little research before making an approach, since the character and culture of individual hunts, as well as the land they have the use of, can vary widely. Some are casual and classless, some are very socially conscious, and some, it seems, are made up exclusively of daredevils! And yes, there is an après-ski set as well. Jacqueline Kennedy Onassis, who hunted with the best of them, was credited for making the hunt breakfast into the elaborate feed it is today. Most gatherings take place at members' houses, preferably after the horses have been properly put up at home.

Happily, in addition to the regular hunts, the sport has spawned a lighthearted competitive tradition, the hunter pace. For these increasingly popular events, a planned course is ridden over in advance to determine the optimal time it would take to complete it while maintaining the pace of the hunt field. Then teams of two or three follow the course and attempt to complete it in that established time frame, which to make matters more interesting is never announced in advance. The team that completes the course in the closest to optimum time wins. An average course takes between fifty and ninety minutes to ride and affords a leisurely round of jumping and the additional pleasure of glimpses of the countryside.

What makes paces popular is that the competition is rather easygoing, and many people simply ride at their own pace, taking the fences they wish or none at all (well-planned paces always have "go-arounds" so that no one is forced to jump, though it definitely saves time). The catered lunch is frequently the high point of the day, and a general air of camaraderie prevails. Again, as in pleasure classes, hunter paces are pleasingly democratic to compete in—everything from vast draft horse crosses to burly Icelandic ponies can make their way around.

Clothing and Equipment

Thoreau (he of the new clothes aversion) would probably have been appalled by the sartorial demands of hunting. Even more than most of the elaborate equestrian sports (such as Western pleasure, sidesaddle, and saddle seat), this sport definitely requires *outfits*.

If you have ever seen old hunting prints, you may be loosely familiar with the "kit," as hunting gear is known, but you may be surprised to hear that standards of dress have changed very little from what they were in the eighteenth and nineteenth centuries. The top hat has become obsolete, and the always-proper bowler derby has virtually disappeared as well, victims of more safety-oriented requirements in riding equipment. But you'll still see the electrifying sight of men (and women who are staff) in those grand scarlet coats, which are nevertheless called "pink" after the tailor who first made them, and trim female members in dashing black with contrastingly colored collars.

Those people have earned their hunt "colors," which takes several years of brave participation (sort of like karate on horseback). You, a nonmember, won't be allowed to dress like that, so don't try it. Instead, you must show up in a black wool jacket, breeches in buff or canary, a stock tie—a long white cravat that wraps round your neck and is assembled into a sort of plumage, fixed by a decorative pin, on your chest—string or black leather gloves, and plain black velvet-covered helmet. A canary-colored wool vest generally completes the ensemble; though these are optional, they add warmth, and they're terribly smart looking. In England, the mens' jackets can be vastly different from the norm—the Quorn, for example, is famous for its bright yellow coats. Generally, more casual and subtle clothes are worn for the earlier autumn cubbing season, when young hounds are trained. You need tweeds and brown boots for that. The severe black-and-canary arrangements are for when the season is in full swing.

Of course, this is America, land of the free, and some hunts have more relaxed standards, allowing you to ride in the same clothing you might wear in the show ring. Some of these requirements, however refined, are simple common sense, and accessories can be borrowed or contrived in a pinch. (I once turned up to a cubbing meet in what I thought was a perfectly credible collared show shirt, only to be informed that I needed proper neckwear, so I grabbed the designer headscarf I keep in my car and contrived a somewhat flashy mock cravat!)

If you are taking your own horse (and you want to get some advice about whether he or she is a likely hunt prospect), there is a range of paraphernalia for the mount, also. Hunting demands more accessories than "normal" riding, though if you're leasing this will not be a consideration. Plunging and jumping boldly through variable terrain requires a breastplate to keep your saddle in place. Protective boots for horses are frowned on by purists but are sometimes necessary, though in wet weather it's best to leave them at home.

Participation Opportunities

One key difference about this aspect of the sport, as I've said, is that it is invitational. The social aspects of riding come more markedly into play than at a simple horse show. But in my experience, many hunts are welcoming, assuming you behave correctly and do not have a troublesome horse. So assuming that there is a club in your region (see appendix B) and you're willing to go through the various rites of initiation, this is one discipline that is definitely not child-centric. However, if you have an older child interested in riding, most hunts welcome and cherish children—the guardians of the sport for the next generation—and have supervised groups in which they can ride safely.

(It is also possible to book hunting holidays—see chapter 28, "Horses on Holiday.")

Training Opportunities

Foxhunting may well be the activity for which the phrase *seat of the pants* was invented—and also, for the foolish, *reckless endangerment.* There's no actual training for hunting, except hunting. You should have a secure seat over a fence (unless you wish only to hilltop), a horse you have confidence in (your own or a good hire), and a willingness to take risks. Until virtual reality is perfected, no academic environment can replicate the pace and excitement of the real thing.

5

Show Jumping

Show—or stadium—jumping is probably the most spectacular and purely artificial of equestrian sports, and the one with the most indelible image in contemporary times. Mettlesome horses soaring over brightly colored fences make great poster art, but there is nothing cosmetic about this challenging sport.

For all we know, the ancient Persians were hopping over dunes in the desert, but modern show jumping evolved from several sources. Nineteenth-century jumper trials were considered tests for hunters and were also a feature of cavalry training. Caprilli, the inventor of the forward seat, was chief instructor of the Italian Cavalry School. Military competitions that eventually evolved into today's national trials were common following World War I. The same daredevil impulse that prompted car races and airplane stunt flying was also at work here. (There are surviving photos of men jumping over cars, wagons, and that sort of thing.) Unlike field hunting, which involves natural obstacles encountered fairly randomly in the countryside, or the hunter ring, which creates modest approximations of these to test a horse's poise and consistency, show jumping is pure mathematics: it asks for speed and dexterity over very challenging obstacles designed to elicit from both rider and horse a combination of boldness and shrewdness. Though no longer military, there is still fierce rivalry among national teams on the international jumping circuit. But most team members today come from amateur and professional show barns, and indeed, jumping has been an established part of many horse shows since the late nineteenth century. The first U.S. competition was held at the National Horse Show in 1883.

Show jumping, like hunt-seat competition, follows an annual circuit in each region of the country. Most midsized and larger shows have some sort of jumper class. (The show circuit has ratings for its shows—"A" is the top tier—relating to prominence, level of competition, and points awarded to horses being ranked in the national standings. Trust me—this is unlikely to concern you.) These classes come in several flavors, each thrilling or daunting in its own way. Most basic classes combine speed and height requirements—the cleanest round in the fastest time wins. Some raise the height of the obstacles to determine jump-offs, and the most sensational class, the puissance, is exactly what its name suggests—a test to see which horse can jump the highest, with the final minutes of the competition consisting of assaults on a single (fake) brick wall. The unofficial world record is eight feet, two inches—almost unimaginable.

Basic Technique

The principles and biomechanics involved in sound and successful jumping are theoretically the same whether you're jumping a tiny cavalletti (low poles or cross-rails used for schooling) or an imposing five-foot fence. A horse's weight displaces forward as he jumps, and it is the rider's job to follow his motion and not upset his balance. As the horse's forelegs leave the ground, the rider folds forward, and his arms follow the extended line of the horse's head and neck. In the hunter ring, you can see fairly exemplary versions of this form, as these straightforward obstacles do little to upset a secure rider.

In the jumper ring, however, everything seems more exaggerated. The horses, swift and volatile, look like contained springs as they travel toward fences. Once released, they leap forward and arch their backs significantly (this rounding is called a horse's "bascule") to allow themselves to clear these high, wide fences. Naturally, it becomes harder to hold a cosmetically perfect position under such circumstances, and show jumping films and photos often show much more extreme postures, with legs thrown back, arms far forward, and the body of the rider barely in contact with the horse.

However, the American Olympic team of the 1960s under William Steinkraus was renowned for its classical form—especially among the women, including Kathy Kushner and Mary Chapot. Look closely, however, and you will still see a balanced rider, one whose position and reflexes allow her to snap back into a controlled position in time to get her mount safely to the next fence—all of which is to say that fairly exceptional skill and confidence are required, not just to excel, but to survive.

Pros and Cons

If you come to love jumping and like the formal challenge demanded of today's courses, or if this was your field when you were a younger rider and it calls to you still, then it is hard to imagine anything comparable for sheer excitement. Also, the level of trust and sense of partnership required for a really successful horse and rider team is intensified here, so profound bonds can form between jumper riders and their mounts. And if you enjoy the excitement and bustle of the horse show experience, you will get plenty of it as a show jumper.

But implicit in the description of what it takes to succeed in show jumping are its disadvantages for the beginning or returning older rider, especially one who, like most of us, rides only on weekends. One challenge is that local unofficial and/or unsanctioned shows often have jumper classes with relatively low fences, but there is no formal tier of competition for beginner or low jumpers, so if you want to compete seriously, you're going to have to take it to a higher level in terms of investment and involvement. Talented show jumpers are expensive, high-maintenance horses who need to be in a regular program of work. The rider needs to be strong, focused, and competitive, too, and to have enough riding time to perfect those skills with the horse in question.

It is hard to do this without considerable investment in time and money, and even then, getting to the point in your riding where you move beyond competence may take more time than you think. (You probably wouldn't even be considering show jumping if your initial jumping experience hadn't gone well, but this is an area where it could be extremely dangerous to try to rush into higher levels of competition before you're ready.)

Also, as I said earlier, successful show jumping is the result of real partnership with a talented animal, and this usually means investing—fairly heavily—in a horse of your own.

Leisure and Competitive Opportunities

If you've got the horse, they've got the fences. In the regions of the country where there are established show circuits, competitive opportunities abound. The key will be to ally yourself with a barn and/or school that is connected to your local circuit. Unless you have tremendous resources and can assemble your own team, your access to focused lessons, schooling, and competitive opportunities will most likely come through an existing establishment. Then, be sure that you're working with teachers and trainers you trust, who will know when you're ready to take this exciting step. To give yourself a treat and a taste of things that might come, arrange to go to one of the big "A" shows in your region. Many are organized by Horseshows in the Sun (HITS); have a look at its summer/winter schedule here: www.hitsshows.com.

This is also in many ways the least democratic of the disciplines. Whereas many kinds of duos can compete at the lower levels in most aspects of the sport, except for courses you might encounter at low-key schooling shows there isn't a formalized lower level in jumping (though some schooling shows have "baby" courses), and real boldness and athleticism in both horse and rider are a prerequisite, not only for success, but for safety.

Clothing and Equipment

Other than basic show ring attire (a black coat—with plenty of give—and dress boots, buff breeches), nothing exceptional is required in the way of clothing for the rider. The horse, on the other hand, can have quite an extensive wardrobe. Advances in sports medicine and technology, as well as the thriving marketplace, have yielded dozens of products—boots, pads, reins, and so on—designed to improve his performance and protect him in a physically taxing environment.

Participation Opportunities

As with the hunter circuit, if you're willing to invest the time and money required, there is no lack of opportunity to compete if you're in an area of the country where competitive English riding has a presence. Your entrée is likely to be through your trainer or barn.

Training Opportunities

While any reasonably well-grounded riding school and, theoretically, any decent instructor should be able to impart the basics of jumping, show jumping, even for amateurs, requires an almost professional level of dedication and a vigorous training regime. If this is the field that wins your heart, you may find yourself shopping, as I suggested earlier, for a training stable and a mount to join you there. Conversely, if you buy a made horse, other than getting comfortable with his/her style, you don't need to overemphasize schooling—these horses have a lot of nervous intelligence, get bored or jaded easily, and usually know what to do on the day. Professional trainers often keep them in light work once they're fit, with occasional schooling sessions to take the edge off.

Unquestionably, there are lots of junior jumpers—this is one of the fields of competition that grooms young riders for the U.S. national teams and a thriving professional circuit—but there is also a strong amateur owner/rider tradition that means you won't be an anomaly.

6

Dressage "Airs above the Ground"

If riding were language, show jumping would be a declamation, and dressage a sinewy poem by T. S. Eliot or Adrienne Rich—a subtle, sometimes indecipherable surface yielding up rich secrets of meaning and technique. Take for example "airs above the ground," the poetical phrase used to describe a sequence of balletic movements performed by classically trained horses at their peak.

In fact, dressage is probably the discipline with the most ancient lineage, deriving from the ancient movements of war and military exercises and the resulting principles of horsemanship that have come to us from the early Greeks (Xenophon's seminal *On Horsemanship*, noted earlier, was written in 350 BC), Persians, and Romans. Various European court masters such as Giovanni Baptista Pignatelli, Antoine de Pluvinel, and François de la Guerniere, whose book *Ecole de Cavalerie* (1733) became the dominant text of the Spanish Riding School of Vienna, began to articulate the principles of dressage that define training and competition today.

Basic Technique

Even putting these principles into words is a metaphysical act, and one that is still the subject of hot debate among dressage professionals today. It's nothing less than an attempt to synthesize how all the natural movements of the horse can be put to the service of a range of formal gestures that paradoxically appear to be both free and controlled. Sometimes it's said that in dressage, the ideal for the horse is to move with a rider as he does in nature. As Xenophon wrote, "If one induces the horse to assume that carriage which it would adopt of its own accord when displaying its beauty, then, one directs the horse to appear joyous and magnificent, proud and remarkable for having been ridden."

In its practical application, the discipline involves pursuing these ends through a progressively more elaborate vocabulary of exercises. But it's not all scholastic drudgery. In fact, dressage's scholarly mien appeals to a great number of beginning adult riders, often because they wish to study riding seriously but simply don't want to do anything too fast paced. Furthermore, dressage's controlled movements fit in with the Eastern-influenced exercises many adults like—it's yoga instead of aerobics, in a way, and can become either an exuberant mode of expression or a private meditation, depending on the personality and ambition of the rider.

One starts simply by learning how to walk and ends—if one is very persistent, skilled, or lucky—by waltzing with the horse in the balletlike *piaffes* and *passages* associated with Vienna's "dancing white horses." As expressed in *Classical Training of the Horse*, the handbook of the U.S. Dressage Federation, "The object of dressage is the harmonious development of the physique and ability of the horse. As a result it makes the horse calm, supple, loose and flexible but also confident, attentive and keen, thus achieving perfect understanding with his rider."[*]

---

[*] The ultimate source for this description is the *USEF Rule Book*, which lays out the standards by which horses are judged in various sanctioned matches in each of the disciplines it oversees.

Training and competition require referring even the simplest movement back to ultimate principles and then finding a purely kinetic way to translate a complex formal lexicon into a vital movement.

Pros and Cons

Dressage involves less physical risk than some other equestrian sports since it takes place entirely on the flat, so it may well appeal to those who don't want their pleasure mixed with peril and don't need speed or elevation to give them a sense of excitement or satisfaction. Don't think this means you can be inattentive. The flip side of the coin is that dressage movements at the upper levels of the discipline can cause a lot of stress to the *horse*, who sometimes gets tense and anxious. Highly schooled dressage horses, many of them large, powerful warmbloods (see part IV, "Choosing a Horse"), often have a great deal of nervous energy, and the concentration required at the higher levels of the discipline can sometimes produce a combustible animal.

On the other hand, dressage does require a good deal of patience and focus, for its excitements and rewards are more nuanced and have more in common with chess or ice skating's school figures (though there are more performance components at the higher levels) than with show jumping or, say, barrel racing. (One official Olympic commentator said he'd rather watch people knitting!)

Dressage is another field where there is a great financial divide between the higher and lower levels. With sufficient patience, perseverance, and some outside supervision, any horse that can move relatively freely and is without hideous temperament and conformation faults can compete respectably at the lower levels. But growing interest in the sport, the aggressive marketing of European warmbloods, and increased competition have made the high end very high indeed. Horses are regularly imported from Europe with price tags in five figures, and even home-grown horses have become virtual investment prospects.

Leisure and Competitive Opportunities

Because dressage is a discipline concerned with formal schooling, it cannot be considered completely as a leisure activity except in the sense that all riding is leisure as compared with work. Like daily barre practice for the dancer, dressage involves slow, incremental schooling of the horse and rider with the aim of testing increased suppleness and obedience by asking for increasingly challenging movements. Of course, it is still possible to do this outside the context of competition, and happily, there are more and more opportunities to do this.

Dressage has enjoyed real growth in many areas of the country in the past decade, prompted in part by international successes on the part of the American teams and aggressive proselytization by warmblood breeders (the U.S. Dressage Federation experienced a 23 percent boost in membership in 2007). This means that it has become much easier to find establishments that either specialize in dressage or at least offer classes. These are often smaller than the tumultuous hunter/jumper barns. Dressage riders take many years to perfect their craft, and responsible instructors undertake vigorous formal certification before they offer to teach at various levels. One reason for the growth may also be that, like ice skating, some freer and more invitingly creative components have developed in recent years. These include a form called musical freestyle, or *Kür*, which is a choreographed pattern to music done by riders at third level or above.

Clothing and Equipment

In thinking about accoutrements for dressage, the analogy with ballet is again useful. When schooling, only neat and functional basic riding garb—the equivalent to the dancer's practice leotards—is required. Breeches, boots, a helmet, and an unconstraining shirt are all you need to practice. In this era of infinite choice it is best, however, to avoid boot and breech combinations like blue and blue or black and black that obscure the line of the leg.

Dressage competitions are organized into progressive levels, each requiring increasingly demanding movements, from the lower training levels to fourth level (competitions are governed by the U.S. Equestrian Federation, the national adjudicating body). Upward from there, we have Prix St. George to Grand Prix Special (competitions governed by the international body, Fédération Equestre Internationale, or FEI). For competition up to third level, clothes are simple and conservative: black hunt coat, buff breeches, stock tie, and dark gloves. But for riders competing at third level and above, an element of theatricality enters in. For example, the rider may wear a top hat, but in the words of one competitor, "If you wear a top hat, you'd better be good!" Bowlers are becoming more popular with a short coat and white breeches at the third and fourth levels, but by the time you get to Prix St. Georges, a top hat and cutaway frock coat known as a "shadbelly" are required. (Note that wearing white breeches or white gloves before you're competing at the appropriate level is a solipsism, rather like sporting a club tie for a club of which you are not a member.)

Participation Opportunities

Dressage is like champagne: it often takes a mature palate to appreciate it. A great many riders, even those who have ridden consistently throughout their lives, come late to dressage, and the steady increase in membership in the U.S. Dressage Federation is one indicator of this. Dressage shows will probably never be as common as hunter or pleasure classes because criteria for both showing and judging is much more stringent. The

USDF requires an elaborate certification process, and even if local shows don't adhere strictly to protocol, the judge still has to be experienced and capable of assessing a wide range of tests, judging them in accordance with a received formal vocabulary. Still, there are more shows, or dressage components within shows—with a range of different classes—than there used to be (this is not counting the dressage phase of a horse trial, which must be considered integrally with the other elements).

There are probably several reasons why dressage attracts more adults. As people grow older, they naturally look for horse sports a little less all-consuming and physically punishing than hunting or cross-country jumping. Some gravitate out of these areas due to accident or injury. One of my instructors, a very promising eventer as a junior, had one accident too many and lost his zest for eventing. Also, unlike the bold surges of jumping, the ambling and rugged pleasure of trail riding, or the showmanship of pleasure or hunt-seat riding, dressage offers the thrill of nuance, and nuance, as we know, is often wasted on the young.

Dressage is becoming more publicly visible as well. American national teams and individual riders at the international level are beginning to hold their own after long lagging behind European riders, and of course, success always adds to a sport's allure.

Training Opportunities

As a result of these demographic and psychic shifts, there are more dressage barns and more stables offering some kind of dressage instruction, even if it's in the form of imported instructors booked for clinics. In this, above all, finding a good fit with a teacher is key. The ability to vividly convey the complexities of dressage in a way that both satisfies the mind and translates to the body is what distinguishes a first-rate instructor from an undistinguished one. As an old television ad used to put it, accept no imitations. (We'll talk further about assessing instructors in part II.)

7

Horse Trials

Eventing is the most demanding of all equestrian sports, requiring an all-round ability. It can also be the most exhilarating and rewarding. The discipline of the dressage ring, the thrill of the cross-country and the challenge of the more formal stadium jumping all require tremendous concentration and sustained effort from you and your partner, the horse.

—Sally O'Connor, *Practical Eventing*

The ancient Greeks have taught us to respect the ideal of a well-rounded person: intellect complemented by action, passion by rationality. If any discipline aspires to this Augustine mean, it is that of the horse trial, which might be considered, for those who love it as I do, the best of all possible worlds.

Like many competitive forms, this one has come down to us from the military. The earliest kinds of horse trials were in the form of endurance rides that constituted part of nineteenth-century cavalry training. Jumping was incorporated in the early twentieth century, and the Swedes won the first team gold medal in the sport at the 1912 Olympics. Oddly, the country that has come to virtually define the sport—England—was not among the original competing countries.

Peacetime has proved even more of an incentive to eventing—a verb derived from the notion of a three day "event" reflecting the three phases in which the horse and rider are tested. The sport grew significantly after World War II, aided by the establishment of such high-profile events as the Badminton Horse Trials. Begun in England by the Duke of Beaufort, the Badminton event celebrated its fiftieth anniversary in 1999 with huge crowds attending. In the United States, the first major event was in July of 1953, so we are past the midcentury point as well, and the country's official teams usually perform well at international events (with David O'Connor, the current president of the U.S. Eventing Association, winning the individual gold medal at the 2000 Olympics in Sydney, Australia).

The basic premise of eventing retains its nineteenth-century military origins. It aims to test a horse's abilities in three types of performance: dressage, cross country, and show jumping. In a sense, what eventing celebrates is contradictions, by demonstrating that a very fit horse can still be supple and obedient through a dressage test, that a dressage mount can have the vigor and stamina to undertake a long cross-country ride over obstacles, and that both can display the focus and form required to complete a show-jumping course even after a series of tiring jumping efforts in rough country.

Basic Technique

At the more advanced levels—for a full three-day event—the demands on horse and rider are high indeed. Dressage tests are stringent, requiring a high degree of suppleness and collection from the same animal who is going to gallop his heart out the following day. The cross-country course can consist of as many as twenty to thirty very challenging obstacles.* On the following day, the horses are tested for soundness (and no wonder!) and then proceed to a show-jumping round. (None who witnessed it can forget David O'Connor's hair-raising ride at the 2000 Summer Olympics, when, weary after months of competition, he nearly lost his bid for a gold medal when he briefly forgot which fence was next on his course. Happily, he recovered, set right by the nearly hysterical crowd of spectators, all screaming, "The wall!")

If you're already turning the page in dismay, take heart. There are now many lower-level competitions with divisions ranging from prenovice to advanced (in the U.S. system). These horse trials, as they are known at this level, usually eliminate the steeplechase and roads and tracks phases, have fewer obstacles, and often take only one or two days.

Pros and Cons

What's not to love? You and your horse get to prove you're the all-around athletes you always knew you were, and instead of having to choose among the various disciplines, you get to combine three of the most rewarding and challenging. And in some ways, eventing is the ideal form for a mature mind: it takes a great deal of time and patience to train up a good event horse, but that patience is amply rewarded by pleasure both refined and bold.

What's not to love? Well, it takes a great deal of time and patience to train a good event horse—to achieve real competence in all areas. Very few horses and, indeed, not many riders are strong in all three forms.

---

* The cross-country phase actually used to have four components: two timed rides across open ground known as "roads and tracks," separated by a steeplechase course, then the actual jumping course, but under threat of losing its Olympic status, the USEA decided to eliminate the roads and tracks and steeplechase components.

The obedient dressage horse is sometimes less bold and confident as a jumper; the ground-eating cross-country mount can all but jump out of his skin in the dressage ring. A fairly vigorous training program is required. It's hard for the weekend rider, and the cost of trainers, clinics, and competition can really add up. Also, there is the element of danger. Eventers (usually, it should be said, at the higher levels) have sustained some serious, even fatal injuries cross-country, and even lower-level riders take spills fairly frequently. However, much has been done to try to improve both rider safety and courses by discouraging people from riding above their level, getting unsafe horse and rider combinations off the field quickly, and creating more yielding obstacles with breakaways.

Leisure and Competitive Opportunities

Strictly speaking, eventing does not have a leisure component—it is a competitive field, pure and simple. However, since the training required calls for the complete mental and physical fitness of the horse and rider, there is much pleasurable—and even uneventful, riding to be had in just getting your horse fit, since this requires work outside over as varied a terrain as possible in your area. Nevertheless, it is unquestionably one of the most adult friendly of all horse sports. A serious review of USEA membership and levels of competition several years ago made clear that adult amateurs were coming to dominate the sport. The organization has risen to the challenge of serving this population, even with limited resources.

In many parts of the country, horse trials are among the fastest-growing additions to the seasonal calendar, and the USEA, the governing body for the sport, has seen a steady increase in membership—up 21 percent since 1997. However, the sport faces several challenges. Because of the cross-country element, it requires land, and private land with willing owners is in increasingly short supply. This means that existing events are inundated with entries, and because of the time-consuming nature of the dressage and cross-country phases, these must necessarily be limited. Also, until recently, the beginner novice and novice levels, where most adult riders new to the sport compete, were low priorities in a system focused on creating future U.S. team riders and professionals. Happily, this has changed to some extent, but there are still far more hopefuls than most competitions can accommodate, so you must be well organized to secure a spot.

Clothing and Equipment

As you might imagine, a three-component discipline does involve three different outfits. (Thoreau's ghost will stir again.) Fortunately for your purse, at the lower levels appropriate dress for the dressage and show jumping phases—regulation breeches, dress boots, black jacket, and stock tie or similar neckwear—is virtually identical, and at some more casual events people even compete in sports shirts. It is with the addition of cross-country that a whole new range of paraphernalia becomes necessary. For this rugged riding, an entire small fashion industry has grown up. Although for one-day horse trials competitors sometimes keep the same breeches they wore for the dressage and stadium phases (hoping they will not have a spill!), these are also often changed for darker breeches with an elastic fit, worn with a tailored sports shirt in summer and a turtleneck in winter. In recent years, following a number of sad accidents, safety regulations for this sport have become more elaborate, and competitors must now wear an approved helmet (see part III for a fuller explanation) and a protective vest. These are shell-like garments, bulky and hinting at mercenary chic, that are designed to prevent—or at least mitigate—chest and spinal injuries. Almost all events require them, and they are really advisable even if one is only schooling. They cost $125–$300, so the purchase of one becomes a sign of commitment in itself.

On a merrier note, the regulation helmets, which come unadorned principally in black or white, have inspired a virtual Aladdin's cave of nylon head coverings in every conceivable shade and combination, from basic primary colors to pastels to extreme sport neon.

The horse is even more burdened by protective gear. These are not the pages in which to dwell on the extensive array of boots and breast-plates, shoe studs, and saddle pads that have been created to refine the performance of the event horse. And the growing influence of the sport reaches well beyond equipment—eventing has been key in promoting the breeding of an entirely new type of horse, the "sport horse" (often a draft/warmblood/thoroughbred combination of some sort), in whom some of this ruggedness is thought to be innate.

Participation Opportunities

As I said earlier, the demands eventing makes on its organizers and on land mean that there are at present far more would-be competitors than openings. In order to make the most of what there is, you need to join eventing's regulatory body, the USEA, and your local chapter as well, to receive mailings and literature relating to exciting competitions. This is also one area where competition is very much linked to training; be-coming attached to a barn that competes regularly will vastly increase your chances of getting your stirrup in the door. The issue here is not so much that there are few opportunities for adults per se, but that there are far more for advanced riders. One additional point of access is the less formal "schooling show." Accredited events are very taxing for orga-nizers, and some facilities have opted to offer competitions that don't fig-ure in the annual point count tracked by the USEA or require formal dress, but that do give out ribbons (nice for your self-esteem) and give you a chance to test your horse in competition. These shows tend to offer only one or two phases—dressage and show jumping, or cross-country and show jumping—for example.

Training Opportunities

Training opportunities have been growing, so your chance of finding a barn—or an instructor—with some knowledge of, and connections to, the eventing world is greater than it was, say, ten or twenty years ago. And at the lower levels, again, well-chosen (safe!) school horses can give you a taste of the sport. However, even more than most disciplines, serious eventing requires a consistent training program and a symbiotic relationship between horse and rider that can be achieved only by having a horse of your own.

Adult pony club teams, similar to those for juniors, compete for championships (usually at the novice level); special clinics and camps have sprung up, catering to lower-level riders, and established events have increased the number of novice- and beginner novice-level competitions they offer.

Concern about rider safety has prompted an instructor certification program, from which will eventually emerge a corps of instructors trained to get you where you want to be safely and effectively. To tap into this growing resource, join the national body, the United States Eventing Association, and its regional extensions, which provide regular mailings on competitions and training opportunities.

8

Western Pleasure and Trail

Western riding developed out of the cattle ranching traditions of the Spanish and emerged in the nineteenth century, as agriculture met machinery in the establishment of the beef and leather goods industries. But even before this, the West, with its ties to Spain, was evolving quite a different riding technique from that patterned on the military and the hunt field.

The Spanish had retained the ornate saddles that derived from medieval equipage. More enveloping than even the early cavalry saddles, these elaborate accessories signal one of the distinctions about early riding in the West—the need to stay mounted for long periods of time, to comfortably cover great distances, to carry supplies and tools, and to provide an anchor for roping cattle.

The actual style of riding in the West evolved similarly. While the original conquistadors must have had their technique shaped by the elaborate traditions of classical riding, their hardworking cattle-ranching descendants had to develop a technique that facilitated long hours in the saddle while moving and managing herds. The 1991 film *City Slickers*, in which two dudes (Billy Crystal and Bruno Kirby) wind up having to move a herd of cattle on their own, pays tribute to this daunting profession.

Basic Technique

All riding disciplines refer to the horse and rider relationship as a partnership, but in Western riding this was more than an aesthetic goal. The traditional Western horse was, and is, a work animal, assisting in cattle herding and in the myriad outdoor tasks related to that work. He needed to be relaxed but alert, capable of the quick turns, sudden spurts of speed, and abrupt stops that cattle herding—and work in an untamed wilderness—required. (This book is oriented toward the United States, but the same style is common to South and Central American cattlemen.)

By the same token, the rider could not always be focused on his horse or even have two hands on the reins. The new, emerging style emphasized control through balance and shifting of weight and a somewhat higher degree of initial collection from a horse expected to be responsive to the slightest pressure of the rein on the neck. Traditionally, the reins are held in one hand and the lariat in the other. (In the so-called Texas style, reins are held in two hands.) Western curb bits appear much more severe and shouldn't be used by beginners, but these horses are trained to be responsive to the slightest adjustment. In any event, these bridles are used primarily for show, and Western horses are usually ridden in the milder snaffle bits (plain rings with joints in the middle) for pleasure and training. In either form, and with either type of bit, a very light hand is required, as well as a light body. Because Western riding relies heavily on shifts in weight, the ideal neutral position for the rider is erect and balanced over the horse's center of gravity. This makes the discipline more challenging than it might first appear for adult riders, with our ingrained slouches and tense lower backs.

In addition to quick starts and stops, the working Western horse had to comfortably convey its rider for extended periods of time. The more propulsive natural gaits of the trot and canter are modified into the jog and lope, which have smoother rhythms.

For all these reasons, Western riding, even while the frontier was receding, gained a firm foothold in the world of recreational riding. (The National Reining Horse Association saw a 90 percent increase in membership between 1997 and 2007!)

Pros and Cons

For the uninitiated, Western riding seems, and at the milder levels probably is, more accessible. The saddle feels safer than the spare English saddle. The seemingly casual position of the rider conveys a sense of informality, and Western horses, the staple of many a dude ranch and trail-riding establishment, seem relaxed and biddable, too.

And if you'd like to go more gently into this new world but still have an interest in showing, Western pleasure is certainly a less aggressive form than show jumping or eventing. The Western gaits, too, are subtler and less volatile than their English counterparts (except the gallop, which is the same exhilarating flat-out run the world over), and a novice rider may feel able to almost relax into knowledge.

Somewhat apart from the traditionally rugged mythos of the cowboy, Western riding has, in recent years, developed almost a New Age face, with the popularity of books like *The Horse Whisperer* and those who were the models for the intuitive trainer—John Lyons, Monty Roberts, and others. This more spiritual face allows the rugged world of Western riding to appeal at a psychological level that far transcends nuts and bolts. Also, this is another area, like low-level eventing and English pleasure, where a modest mount can yield considerable fun and be brought along with patient training, and many school horses of just this type are available.

As with any form or product, however, popularity in riding styles can lead to profusion without regard for quality. There are many, many stables offering Western-style riding, and at many of them you will be paying for substandard teaching or even trail riding disguised as teaching. But as with show jumping and eventing, the upper end of the discipline offers the opposite scenario—a wealth of trainers and competitions requiring an investment of considerable time and money. Even at the more casual show levels, the degree of sartorial glamour required of both horse and rider is enough to either beckon or give one pause. (See "Clothing and Equipment," below.)

Leisure and Competitive Opportunities

For the reasons just discussed, Western riding is firmly embedded in American equestrian culture, and opportunities to participate abound, though naturally to a lesser degree in the East.

If trail riding appeals to you, you're limited only by the resources— in terms of horseflesh and land—of the stable you ally yourself with, so it is worth inquiring about an establishment's access to trails. For insurance reasons, many stables will not allow riders to ride out alone, but do organize regular rides for participants.

Even if leisure is your goal, don't make the mistake of thinking you don't have to take your riding seriously if you ride at this level. Without proper fitness, control, stamina, and technical skills, trail riding can be anything from tiring to alarming. Properly pursued, it's one of the great private pleasures, giving the rider glimpses of unfolding nature and the intricate beauty of the landscape, and time to think and dream (while still paying proper attention to your animal, of course).

The show ring becomes, in effect, a stylized version of experiences in nature and of the horse's response to them. Western classes are a staple of many breed shows, including Morgan, Arabian, Saddlebred, and Paso Fino, as well as being common at local shows with mixed classes. Of course, in the many rodeo and related events, the quarter horse remains the king of the American West, but I cannot seriously recommend taking up rodeo riding. As in English pleasure shows, trail classes ask the horse to negotiate a series of obstacles or challenges—flapping debris, gates to open and shut, simulated streams—of the kind he might actually encounter. He also has to perform turns and reinbacks, which are just what they sound like: the horse must stop and back rapidly and straight, perhaps through a grid or an arrangement of ground poles. If you have a little more time to spare, there are also competitive trail rides over distance, usually taking one to three days.

Pleasure classes look for a horse and rider combination that evinces relaxation with panache, as well as a capacity to perform the three basic gaits (walk, jog, and lope) obediently and with suppleness, with the horse coming back quietly after each transition to demonstrate that he would not tear away from you in a field. Horses are also asked to back up. Since this is one of the most practical skills a horse facing unknown circumstances can have, it is a common feature of both trail and pleasure classes. (Collapsed bridges, recalcitrant gates, and unfriendly livestock are common hazards in trail riding.)

And as with the hunter/jumper circuit, Western shows also include equitation classes, in stock seat (which involves a mock herding exercise with actual stock) and reining, though the distinction is beginning to blur. These judge the form of the rider through an increasingly demanding set of movements and patterns that test both form and the practical application of techniques.

Clothing and Equipment

I've mentioned the potential Las Vegas aspect to high-end Western showing (one woman I know used to agonize about whether she had "this season's" earrings or not). But generally, Western riding is the perfect sport for either end of the fashion spectrum. If you hate dressing up, jeans and sensible boots are considered appropriate, though you probably will want to invest in a pair of chaps, the real cowboy kind that cover your whole leg and zip up the side. A basic training helmet is fine for riding out, although the most identifiable component of Western dress, the cowboy hat, is still de rigueur in the show ring. Some companies are even working on models that incorporate some of the same safety features that are in riding helmets.

At the other end of the spectrum is, well, Las Vegas. Western show gear includes, for both men and women, resplendent shirts in bright colors, like brilliant red and turquoise, with silver snaps, gaudy kerchiefs, and bolos for men and big, noisy, fake gems or vast abstract pieces for women. In the transition from the range to the ring, Buck Owens and Glen Campbell or other flamboyant rhinestone cowboys on the entertainment circuit supplanted the type of weathered, sage, salty cowboy portrayed by Jack Palance. Tack for the horse follows a similar pattern, with relatively unadorned saddles and bridles available for trails and fabulous pieces covered in delicate scrollwork or bedizened with silver that would dazzle the original conquistadors.

Participation Opportunities

As mentioned earlier, Western riding is more heavily concentrated in the West and Southwest, but there are still many stables that offer lessons. The link to traditional trail and holiday pleasure riding means that many barns will be especially hospitable to adults; after that, there's only the challenge of distinguishing the wheat from the chaff. And while this book assumes that you are contemplating a long-term relationship with riding, it is also true that the upside of the dude ranch industry is that there are a number of pleasant and responsible holiday opportunities that will give you the Western pleasure experience. (See chapter 28.)

Training Opportunities

Once you have distinguished the tourist traps from the training barns, you will find serious Western riding enjoying new celebrity. And once you have learned the rudiments, many establishments offer both trail riding and show opportunities. As with eventing, trail riding is part of the training regimen of any accomplished pleasure horse, so you can get the best of both experiences. As befits the spirit of rugged individualists, there are also a lot of private trainers in this field who, like consultants, can sometimes be allowed to train at your barn. Arrangements of this kind are more common among riders who have their own horses, but worth looking into if you feel you'd like to get more focused attention.

9

Western Kicked Up a Notch
Reining, Roping, and Barrel Racing

With cutting horses, you have to find a harmony with the horse. You have to reflect that horse's energy, and he has to reflect yours. You have to be sharp. You have to react. But the thing you have to have is the feel. . . . And the feel could come from anywhere. . . . You could never be sure who had that feel. It might well be somebody's grandmother.

—Thomas McGuane, *Some Horses*

History

The thrilling and exacting cousins of Western pleasure and trail riding—reining, roping, and barrel racing—descend from the same source: the Western frontier. The skills required of the working cowboy to herd and drive cattle to market—chasing down errant cows, roping, and herding—called for a remarkable level of responsiveness and coordination on the part of horse and rider. These skills, isolated from their practical origins, gave birth to the culture of rodeo and the more sensational elements of the Western pleasure circuit, such as reining. If Western flatwork and trail riding is a warm bath to the beginner or returning adult rider, this is more like choosing to go down the rapids and over the falls.

Basic Technique

Reining has been described as the Western equivalent of dressage and requires a deft mastery of the basic Western aids. It uses one of the two methods of holding the reins: coming up through the top, or down through the bottom, of the hand. The rider then executes a prescribed series of rapid turns and stops (known as pivots, spins, and rollbacks) that require both balance and collection on the part of the horse. If classical dressage can be rudely likened to knitting, as it was by the imperceptive sports commentator I mentioned earlier, then this is more like a runaway sewing machine!

Cutting and roping competitions may seem to be the province of professional rodeos, but cutting, at least, has developed a show ring equivalent that is rapidly gaining in popularity, at least among junior riders. The horse and rider are asked to "work" a cow for a timed period and are then judged on their effectiveness.

Barrel racing is exactly what it sounds like, a robust and exciting form that makes use of the basic Western techniques—balance, quick changes of collection and extension, and quickness, to guide the horse through an obstacle course. It is part of the tradition of mounted games, or gymkhana, that is among the oldest form the sport takes and, to add to its colorful effect, is done only by women. The sight of the horses leaning almost sideways, like ships keeling over, into the barrels, is thrilling to the spectator, so just imagine how it must feel to the competitor.

Pros

There's a unique satisfaction to be had in perfecting a practical skill with flair. Cooking and carving, rowing and woodwork—all bring this sense of core accomplishment, and it seems to be the soul of reining, roping, and barrel racing. Then, of course, there is the inner child to be considered, the one who wanted to be a cowboy, or go really, really fast, or liked the twists and turns of barrel racing as a child.

If part of your entry or re-entry into riding has to do with wanting to plunge into new worlds, then the Western circuits, like the hunt world, are a unique, spicy, hearty culture unto themselves.

You could hardly come to grips more directly with the best and boldest of original American riding than by entering into this exciting field, and if you've only glimpsed it from afar, you really will be encountering a range of very different characters, as writer Thomas McGuane, quoted at the start of this chapter and a reining competitor himself, can attest. When you ask this much of an animal, you get a lot back, a real partnership forged by the two of you. And when you ask this much of yourself, you are enhancing your skills in a thrilling and satisfying way.

The three Rs, reining, racing, and roping, require both precision and boldness, and if you demand that your sport have these characters, either because they complement or contrast with the life you're currently leading, you'll be well rewarded.

Cons

A successful plastic surgeon I know, now in his sixties, discovered riding about a decade ago, along with his wife and partner, a small, slender woman. Although they live in hunt country in upstate New York, when they thought of riding they thought of the romantic West, and they began to teach themselves reining and barrel racing. Several injuries later, they decided that this was not, after all, the wisest leisure pursuit for middle-aged amateurs. All of this is to say that we're breakable to begin with and become more breakable with age. While cowboys as depicted in the media seem to dwell in some perpetual grizzled twilight, aged but ageless, in reality, most rodeo riders and cowboys learn young. It's not just their strength, but the whole lightning disposition of muscle and sinew, the quick reflexes, they exemplify. These are harder to develop later in life, as is the sheer nerve required for some of these maneuvers.

The term *weekend warrior* has come to define the late twentieth–century to early twenty-first–century leisure experience but might turn out to have truly savage implications in the context of Western competitive riding. More than almost any discipline other than hunting and all-out three-day eventing, roping, reining, and barrel racing call for more fitness and focus if you're to participate safely and pleasurably.

And the degree of skill required means, almost certainly, a seasoned mount, ideally your own, and regular work with a trainer. My rather mad friends taught themselves but would now probably be the first to say that this was foolhardy. (Actual rodeo riding remains a professional sport and a very competitive one to breach; unless you're having a serious midlife crisis, this is probably not a practical option.)

Leisure and Competitive Opportunities

Reining

With the slow dissolution of boundaries between the East and West Coast, more and more disciplines are practiced around the country. You're not going to find a plethora of rodeos in the eastern states, but, as noted, many local shows with a Western component and breed shows for Arabians, paint horses and pintos, and quarter horses usually have reining classes. The discipline has recently been recognized as an official USEF show sport, which should help it to establish an even firmer hold on the show world and open up more regional prospects.

Cutting

Opportunities in cutting are somewhat less common than those in reining as they involve work with real cattle! Some facilities do offer lessons using a simulated, mechanical cow, or lessons combining a mechanical cow with real cattle.

Barrel Racing

Barrel racing classes are hugely popular in the American Southwest and gaining ground elsewhere. There are crowded show calendars and many regional organizations.

As we've seen, other than the dexterity and fluency of motion given by trail riding, there really is no leisure side to these energetic pursuits. But there are equestrian classes which recognize that the form has become a refined discipline, calling for precision and focus from the rider, and that it's not just an imitation of life transferred to the show ring.

Ranch Riding

A new branch of Western competitive riding, ranch riding, has grown up recently, with an emphasis on all-round practical skills, including trail, cutting, and working ranch horse segments. The competitions are overseen by the American Quarter Horse Association; see this link for a more detailed explanation: www.horseshowcentral.com/flex/ranch_horse_competition/446/1.

Clothing and Equipment

As with Western pleasure classes, reining and rodeo attire hints at the Wild West, though with less of a nightclub patina. Dressy shirts, bandannas, and cowboy hats are the costume of choice, but need not be elaborate.

Participation Opportunities

Stock riding—the practical work with livestock from which many of these contests derive—is something a lot of people who participate grew up with and later decided to take up competitively, rather like musicians in New Orleans or circus performers. Still, with interest and determination, it is possible to break through the calico ceiling. As with eventing, your most likely source of information is your trainer or barn.

Training Opportunities

Like many of the disciplines, stock riding is gaining in recognition and participation figures, and this is the sort of trend that drives and shapes a training industry. Instructors focusing on these areas may be fewer and farther between on the East Coast, but those that are based in the eastern states are eager to proselytize. Again, beware of the stable that just offers "Western" riding without seeming to know or care about the distinctions, as this label can, regrettably, mean nothing more than a Western saddle slapped on the back of a jaded school horse.

10

Endurance and Competitive Trail Riding

History and Overview

There have always been adventurers, but for most people, life itself, until well into the nineteenth and twentieth centuries, was perilous enough. Travel was arduous. War and pestilence were common; untamed nature and brigands plagued the roadways—when there were roadways. Blink the camera's eye, and we're in the early twenty-first century, where, for mechanized countries at least, our most significant day-to-day hazard is the traffic jam.

It's no wonder, then, that the last decade of the twentieth century produced the burgeoning of adventure travel and extreme sports. Even riding, which had evolved fairly elaborately from the battlefield to the arena, had to have its representative extreme sport: endurance riding.

The American Endurance Ride Conference was founded in 1972 and sanctions more than seven hundred rides per year. It is the companion and successor to the many trail riding associations that have been in existence since the 1920s, when the U.S. Cavalry helped impel the sport by conducting endurance tests for its horses.

Basic Technique

Endurance riding is to trail riding as competitive swimming is to wading. The technique used to elicit the basic gaits (walk, trot, jog, canter, lope, depending on your discipline) becomes a refined strategy for creating sustained fitness and peak performance over a long distance. Endurance rides range from twenty-five to one hundred miles, usually take place over several days, and often involve marked trails and time limits.

The rider's position in the saddle needs to be balanced and relaxed. This pursuit (along with trail and trekking holidays) probably offers the closest approximation to a world in which people once rode everywhere, and the endurance rider is more likely than most to encounter mountainsides, running rivers, and rugged terrain—think of it as trail riding with a sting in its tail. The whole of endurance riding is the culmination of an extensive fitness program, and in that sense, your riding is both always and never casual. It's also a discipline that has melded the various riding techniques. Practitioners derive from both English and Western traditions, so this might be a venturesome next step for you regardless of how you first come to riding.

Pros

While Arabs—the original long-distance horses—dominate the sport, people compete on all manner of mounts. Unless you're dead set on winning (and if you are, there's an Arab somewhere with your name on it), endurance is a sport where refined antecedents and vast expense matter less than good heart, good legs, and sound training. While it requires plenty of stamina, it is not especially risky, except for the toughest terrain-covering rides. And the opportunity to see the outdoors in this intimate and challenging way is rarer and rarer in everyday life. Now a world-class pastime, rides can take you as far away as Australia and

South Africa. Endurance rider Patty Katucki, a concert musician by profession, says that she enjoys it because she can "ride hard and fast"—as neat a sentiment as ever appeared in a John Ford movie.

Endurance riding is also grown-up friendly. According to sources within the community, a significant proportion of participants are over forty.

Cons

Endurance means just that. This is tough work and requires months of dedicated riding to get you and your horse fit. (The physical examination of horses after rides makes it impossible for somebody with an unfit horse to win.) Its advantages are also its challenges—exposure to inclement weather, potential discomfort, and anything else nature has to offer. For the serious competitor, travel and specialized tack are a necessity. The tack, at least, isn't as expensive as English equipment and is frequently made out of easy-to-clean synthetic material.

Leisure and Competitive Opportunities

Endurance riding faces some of the same challenges as eventing in terms of access to land, and it is not yet so well established that you'll find quite as many endurance rides as ring shows. But the field is growing. It was recognized by the Fédération Equestre Internationale (FEI), the international supervisory body, in 1978 and became the fifth U.S. team sport in 1993. While international team competition is not, of course, the likely goal of the average adult rider, it does mean that interest and awareness levels get raised, which often helps a sport at the local level. However, because endurance rides can last for several days, during which you have (relatively) unsupervised responsibility for the animal, this is a difficult field to pursue without your own horse.

Clothing and Equipment

Gear for endurance has become increasingly specialized, reflecting the need for comfortable, lightweight, flexible all-weather gear and saddles (reverting to some of the older forms) that are comfortable to sit in for long periods of time. The assumption, as with skiing or mountain climbing, is that the participant will be willing to spend a little extra to secure a comfortable and effective ride, and this is one area where economizing too much goes against the grain of common sense. A good endurance saddle can list for as much as a good all-purpose saddle, in the $750–$1,400 range. For the economy minded, lots of people also do the shorter rides (twenty-five to fifty miles) in dressage saddles (which are squarer and flatter than jumping saddles). A synthetic saddle brand called Wintec, which is waterproof, is also popular.

Participation Opportunities

This field is dominated by adults, many in their mature years, and many sanctioned events make it easy to at least make contact. The American Endurance Ride Conference is proactive about the establishment and maintenance of trails, which helps to promote growth in the sport. The AERC has information on its many regional events and links to the international community.

Training Opportunities

Training in this field is less formal and requires more perseverance and self-motivation than fields such as hunt seat and dressage, with their strong academic traditions. Mentoring is a common form of learning here; fortunately, as long as you don't abuse the privilege, dedicated riders are generous with their time and knowledge.

Competitive Trail Riding

A related field to endurance, though under different auspices, is that of competitive trail riding, also known as "judged pleasure," "judged trail," or, wittily, "trail trials." Like Alice's looking glass, this discipline has magnified the show ring trail class with its set obstacles and returned it to the outdoors, thus bringing the sport full circle. The competitions range from endurance-type distance rides to funfests with artfully placed fallen logs or manmade obstacles and distances ranging from ten to one hundred miles.

As with endurance, training and resilience count most, and at the lower levels many of these competitions (again, most are concentrated in the West and Southwest) are both informal and inexpensive. Key elements for entry are a secure local base in an area where such rides are offered and a training environment, both in the ring and outdoors, that allows for the dedicated hours you need to put in with your horse. A horse of your own is almost a must here, and many types of horses can successfully enter into this sport.

11

Polo

A polo handicap is your passport to the world.

—**Winston Churchill**

History

Racing has always been known as the sport of kings, but for many years polo has been the sport of princes—Arabian or the potentates of commerce who could afford this pricey sport. Think of it as some combination of golf, tennis, and croquet, but on horseback. Versions of the game (some involving dead animal carcasses) have been around in remote Eastern regions for thousands of years, with the first recorded match taking place (Persians versus Moguls) in 600 BC.

The modern game as we know it today was codified in the mid-nineteenth century by an Irish cavalry officer, Captain John Watson, and was taken up enthusiastically by the British merchants and military men living in India at the time of the Raj. Polo traveled to America at about the same time; this was the era of the Grand Tour, and wealthy Americans were eager to bag European culture in all forms. (Improbably, the first recorded American match took place in the middle of New York City's Fifth Avenue.)

Today, it has inspired an entire equestrian subculture. It is played internationally, of course, but in the Americas is dominated by South American pros who travel to various parts of the United States to help manage the teams of wealthy *patrones* (pronounced pa-TRON-ess) who keep strings of polo ponies and play matches throughout the May–October season, culminating in end-of-season tournaments. Players are ranked according to an elaborate numerical system (ten is highest), like golf handicaps, and low-ranked *patrones* usually play flanked by their dazzling pros. This tactful cadre tries to orchestrate play so that the wealthy backer gets a chance to hit the ball occasionally, before taking matters into its own hands to bring a chukker (the playing period of polo) to a thrilling conclusion.

Why am I telling you all this? Well, I'm telling you because there has been a slight softening of the upper crust, and some polo clubs are packaging affordable lessons for people other than those knee-deep in sources of unlimited wealth.

Basic Technique

In some respects polo is a sport most easily taken up before your own riding style has had a chance to conform to one of the other disciplines because it is the least traditional of all riding styles. Most horse sports emphasize the rider's control over the animal, a centered position with direct and even rein contact allowing the rider to direct the horse, to push him to adopt a particular gait or rhythm, or to clear a fence. In polo, your sole focus is on the ball—hitting it yourself or preventing others from doing so—and your riding must be adapted to this end. A secure seat is important so that you can more confidently and safely lean over to swing your mallet, which moves in an arc over your shoulder (a motion rather like bowling, but quicker and more exaggerated; croquet is another good model).

Your stirrups are likely to be longer for polo than for the English hunting-derived sports, and your leg farther forward than for any style of Western pleasure or stock riding. Added to this, you must eventually be able to perform this swinging maneuver while cantering, or galloping, down the length of the polo field in the face of opposing players.

Indeed, the other key distinguishing feature of polo *is* that it is an aggressive team sport, with all that implies. You must be able not only to accurately secure the ball when the opportunity presents itself, but to move it along the field quickly and efficiently and know when to pass it to another player. And you must do this without endangering yourself, your pony, or other riders.

While all competitive equestrian disciplines have certain protocols, polo, being a competitive team sport, has more than most, and in addition to learning to play, you will need to learn the history of the game, how teams are organized, and rules of the field in order to play effectively and correctly.

Pros

As a recent convert to polo, I cannot begin to tell you how much sheer fun this somewhat helter skelter sport is. At the modest level at which I was learning, a kindly pro shepherds you around a ring or field, helping you refine your swing, and then lets you loose with other class members for a mild game known as "stick and ball." The mock ferocity and skirmishing are exhilarating, as is the moment when you actually score a goal or prevent someone else from doing so.

This zestful game is also community building; it is fun to play with friends, and new polo "families" quickly develop, according to the United States Polo Association (see below).

Ironically, although polo is billed as one of the world's most expensive sports because of the costs associated with maintaining teams and a stable full of ponies, for the lone amateur it requires little investment; horses and equipment can be provided by training stables (although if you become seriously enamored, you may want to acquire your own mallet), and you can ride in jeans, with flexible gloves and a good helmet. (Teams have their own colors, of course, but it will probably be some time before you have to worry about this level of investment, and even then, the expense is on the order of outfitting your teen for baseball.)

Cons

For the traditional rider or anyone who is tentative, polo is at first disconcerting, as the focus on hitting the ball and on running and blocking means that you are often sitting lopsidedly in the saddle and moving at a variety of ill-regulated speeds.

And even though there are polo clubs in many areas of the country, they are still not as generously seeded about as regular riding establishments; you can wind up driving quite a long way to a lesson. Clubs are also variable in their culture and orientation. While some are clearly designed to give anyone interested a crack at the game, others are unquestionably dominated by wealthy *patrones*, their entourage of Argentine pros, and aggressively fashionable women dripping with name-brand accessories—a society not easily breached by those of us with more modest means and habits.

Another thing to bear in mind, as noted in the technique section, is that the sport, curiously, is not actually about horses at all. While the ponies (a term used for any equine team member, although many are above the maximum pony height of 14.3 hands) are your means of conveyance and while you wind up with a healthy respect for their energy and dexterity, you are not really focused on your mount during a game. You are not there to develop a bond or relationship, or to worry about what they are thinking and feeling—some of the key pleasures of other types of riding. (The pro with whom I took lessons was somewhat bemused when I asked the name of my pony.)

Training and Competitive Opportunities

As of this writing, the United States has just elected its first African-American president, despite the popular assumption that such a moment was a long way in the country's future, so it is not such a leap to see other long-held assumptions toppled at the same time. The U.S. Polo Association is working hard to correct what it perceives as the many misconceptions surrounding polo—that it is only for the rich, for those with horses, for men, or for the young and glamorous. Instead, it points out that there are polo clubs all over the country within the reach of ordinary folks and forming low-level teams for intramural competitions. And, particularly relevant to your concerns, the association points out that people can learn to ride and learn to play polo at the same time. The association is listed in appendix B, "Resources," and its website includes a detailed description of the game and its history, a directory of clubs, and a section targeting adult riders.

12

Out of the Saddle Driving, In-Hand, Minis

I'd like to say that there is no age at which riding is not a possibility and a pleasure, but in truth, your heart may have been stirred by horses when you're past the age when actually being in the saddle is practical or comfortable. Or you may suffer other infirmities of the type that creep up on one with age. I've always been of the opinion that before twenty, all physical ailments seem to be the invention of commercials.

Happily, none of this will keep you from enjoying horses. Age and infirmity are not the only issues, after all. It would be doing a great disservice to the variety and complexity of the horse world were I not to introduce you to some of the disciplines, events, and communities that partner with the animal other than as a mount. (Also see chapter 29.)

Driving

The history of driving may be older than that of riding. Once horses were domesticated and mobility became increasingly important to early tribes, the horse's other potentials were soon explored.

Of course, the other, more spectacular use of driven horses was in war and such war-derived games as chariot racing. The passage of time removed the horse and chariot from the battlefield to the road—a boon to both commerce and social life—and from there to the park and track.

Driving competitions were commonplace in Europe by the end of the nineteenth century. Now one of the fastest-growing of the equestrian sports, competitive driving has come full circle, enacting exciting mock battles against nature and other competitors in combined driving events. This is, of course, in addition to the long history of professional harness racing, which is not relevant here.

Europe's "golden age of coaching," from which many of the driving styles, carriages, and competitions originated, was between 1750 and 1850. First mail coaches (like Wells Fargo) and then public stagecoaches served travelers, literally paving the way for commercial long-distance travel. At the same time, a tradition of private pleasure driving grew up, becoming the hub of genteel social life in both environments.

The last carriages were on the road as functional vehicles in both the United States and the United Kingdom up to World War I. These then receded to museums, private collections, and shows as the luminous ghosts of a vanished world.

In social life, horses and carriages were common in both urban and rural landscapes. They conveyed neighbors to luncheons, teas, and dinner parties (think of Jane Austen—the many film adaptations of her novels of genteel eighteenth-century life have called for the re-creation of a vanished equine culture). Well-born young men had a chance to show off their status in amateur driving clubs. In the cities, driving in the then-extensive parks offered an opportunity not only for fresh air and novelty, but for flirtation and courtship. Indeed, carriages were the precursors of all the forms and functions we now associate with cars, with heavy broughams conveying long-distance travelers from inn to inn, and at the opposite end of the scale the flashy phaeton, plaything of gilded youth, acting the role of the Jaguar, MG, or Hispano-Suiza. Vehicles, now lovingly cherished by collectors, were also crafted to accommodate class and gender distinctions. There were dainty ladies curricles (not for driving themselves, of course, which was a rare and daring phenomenon) and "governess carts," which were modest and boxy and designed to be pulled by a pony. The gig and the surrey were more in line with the basic Subaru or Toyota, and there were plenty of precursors to the pickup truck. While competitive driving evolved into today's driving trials, social driving has engendered show, exhibition, and "park" driving classes.

Basic Techniques and Context

Driving styles don't differentiate quite as much as riding techniques and positions, but considerable confidence, strength, and dexterity are required to keep one or more horses balanced in a rig. The basic hand position for driving is like an inversion of the hand position in English riding, with the palms resting upward and the reins running freely, but not loosely, through the hands. It's almost as if you're at the end of an exceptionally long bridle.

The real challenge and science of driving is, of course, that you're directing the horse to maneuver a wheeled vehicle that has to be kept steady and balanced, and you're doing this not with aids transmitted through the body, but with hands, voice, and whip only. As Sally Eckhoff observed in an article on driving classes for the *New York Times*, "Without being able to touch my animal the way a rider does, it took longer to communicate the need to turn or stop." In addition to the traditional coaches and carriages historically established, competitive driving has created its own class of vehicles, and each of these demands its own approach, from farm wagons and small governess carts to the massive marathon competition vehicles for cross-country driving. Basically, however, you're dealing with one or more pairs of reins, and handling, as a rule, one to four animals—ranging from mules, miniatures, and ponies to some of the driving breeds such as Morgans and Hackneys to vast and magnificent draft horses.

Pros

While competitive combined driving events call for considerable strength and stamina, single-horse driving, either in the show ring or on prepared paths, doesn't require the same all-out physical effort and is enjoyed by many participants well into their senior decades. And as horses of almost every scale are included in the tradition, you can wind up with a size and type you feel comfortable with if the opportunity presents itself. Even the tiniest pony can compete.

A related pleasure is the fascinating culture of driving and the intricate beauty of many of the rigs. Participating in a driving competition is like getting a chance to relive a portion of history, with the appropriate etiquette and apparel. Carriage driving in period classes requires tremendous attention to detail and gracious elegance. At the same time, the experience, even just the look of the carriages, is a reminder of the courage and determination it took to convey people, goods, and livestock through uncharted, often perilous lands without locomotion.

And there may be a place for you even if you feel timorous about actually driving. Some competitive classes call for a navigator, and others require human "props" to round out the picture of a vanished age. Like being the guest of a restaurant critic, you get to dress up and sample the fare without being responsible for the critique or outcome.

Cons

The stable up the road isn't going to have a driving rig for you to try out casually. This is a discipline that must be actively pursued. It is absolutely essential that you be taught by someone competent, but driving doesn't have the reach or saturation of riding, so there aren't dozens of trainers in every region available to teach you. Nor is it easy to maintain at one remove—there are recreational driving classes, but if you want to keep it up, you're probably looking at a real investment. Of course, there's still an element of danger—it is hard to go abroad these days without encountering the noisy evidence of civilization, and there is always the possibility of animals bolting where there is traffic, noise, farm machinery, and the thousand and one perils the horse in its atavistic mien is prey to. This is always the case, but a carriage, with its wheels and spokes and weight, adds to the challenge.

Clothing and Equipment

Driving, like pleasure and hunt classes, is another one of those fields in which the whole history is encapsulated. In both leisure and competitive driving, every social stratum is represented, from farmers driving plows or market carts to grandees driving phaetons, so dress for park and pleasure classes is dictated by the vehicle. A key component to your kit will be a really good pair of gloves. Casual pleasure driving, or driving teams, is usually done in whatever you would wear around the barn, with the usual cautionary rule that sturdy boots are important for both comfort and safety.

One step up, sartorially speaking, is clothing for competitive combined driving events, where the "school figures" stage requires something akin to dressage, while the field components call for more rough and ready protective gear, including approved safety helmets. The marathon phase of a driving trial is rigorous work over varied terrain.

Then there are the competitive pleasure classes, where an attempt is made to re-create the whole lifestyle suggested by the vehicle you're driving. A "gig" might find you in a tweedy travelling costume suited to a well-bred nineteenth-century lady, and if you were in a governess cart, you would be dressed like Mary Poppins. Like hunt and pleasure class outfits, these reflect the greater detail and complexity of eighteenth- and nineteenth-century dress.

As you might imagine, this type of dress code calls for a bit of antiquing, which can be fun in itself. Your search would not be just for clothes, but also for props. Pleasure drivers can amass wonderful paraphernalia—dainty gloves, elaborate bonnets, flasks, and picnic baskets are among the items that can add verisimilitude to your presentation.

Correct dress is one of the elements on which individual drivers and teams can be marked, and judges can be insanely picky—one I heard about didn't like argyle socks and demoted competitors accordingly!

And then, of course, there is the harness, about which a whole history in itself has been written. Both functional and decorative, harness varies depending on the number of horses, the weight of the carriage or wagon being pulled, and the context. Often studded with decorative metal, driving harness needs to be both strong and supple, and is *not* inexpensive. Synthetic harness is making inroads for light-duty driving, however, and is a good idea to start with if you are not sure what your level of commitment will be.

Leisure and Competitive Opportunities

After almost vanishing from day-to-day life, driving is making a comeback as a sport. Many agricultural fairs around the country feature driving classes for draft horses, and breed shows for Arabs, Morgans, and Saddlebreds also include these classes. There is a competitive driving circuit, as there is for hunters and jumpers, offering a wide range of classes in and out of the ring. These shows have faced some of the same challenges as horse trials—dwindling land, financial constraints, and a constant need for volunteer labor. There's even an activist group that has been lobbying for the opening up of driving roads for pleasure.

Participation Opportunities

Driving is one of the few areas where riding is not naturally prejudiced toward children. The subtler pleasures of driving—the formality, the technical intricacy, the sense of calling up one or more pasts— simply resonate more fully in the mature mind. All of this is to say that the driving community eagerly welcomes adult additions to its ranks. And being adult sized is a great help. All-breed shows for horses with a driving legacy such as Morgans, Saddlebreds, Arabs, and Missouri Foxtrotters, have also kept driving alive. The American Driving Society has over sixty affiliate local driving clubs.

Training Opportunities

Like cooking or sewing—domestic skills that are often passed on through direct transmission—driving is something a lot of equestrians learned informally because they grew up on a farm or near one, or knew someone who loved it and kept the form alive. Consequently, most people's memories of learning to drive horses are a pleasant mixture of the concrete, the euphoric, and the nostalgic. This does not, of course, mean that you cannot come to this pleasure later in life. Local driving clubs offer lessons, and if the sport continues to grow, there will be more and more trainers drawn to it; like savvy ingenues and Wall Street traders, trainers follow the money. At least at present, driving is a peculiarly bifurcated discipline that traditionally has drawn almost exclusively from moneyed participants at its highest level and from land work at its lowest. It doesn't claim much middle ground at all, though this gap in its participation level is changing quickly. Now that the field is widening, however, there are more opportunities for formal training, but since driving is not yet as entrenched at a professional level, this is still a field where a little proactivity will go a long way. Contact the American Driving Society for a list of clubs; look for, and place, advertisements in your local papers; go visit people you see at shows; check bulletin boards and local tack shops; and look for mentions in such printed sources as *Rural Heritage* and *Small Farmer's Journal*, which cater to this generation's version of the gentleman farmer. Look for Morgan or miniature horse farms in your area—these often have a driving focus. And make a point of attending some of the dramatic draft horse pulling competitions at agricultural fairs. Though it takes years to develop these stupendous teams, some of these working farmers also give lessons. If you choose to buy your own horse, you may wind up with one of the breeds that has traditionally excelled at driving.

For those who crave a glimpse of real-world excitement, the United States Trotting Association even offers a hands-on seminar on professional harness racing, a sport with a growing amateur sector. I list this course in appendix B.

Out of the Saddle: Showing in Hand

In halter or "in-hand" classes, the conformation and movement of the horse are being judged. Unencumbered by tack or a rider, the horse stands at the end of a lead line held by the exhibitor, while the judge assesses physique, skin tone, musculature, and the relation of your horse to the breed's standard.

While any display of talent may reflect favorably upon a horse's background, it is in these in-hand classes that the focus is entirely on form, lineage, and potential. The casual observer may see only a display of talent and beauty, but interested parties see bloodlines and money.

There are classes for mares, stallions, colts, and fillies. In breed shows, these are for registered animals of the breed or accepted half-breeds. In open shows, halter classes are handler classes, where exhibitors' skills at presentation are being assessed, and any breed or mixed breed many be shown.

For these classes, it is the job of the presenter to show the animal (usually to walk and trot) to its best advantage. The rules vary somewhat, depending on the type of show and type of horse being shown, but this is the general rule. Young horses, like, say, young dancers, have few formal skills, but it is already possible to get some sense of overall conformation, line, freedom of movement, and spirit.

Historically, in-hand classes have been an extension of the big agricultural fairs where, depending on the economy of the region, everything from quality bloodstock to local 4-H projects were put on display. (See chapter 29, "Beyond Lessons.")

Then, as horse shows became more specialized, the proliferation of breed-specific shows began. In-hand classes became a regular feature, subtly re-emphasizing the way that breed shows, at least, are both competitions and trade shows. Breeding stables advertise their sires, dams, and offspring to other breeders and stimulate the interest of riders on the lookout for a quality animal.

Basic Technique

Horses are not large dogs, and *The Horse Whisperer* and similar volumes notwithstanding, it still requires skill, strength, and coordination to handle a horse at the end of a lead line. While a rider has a panoply of aids, body weight, and the benefit of close contact with which to telegraph commands to a horse, a handler has only hands, voice, and a schooling whip. And while conformation rather than performance is being judged, it is still the task of the handler to keep the horse (or foal, filly, or colt, as most classes are for the younger generation) both calm and obedient, and alert and compelling to the eye. At rest, this is done by keeping the animal standing square, usually with the head raised and attentive. In motion, you need to be able to trot beside your horse and have sufficient fleetness of foot to let a horse run at the end of a line without your getting run over or overpowered. The challenge, of course, is that you're continually dealing with the exuberant temperament of young animals, which is like leading 1,000-pound teenagers. (Foals, while lighter, are more skittish and can be quite a handful.)

Pros

I expect that somewhere in all of us who ride or wish to, is nevertheless a love of the untrammeled horse, displaying its natural beauty without the encumbrances that involve us as passengers. And while, as we see, considerable art goes into showing in hand, you're still fundamentally helping a horse, without the burden of tack or rider, be radiantly itself.

Possibly, too, as we've said, because of disposition—or indisposition—you no longer see yourself in the saddle, or riding is no longer a viable option for you. If you have sufficient physical confidence, here is another way to relate sensitively to horses.

Cons

While local shows often have in-hand classes to test horsemanship, competitions at breed shows are really a marketplace mechanism. Handlers are usually staff or owners of breeding operations, so it is hard to become an insider in an essentially professional world. Without some kind of entrée or the wherewithal to establish your own breeding and showing program, this may not be a practical choice. And while riding offers the twin attractions of schooling a horse and learning all the nuances of a particular discipline, showing in hand has limited application outside the show ring, thus limiting your options and potential relationship with the animal.

Leisure and Competitive Opportunities

This is another area where it will be helpful to be associated with a barn that is part of the community's network of shows. Stables that like to offer showing opportunities to their clients may well have horses that you can try showing in halter. However, for breed classes—for the very reason that halter and in-hand classes are meant to show off young livestock, thereby increasing their sale value and the reputation of their breeders—it is not always a realm that welcomes amateurs, unless you're willing to risk some disposable income on a single well-bred but unproven young animal. And riding stables, with the emphasis on—well— riding, don't have a stock of young animals available to train with. You may need to take the initiative and craft your own program here.

Clothing and Equipment

This may be as close as you'll get to a nine-to-five look in the horse world. Many handlers show in a suit, the theory being, no doubt, that the less you stand out, the more your horse will. In any event, this is certainly not one of the dress-up fields—a suit, breeches, and boots, even neat blue jeans at less formal events, are all appropriate. Women, inevitably, are a little dressier—chic trouser suits and slit skirts abound, as if the handlers were CEOs who happen to be conferencing with a horse.

For the horse, equipment is rarely more elaborate than a very good-quality halter and leather lead with a chain. In some classes, there are quite elaborate grooming requirements to highlight this or that feature of the breed, even if they're not wearing much more than their skin (oiling the contours of their faces, for example, so that they catch the light). These are high-strung youngsters, remember. Most trainers also carry a whip, which, like the liver treats and squeaky toys used at dog shows, are meant to get the horse's attention, to "set her up," not to chastise. (At most responsible shows, striking a horse will lead to at least elimination and sometimes more severe professional censure, such as the suspension of a license, though there are always an unscrupulous few who get around the rules.)

Participation Opportunities

As we've seen, age is less the issue here than experience or aptitude. Your best bet is to form an alliance with a barn, the kind of relationship that may grow naturally out of either your riding lessons or your purchase of a horse.

Training Opportunities

Here again is a gray area, one in which formal training mechanisms are not really evident. For the breed show circuit there is actually a potential dichotomy: many trainers also make their livings showing in hand for clients. What training in this realm does offer is an opportunity that's so often missing in more formalized and crowded equestrian environments: a real mentoring relationship. Unless the horses are your own, no one is likely to lead you through a trial-and-error period of handling horses without guidance. And this is the sort of guidance, compounded of technique, tradition, and sagacity, that makes romantic the notion of horse whisperers and their ilk. Here's where your local grapevine is going to work to your best advantage. Find out about breeding farms in your area; they may well offer opportunities.

Part II

Choosing to Learn

13

Learning to Learn

The noblest task of the riding teacher is to form the mind of the student as well, so that the latter comes to depend on the teacher less and less.

—Waldemar Seunig, *Horsemanship*

Choose your slogan: "Woodsman, mind thy axe," or "garbage in/garbage out."

Any way you describe it, when you're in the early stages of introduction or reintroduction to riding, the quality of your instruction dictates more than any other single element whether your enterprise is going to succeed. Everything from your understanding of the basic principles of riding to your sense of pride and accomplishment to your safety will depend on your relationship with your teacher. So don't, for goodness' sake, make this decision casually, by just wandering up the road to the nearest place that offers lessons.

One thing that makes this a crucial decision for mature riders, especially if you're coming to the sport for the first time, is that adults learn differently than children learn. Like our aging bodies, our minds are sometimes less supple, and our brains, laden with a lifetime of memories, anxieties, responsibilities, and thought patterns, may need to approach this skill, a fascinating combination of the mental and the kinetic, differently.

Then, too, this is a splendid period in which to enter or re-enter the sport. Riding has benefited from the revelations of sports psychologists and cross-fertilization from experts in many fields. We've also progressed into a much-improved potential for tracking who is teaching what. With so much potential, don't settle for a school that treats you like a lady who lunches or a football fan on horseback, and never settle for an instructor who thinks of you as a slovenly military recruit or an outsized Pony Clubber.

How Adults Learn

The attributes of the adult learner have come miraculously into focus in the business and education environments. Issues and challenges as disparate as job training and illiteracy, as well as the growing number of seniors returning to serious schooling, have affected a new awareness of how mature minds take up new knowledge.

Teaching and learning styles today are divided into two general approaches. (Professional educators have, of course, addressed this subject in depth; this is not meant to be more than the baldest summary.) Pedagogy, the type we're all familiar with from the schoolroom, derives from Greek words meaning to *lead* a child. In the late 1960s, theorist Malcolm Knowles is thought to have coined the term *andragogy* ("to lead a man") to define a different, adult-oriented model.

The two models are easiest to contrast by generating a corresponding list of opposing characteristics. It becomes obvious how much these might affect your experience as a rider.

Children versus Adults

Children are reliant; adults are self-determined. On the good side, this means that you've really chosen to devote yourself to riding and have come to your lessons already motivated. It also may mean, though, that you'll find it difficult to be told (by your pedagogical teacher!) to focus on the basics when you want to devote the hour to discussing the finer points of horsemanship or how stress always makes you cramp up.

Children expect to be taught; adults enjoy control. Even when you've placed yourself in the position of student, it can be harder to relinquish control than it was when you were young, whether you're a successful professional, a successful parent, or both.

Children accept what they are told; adults need valid information based on experience. Again, the upside is that any new idea a trainer presents may have myriad ways of making sense to you, of linking up with other beliefs and concepts. But if it doesn't, because you can't put the idea or instruction in context, you may be resistant to it. Adult learners are more likely to say, if only to themselves, "Prove it!"

Children expect learning to be useful eventually; adults, immediately. For children, the act of learning *is* the experience. For adults, it is a means to an end. You want to be in the show ring by the end of the season, say, so it's natural to expect every moment of your training to clearly be serving that goal. If the teacher can't explain the connection between opening up your hip joint and doing well on a dressage test, she may well lose you.

Children have little experience; adults have much. If your instructor views your life experience only as chatter and white noise that gets in the way of riding and teaching, she may not be resourceful enough to let you use your own capabilities fully.

Children are eager sponges for new knowledge; adults are used to being re-sources. If you are accustomed to being the sought-after authority or are simply a product of today's more team-oriented workplaces, you may be looking for a measure of reciprocity in your learning environment. If your teacher doesn't seem able to engage or feels flummoxed by a give-and-take approach, you may wind up feeling demeaned and rejected.

All of this is to say, despite your determination, you will not learn from those from whom you cannot learn.

14

Finding a Riding School

There are thousands of riding establishments in this country, from mom-and-pop trail riding operations to multimillion-dollar professional barns. Somewhere there is the right place for you, but you will need to put in some time identifying likely prospects and then arranging to visit them. A phone book, an ad, or a database entry tells you about location, financial health, or number of horses, acres, or staff. Unfortunately, there's no screening for bald or inflated language or outright misstatements that lead you to dull, distracted instructors, jaded, careworn mounts, and overcrowded schooling rings. So preliminary research is only a first step on your careful quest. Especially if you want to comparison shop and have a chance to see how different schools and instructors operate, a combination of old-fashioned and new-fangled approaches may give you the widest range of choices.

Here are some common research tools—low and high tech—and how they might work for you.

Word of mouth. "The friend of my friend is my friend." As with books, tastes in teachers and environments differ, but in such a goal-oriented field as riding, a positive recommendation from someone you know is at least worth investigating. This is especially true because so many aspects of what makes a school or trainer strong can be charted only by direct experience. By the same token, even superlatives can be fleshed out. The clichéd "experienced instructor" in the mouth of an enthusiastic patron can turn into the one who's "great at explaining how you can relax your back and lower leg," who leads the way to *finally* understanding canter departs," or—best of all—has you announcing, "I'm not frightened anymore." And friends aren't the only primary sources. Tack shops are often good sources of information. They should have a regular client base of people riding in the same area, and shopping and gossip make good bedfellows. Like bartenders, an amiable tack shop owner is the recipient of confidences about frustrated lessons and disappointing clinics, and is also useful just for identifying stables in your area.

Riding publications and local papers. There is a profusion of horse magazines for every type and temperament. While national publications tend to have advertisements for major brands of horse feed and gear, you might also see announcements for schools, especially those that have special programs such as summer camps for adults or clinics. In addition, many regions have local horse publications, often free and lying in piles at the tack shop. These are a particularly good source because in addition to their listings, their coverage of area competition could highlight a particular trainer or facility. Most of them, however, are casually produced. You won't find many back issues. You might not even be able to find the index, so there is a certain element of serendipity about these journals as a resource.

The Internet. The Internet can be a great resource as well, now that low-cost software has put the technology within almost everyone's reach. Many riding schools now have full presentations on their sites—location, driving directions, lesson schedule, instructors and their backgrounds, classes and special events, and a glimpse of the on-site horse population. You can get a good sense of the barn's orientation and culture even before you visit it.

Don't skip that all-important visit, though. Even the best graphics can't really convey the feel of a place. By the same token, don't be a cybersnob. The modest dressage barn where I took lessons for a year is a brother-and-sister operation with little extra cash to spare on things like a website, but these thoughtful and articulate professionals were at the center of their discipline and certified to teach at very high levels.

Telephone directories. The old Yellow Pages advertising slogan, "Let your fingers do the walking," points up one straightforward way to begin your quest. This, however, does present some disadvantages. Basic telephone directory listings (providers vary by region) don't tell you much, and many are now exclusively online. They simply supply telephone numbers under generic business and consumer headings. Display advertisements, a feature of many phone books, and Internet sites will give some sense of orientation and perhaps physical circumstances ("Olympic-size arena, five miles of trails," etc.) but are sometimes opaque or misleading. And there's another problem: they tend to be far from comprehensive because the riding community, often eccentric and clannish, doesn't necessarily think to advertise itself.

Databases. For the purely quantifiable approach, business database references are better because they're created by independent publishers who research a variety of sources—business name registrations, tax filings, Yellow Page listings, and more. These database programs, which are available for purchase (online or in CD-ROM formats), are common in business and well-endowed public libraries. You might have access to them through your company's library or information center. They are searchable by a variety of useful fields, including SIC or SSC numbers assigned by the government to all business categories and service organizations. There are two that are relevant to riding stables. One identifies places that define themselves principally as boarding establishments, and the other, those that define themselves principally as schools. There are also fields for number of employees and income, which help to distinguish large from small establishments. Once you have identified a list, you can even sort by zip code to find the ones nearest to you. (This is how I found my dressage instructor.)

You might be lucky and find the riding school of your dreams on your first foray, but as with any other kind of shopping, don't persuade yourself that the first place you see will "do." If you feel as if something is missing, keep looking. You're going to be spending a lot of time there, so it should be a good fit.

15

Choosing Your School

Let's assume that you have identified two or three places you'd like to consider as your lesson barn. Next comes the crucial step of knowing how to assess them, to evaluate what you see. As with nannies, caterers, schools, and other instructional and service-oriented relationships, or all pet purchases, you're likely to proceed with equal parts common sense and emotion. This is a meeting of an individual (you) with the temperament, regimes, and rhythms of a place (and of course its teachers, about which more later).

Planning Your Visit

Allow plenty of time for your site survey. If possible, try to see more than one school in a day—it will help you to make comparisons (if you have arranged to have a demonstration lesson, this may not be practicable, of course). And you might want to bring a (patient!) friend. Sometimes two impressions are better than one.

It goes without saying that you should call in advance if you plan to visit a school so that someone will be available to speak with you.

During the busy season instructors often have lessons back to back starting early in the morning and running well into the evening. Some facilities have managers, but they, too, will be pulled in a dozen directions, and you want to be sure you don't get short shrift in a day full of crises.

Don't worry that making an appointment in advance will mean you won't get a candid look at the place. Riding schools—indeed, any working stables—are far too busy to institute cleanup sessions just for potential clients.

First Impressions

First of all, how does the place strike you at first glance? Start with the trip itself. Is this somewhere it will be easy and convenient for you to get to and from? That forty-five-minute drive seems like an adventure when you are in quest mode, but do you really want to make that effort once or twice a week in all weather?

Then assess the physical characteristics. Are the buildings well maintained? Is there light and air, or does everything seem dark and cramped? Is there pastureland? Why should this matter to you? Because it matters to a horse, whose physical surroundings and comfort help to shape his health and spirit. Do take a moment to walk around the barn before announcing yourself if you can, since you can't be sure how much of a tour you will get as simply a possible student. Stables devote more time, naturally, to displaying physical amenities to potential boarders. While most stables sell lesson packages to help create a steady stream of revenue (imagine a subscription series for horses), boarders—at anywhere from $250 to $1,350 a month, depending on where you are in the country—are where the money is.

Site Seeing

What kind of appearance should you expect? Not necessarily glamorous. Large, well-ordered show stables have hordes of staff to keep their brass polished, their flowers fresh, and their floors swept constantly. Smaller establishments usually don't. Instead, a single barn manager, if there is one, or the owner or owners, commands a motley assortment of immigrant labor, teenage girls, and part-time professionals (this mix will vary, depending on what part of the country you're in), and it's often a challenge for them to keep up with basic chores.

You may already have some idea of the sort of place you'd be most comfortable, especially if you are a returning rider, but if not, be sure you are thinking about that as you begin to look. Do you prefer intimacy or bustle? Do hordes of teenagers raise your spirits and your energy level or make you feel ancient and invaded by Visigoths? (Or perhaps you have several at home and would rather like to get away from this age group for a while.)

And, as I've said, physical appearances can be deceiving. A short-lived equestrian center in New York City had an Olympic-sized arena, a waterfront view as gorgeous as an impressionist painting—and the service standards of your basic gym franchise.

Creature Comforts: Horses

How are the horses kept? Do the stalls have windows, and are they open? Does the bedding seem to be deep and relatively clean? (Mucking out stalls usually starts early in the morning and continues into the day, depending on the ratio of horses to staff.) No barn is truly perfectly sanitized, horses being what they are, but you can easily recognize the rank smell of neglect.

Is there fresh water? This is a key element to horses' well-being, so a barn that neglects this may well be neglectful in other areas, too.

What is the condition of the horses? The appearance of the horses themselves is also important but may be difficult to assess. Horses look as frowsy as the rest of us first thing in the morning, and even later in the day a grubby-looking animal may be awaiting a laggard owner rather than suffering from substandard care. You should, of course, keep an eye out for obvious signs of *real* neglect—very thin horses with dull coats, runny noses or eyes, or sores. (In some cases, such places, and there are such places, are not only worth avoiding, but worth reporting—see appendix C, which lists a number of animal welfare organizations.)

Creature Comforts: People

In most barns, the horses come first, and that's as it should be. Nevertheless, you're going to be spending time here, too, so it's worth considering the amenities. Is there a bathroom? Heated offices? Heated ring? Heating—period? If you are visiting in spring or summer, you may not be thinking about what it will be like to ride in the real cold, so ask. Mind you, an unheated barn is *not* a sign of neglect or an indication of a substandard establishment. Central heating is expensive, and horses can be rugged up in cold weather, so many barns don't bother to heat their rings. The real issue is your comfort level and hardihood.

Next, is there a gallery that allows for the observation of lessons? (This is usually a corridor along the back or side with a low wall separating it from the arena.) While not an essential, watching lessons can be terrifically educational. If you're in an urban area, where you might be coming back and forth on public transport as opposed to having a car you can lock, are there secure arrangements for valuables?

Check to see whether there's somewhere to make tea or coffee—this can be a godsend on a cold day or when you have early morning lessons.

The Lay of the Land

One of the most important features of a riding school, other than decent accommodations for the horses, is the riding arena or arenas. Indoor arenas usually come in a range of standard sizes. Outdoor rings tend to be more variable in size, and sometimes come in more than one form—an enclosed arena for jumping and basic lessons, for example, and a rectangular dressage arena for practicing tests in this discipline, or an additional large, unenclosed area for jumping. Schools affiliated with particular disciplines sometimes try to replicate competitive environments as much as possible, so one whose students do competitive trail riding might have a ring with a mock obstacle course set out.

Now you want to get a sense of the physical, as well as the psychic, environment. Stables come in quite a few styles, and while you're not making your choice based on architectural merit, some designs contribute significantly to atmosphere. French stables, for example, are often built around a courtyard, which makes for great spaciousness and elegance and easy access to all parts of the building. The traditional model is a long corridor, or parallel corridors, with stalls facing one another on both sides (so that the horses can see and talk to one another). Though not always possible, it's a particularly good sign if the horses have stalls with windows facing outward—it's a sign that the comfort of the horses, as well as the people, has been considered.

"A Clean, Well-Lighted Place?" Glancing down the aisle in a large or midsize barn, you are likely to see a lot of bustle, and possibly wheelbarrows, buckets, shovels, brooms, and so on. Again, you're not seeking decorum, but signs of carelessness or negligence—pitchforks with their dangerous tines lying in the aisle (anything lying in the aisle really poses a danger to volatile animals), coils of wire, protruding nails. I'm reminded of an essay by the food writer M. F. K. Fisher about what you could tell about a restaurant from the way its dishes, floors, and kitchen smelled.

What about the tack? The tack room (where equipment for the horses is kept) is also worth a look. There is always a certain amount of chaos in the jumble of saddles, bridles, and other equestrian paraphernalia, but each item should be racked or hung in some fashion, and it should smell clean and leathery, not damp and musty. Again, why do you care if you are only coming for lessons? Because badly maintained tack is uncomfortable for horse and rider.

Now that you've done your own private site seeing, you are ready to announce yourself if someone has not already asked who you are. If they haven't, this isn't necessarily a sign of poor management. Most people at working barns are overworked and task oriented; if you're not their business, they won't add you to their list of concerns—another good reason for phoning ahead.

Your Type of People?

If you arrange your barn visit for a weekend, you'll probably get a good look at the clientele, another important factor in your selection process. Barns have demographics and personal cultures, just like any other organizational milieu, and you want to be sure that you will feel at home. (Remember those thirteen-year-olds I mentioned earlier?) Don't necessarily expect to find only adults—children and teens are the bread and butter of many barns—but do check to see whether there's a reasonable mix of ages. As I'll discuss in the chapter on choosing an instructor, this is not just to soothe your vanity, but because teaching children is different from teaching adults. Instructors accustomed only to toddlers and 'tweens may not know how to bring out your best, and instructors accustomed only to tourists may not realize you have a best to bring out.

Lesson Plan

Now we come to the real basis of your choice of school: the lessons and those who teach them, both human and equine. In riding, just as in martial arts, dance, or music, lessons are not just a means to an end, not just meant to get you from here to there in one piece. Lessons, with their discipline and focus, are part of a journey in which you and your horse or horses draw closer together. Your classes are part of the ritual of horsemanship that will soon become part of your life, both physically and psychologically. I used to scoff at those metaphysical running books about endorphin highs and glorious "burns," but there is something in it. (Keep this in mind on those mornings when you can't see the point of trading your warm bed for a cold barn.)

And with horsemanship, you get not only the immediate sense of pleasure, but the knowledge that you are part of a tradition that is as old as civilization itself.

This is why the next step in your investigation is to arrange for a sample lesson. This will give you a more intimate glimpse of the workings of the school, and most importantly, give you a feel for the character and personal style of the instructor or instructors.

Classes and Structure

Most places offer three tiers of lessons—individual, semiprivate (two people), and group (three or more). Which is right for you depends on finance, temperament, and learning style, as well as what kinds of classes are available from a particular school.

If you are a first-time rider or a tentative returning one, you may want to start out with individual lessons, and indeed, it's quite common for a school to ask that you do so while you get familiar or reacquainted with the basics. After that, though, there's much to be said for larger classes. You can learn from watching others, you develop some camaraderie, and you're not the sole focus of the instructor's attention, which can be stressful. Those times when he or she is focused on another rider are opportunities to quietly solve problems and get to know your mount. Semiprivate lessons work especially well if you and the other rider are at the same level, and one of the questions you should explore initially is what groups would be available to join and whether anyone's looking for a lesson partner.

Cost is another reason for exploring these options. As with any discipline, consistent practice yields the best results, and costs can really mount if you are riding once or twice a week. And, speaking of costs. . . .

How Much?

Lesson prices vary dramatically around the country, not just state by state, but region by region. A working average scale might be forty-five to eighty-five dollars for private lessons, thirty-five to sixty dollars for semiprivates, and thirty to fifty dollars for groups. Rising fuel costs have impacted riding schools as they have other businesses; increases in the cost of feed and supplies are being passed on to the customer. If rates are way above the ranges I've indicated, you should definitely shop around before committing; if way below, instructors are not really being adequately compensated, and quality may suffer. If you're committing, as you should be, to a course of lessons, most schools offer a discount if you buy a package. Ten lessons is common; some even having yearly rates.

This is for average, day-to-day instruction. Clinics and master classes with distinguished professionals usually run more like eighty dollars. Oh, not bad, you say. But if you are serious about your riding, don't approach your lesson as if they were a diet you were cheating on ("Just one, one's not so much"). You should be riding at least once—ideally, twice—a week during the full season. In colder regions, unless you have access to an indoor ring, instruction follows the law of diminishing returns for you, your frozen instructor, and your resentful and unlimber mount—this, however, is one of many variables. Assume, though, that you will be budgeting anywhere from forty to sixty-five dollars for lessons, and that doesn't count the cost of travel, clinics, or competitions. Costs can be reduced in two ways, as we've seen: by buying lesson packages, which are usually discounted, and by considering semiprivate or group lessons. Some establishments, like clubs, also have base membership fees that entitle you to a discount.

How Often?

Kinetic skills are learned only by repetition, for not only your brain, but your whole body must become patterned to the rhythm of the horse. The sequence of the aids, and the host of other adjustments that make you a rider and not a passenger, rely heavily on muscle memory, and that means practice. Also, you will get to know your animal and your instructor much better if you've got some continuity. Regularity also helps to maintain a general fitness level—while riding is not a matter of strength per se, general muscle tone and coordination do matter (see part III, "Choosing Safety"). Commitment also sharpens your focus and desire to learn, as I said earlier. You should ride at least once a week, twice if you can manage it.

License to Teach?

I'll talk more in the next chapter about how to determine whether you and your instructor are a match made in horse heaven, but in your preliminary conversation with the school's management and/or instructors, you'll want to find out something about the teachers' backgrounds.

In England, there is a rigorous certification program for riding instructors. They must, at least to set up as a business or work for an established school, be accredited by the British Horse Society. (Even this isn't always sufficient to screen out the oddballs—I was first taught by a mad Scots show jumper with dubious military credentials whose skills seemed to have derived from the early daredevils. It took several years of Pony Club to undo some of his harmful techniques.) In the democratic and decentralized United States, there is no such system nationwide. People's credentials and expertise, not to mention their teaching skills, come from all over.

Many trainers have evolved in communities where riding is a strong tradition. They have trained with other professionals, have often had long show careers, and have slowly moved into teaching. Many riders in the English discipline came up through the Pony Club system—a young riders' training program with regional chapters all over the country where juniors are taught both riding and stable management. (Think of an amalgam of "shop," Boy Scouts/Girl Scouts, and 4-H.)

Most of these instructors have mixed competition and training backgrounds; in place of certification, they offer alliances and connections and achievement—well-known riders with whom they've trained, or competitions they've placed in. Some disciplines, such as dressage, have begun to institute more oversight and do certify trainers to teach at various levels corresponding to the competition structure. And in an attempt to replicate the overall training and certification components of the British Horse Society, the American Riding Instructors Certification Program was established in 1984. The organization doesn't have the reach and influence of the BHS, but it's worth contacting for its list of certified instructors. (Quite a number of English and Irish expats work in the United States, and many are certified.)

One problem with this system is that the shaping of teachers is rather inadvertent—a splendid competitor doesn't necessarily, without guidance, make a skilled instructor. But the obverse is also true—competition sharpens skills that otherwise become rote repetitions of basic principles and give rise to insights that can become the foundation of new riding skills. And a maverick universe can give rise to truly visionary riding theoreticians such as Sally Swift, creator of the celebrated Centered Riding techniques. It's worth exploring the instructor's background a little, even if some of the techniques and disciplines that might be referred to are foreign to you now, at the early stage. Once you get the bug, believe me, you are going to begin to read voraciously, and you'll be able to link an instructor's commands or perspective to your newfound knowledge of the field.

Although you can't tell how a rider's credentials will translate into the ring, at the very least, hints of evasion or bluster should be your clues to beware.

What You Will Be Riding: Schoolmaster, Soured, and Everything in Between

Schoolmasters

Sentimental movies about revered schoolteachers are a cinema staple: *Goodbye Mr. Chips*, *The Prime of Miss Jean Brodie*, *Mr. Holland's Opus*. Mr. Chips especially was the quintessential schoolmaster (Robert Donat if you're older; Peter O'Toole if you're younger), gently but rigorously seeing generations of young men into adulthood. Well, there's a reason why certain school horses are known as schoolmasters and are every bit as beloved in their way.

These sage mounts—often older horses with distinguished competitive careers behind them—patiently and instinctively support and guide novice riders through their paces. (In her novel *Horse Heaven*, Jane Smiley has created the racehorse equivalent—a steady, equitable claims horse aptly named Justa Bob, who guides a nervous young jockey through his first races. When I did my first cross-country jumping schooling show in twenty years, my gentlemanly mount was a seasoned quarter horse called Bob.)

A schoolmaster is forgiving, but responsive. As Leslie Webb wrote in an article on buying schoolmaster horses, this is a horse you can learn on because, "He's safe and sane, reasonably easy to ride, well schooled, and responsive. He's not so sensitive and touchy that he can't or won't tolerate an amateur's honest mistakes. Yet he's not so totally push button that he'll do it right if you ask him wrong."

What's really remarkable is that good school horses are able to do this for dozens of different riders, but only if they are properly maintained. One key question to ask is how often each horse works each day. More than three lessons a day, ideally with some breaks, and they're moving toward burnout.

At their best they will school you, teaching you what a correct movement feels like, and give you the confidence to advance. A good school is serious about the selection of its mounts and will have horses at different levels ready to let their students progress. This alone can give you an exciting sense of accomplishment, for instance, the day you arrive for your lesson and have been assigned not Justa Bob (bless him), but the slightly more animated chestnut you've been admiring.

Be prepared, too, to fall in love. Riding is a lot like psychoanalysis, especially for stress-ridden modern adults, so there is a certain amount of transference. When you begin to make riding a regular part of your life, it becomes a therapeutic refuge, and you can develop terrific affection for the creature, be he gorgeous or humble, who has helped to make this possible. In an engaging piece for *Equus* on taking up riding at age fifty, Debbie Springarn wrote, "Turning 50? It's not so bad as long as you share it with someone special—like a gentle horse who will help you through your midlife crisis better than a red convertible ever could" ("No Better Time to Ride," January 2008). We'll consider this phenomenon again in part IV, on buying a horse.

Soured

In the early stages, all horses are going to seem large, with moving parts for which you have not been given the manual, which in turn makes you feel as if your own moving parts are somehow foreign as well. But eventually you will be able to distinguish between a horse who is not responding because you haven't asked the question correctly and a horse who is not responding because he's in a perpetual snit.

In a very real sense, horses are your other teachers in a riding lesson, and tired, jaded, or ungenerous horses can do as much to spoil the experience of riding as an inadequate instructor. Unfortunately, it may be hard to spot the plugs or pigs when you are a beginner.

This means that you may have to experience a cycle of lessons before deciding whether a school is right for you in the long term . . . and why it's worth taking lessons at several establishments and observing lessons if you have that option. If you're a rank beginner, the management is going to assign you relatively stolid mounts, so watching riders and school horses at a slightly higher level than your own may give you a more accurate picture.

Indoors or Out?

Many schools, especially well-established ones, have both indoor and outdoor rings, and more ambitious and fortunate ones also have additional land for outdoor training or trail riding. While natural amenities are not the only reason to choose a barn, you do want at least to feel comfortable and safe. One especially important component is footing—if the practice rings are rock filled or doughy and treacly, you are going to have a difficult time getting a horse to move smoothly through your lessons. If the ring is outdoors, are the fence lines well maintained? Does the ring border on a road (increasing the likelihood of spooking)? If indoors, are there mirrors (useful for assessing position); is it well lit and comfortable or gloomy and drafty? Is the ring a reasonable size? (Rings come in various proportions. Some that follow the guidelines for Olympic competitions have space to accommodate four to seven horses all working at once, while others are more, shall we say, intimate.) And how is the space being used? Are lessons given one at a time, or is the ring shared? Dividing up the ring and teaching more than one class in it at once is a common practice, as it helps to maximize the income of a stable and keep its instructors employed. It shouldn't pose a problem as long as the ring is of decent dimensions and the instructors can be heard above the inevitable background noise. More than two classes leads to cramping and confusion, however, and is a sign that the school has put its bottom line ahead of the well-being of its teachers or students.

The Barn Weltanschauung

As we saw in part I, what kind of rider—and competitor—you become will inevitably be dictated by the orientation and mission of the barn at which you ride. You'll want to know, if your initial research or the contents and layout of the facility doesn't make it clear, whether you've found a place that can give you the tools and opportunities you need, whether you want to study dressage or driving. This is also another way to find out something about the school horses—barns tend to look for animals that have a background in the areas they teach. Sometimes these older animals have had quite distinguished careers and can be excellent schoolmasters. Ask, too, about competitive opportunities if you think that somewhere along the line you might want to give showing a shot. If the school offers no opportunities, you don't want to feel discouraged or left out after you have formed attachments and ambitions. If you think you might be interested in trail riding, be sure to ask whether the school participates in or organizes these. Once you've got your "horse legs" you don't want to be stuck going around in circles when you long to be outdoors. Some barns will have literature in the office or posted on a bulletin board if they are involved in an event, which is common to barns that cater to children and junior riders, though adults are getting more attention than they used to.

Even if a barn doesn't have a lot of bells and whistles, it might still feel like a comfortable place for you to get started, to develop a feel for your new sport (or old sport revisited). You can always move on if you mature.

Bear in mind that I am outlining an ideal scenario. Many busy stables will propel you into an initial lesson rather than sit down to talk with you, and you'll have to garner the information you need from around the edges of a workday. But one way or another, be sure you come away with some information about the points I've outlined.

16

Your Teachers—Human and Equine

"No one can teach riding so well as a horse."—C.S. Lewis

The Sample Lesson

Once you've toured the barn, had the (hoped for) interview with the manager or instructor, and discussed prices, you've probably learned as much as you're going to from the ground. Next comes the all-important sample lesson.

This is a key moment of mutual assessment, and a test, too, of your own pluck and determination. I can tell you from painful personal experience that a first riding lesson may not be as exhilarating as you imagine. Your body has to adjust to a new frame and new rhythms. Oddly, the experience might be even more disconcerting if you are a returning rider because your mind remembers a degree of competence and suppleness that your body can no longer equal.

Momentary discomforts aside, this is the time to get a sense of your potential instructor. If he or she has asked you as many questions as you hope, that's a good sign. For example: Have you ridden before? How long ago? What sort of riding did you do? Did you compete? Did you own a horse?

But even more important than your past is your future—what you hope to get out of your riding now or, if you're too new to the sport to know yet, what kind of experience you envision.

What to Expect

For a sample lesson, your horse will probably be readied and brought out to you. (Once you're a regular, many barns expect you to do this yourself.) The first thing the instructor will (or should) do is check your tack (saddle, bridle, any pads, etc.). Even if the horse has been tacked up by a groom, you are an unknown factor, and they'll want to be assured of your safety. Also, many horses have a habit of "blowing up" when the girth or cinch is being tightened—taking in air and distending their bellies. So the saddle that was snug in the barn aisle might be loose enough to slide right around by the time you mount. Your stirrups may need adjusting as well, so that your leg has secure contact with the saddle but you are not trussed up like a jockey or dangling like a ragdoll.

If he or she has been told that this is your first ride, some time should be spent putting you at your ease with your horse and he with you. Learning to approach a horse carefully and calmly, how to stroke and reassure him, how to move around him efficiently, but not hastily or dramatically, has as much to do with horsemanship as any aid or position you'll learn.

If you're a complete beginner, the instructor will go over the basics: how to mount (from a mounting block, which saves wear on you, the horse, and the saddle); how to sit (the variation on the seat depending on whether you are riding English or Western); how to hold the reins (ditto); how to gently move the bit in the horse's mouth; how (theoretically) to use your hands and legs in concert and independently to apply signals (known as "the aids") to achieve the results you want. Which, at this stage, is basically, "Go" and "Whoa."

If you're a returning rider, the instructor will probably observe you going through the preparatory motions on your own, to get a sense of what you remember and what needs to be retaught or unlearned.

A memorable moment occurred during one of the earliest lessons I took after returning to riding. I was of a generation of riders many of whom were taught to grip with their knees for security. My instructor— an uninhibited woman with the lifestyle of a biker but the instincts of a classicist—pulled my knee firmly away from the saddle, where I had been gripping as I'd been taught, and said, "We don't do it like that anymore."

With one motion, she'd shifted both my position, and my paradigm, so from my very first lesson with her I had to rethink all my old assumptions.

What's after "Go?"

Beginners, you'll probably stay at the walk, getting used to the feel of the horse, an unfamiliar body position, and—steering. (There's a lot of drift in the early stages. You'll probably be in sensory overload, but try to be aware of the instructor other than as a source of commands, since I'm going to review a range of behaviors by which to judge that instructor.)

Returning riders, the instructor will probably take you through your paces—literally—to see how much you remember and to work on basic corrections.

For both classes of rider, the instructor should be monitoring when you seem confused or fatigued. If you're feeling this way and the teacher hasn't observed it, speak up.

If all goes well, the class will finish on a positive note, with you feeling, for example, that you've understood how to hold the reins, or that your rising trot is not as horrible as you thought it might be after a fifteen-year hiatus. Then, if you're a novice, the instructor should be close by to teach you a safe, correct dismount.

If they've gotten a sense that you're knowledgeable, many barns will show you where to put the horse away yourself. Otherwise, someone will come and collect him from you, and you'll be on your way, aching, fragrant, and it's hoped, ready to be hooked.

Your Horse

Let's face it, your first time out, or your first time out in a number of years, you aren't going to be riding Seabiscuit or a retiree from the Spanish Riding School. A responsible (and chary) school's first consideration is for your safety, not to mention its insurance. Your pleasure is secondary. In a sense, the early stages are the time for your measure to be taken as well as the school's. Your instructor knows what your horse is capable of, and how much you can chart those responses is a gauge of how efficient a rider you are, all of which is to say that it may take more than one lesson to determine whether a school has seasoned schoolmasters or jaded plugs. And there is a difference. Like children, any horse might take advantage of your tentativeness or inattentiveness, but a sour horse takes delight in responding badly—or not at all—to any overture. This can become dispiriting, just as absence of positive feedback from your instructor might.

Schoolmaster horses are frequently seasoned campaigners—veterans of the competitive circuit who know all the moves but haven't the elasticity and stamina for high-level competition anymore. They're reliable old souls who won't fuss too much at your less-than-perfect attempts to guide them. Most importantly, they will reward you when you get it right by allowing you to feel a gait or movement as it *should* be. If they are jumpers, they're steady to the fences, so you can concentrate on refining your position without worrying about whether you're going to get over the obstacle. If they're dressage horses, they'll often have a fantastic vocabulary of movements—possibly creaky movements, but that comes with the territory—and are just waiting for you to learn their language.

When I was at the Potomac school, I was fond of a big ex-hunter called Grenadier. He had a filthy temper (*not* usually a good thing in a school horse) but over a fence made me feel like the Olympian I was hoping to become.

Years later, at the Chelsea Equestrian Center, I fell in love (see, I told you so) with a big thoroughbred called Boston. He was a little stiff, but as my first mount in fifteen years, he made me feel elegant and competent.

The Right Teacher for You

Horsemanship is a little like wine tasting. There is a technique and an established vocabulary, but enormous room for individuation. And common to both pleasures is the tendency to use the vocabulary as a barrier or mechanized tool to disguise a lack of knowledge, imagination, or perception.

If you're a returning rider and remember some of the basic tenets of your discipline such as "Heads up, heels down," watch out for instructors who talk only in clichés, who seem to be reciting by rote a list of what *should* happen without explaining why or how. Just as we might label pretentious the wine writer or enthusiast who speaks only in terms of "thick legs" or "nose" without ever linking the arcane terminology to real-world experience, so we must look beyond the familiar lexicon for instructors who've made the language of riding their own. There are some interesting examples that you might well encounter at the schools you look at. Formerly, riding was taught in terms not of how it should feel, but how it's supposed to look. Two of the most interesting and well-regarded equestrian trainers and writers of the past twenty years, Sally Swift (*Centered Riding*) and Mary Wanless (*Riding on the Right Side of the Brain*), jettisoned the language and assumptions that have dominated

English riding for generations in favor of thought-provoking imagery and radical re-examinations of the body and its learning styles.

Swift in particular has been very influential in English riding circles. Many have adopted her specific, imagistic vocabulary to get across such points as the one that a relaxed gaze produces a relaxed body (what she calls "riding with soft eyes") and that an independent seat can be gained by an exercise in which you pretend that you are legless.

I am not, of course, suggesting that you rush out to buy all these books to figure out whether you're being taught by a disciple (though a Centered Riding advocate may well mention this), but that you be attuned to imaginative, articulate phrasing that helps concepts to come alive.

As I mentioned earlier, I'm particularly struck by vivid conjoining of riding terminology and real-world imagery, but sometimes the arresting phrase can be as simple as this pearl of hunt-seat instructor Linda Mc-Claren's: "After you use an aid, put it back."

You'll soon find out for yourself what sort of teaching style suits you and your goals. Choosing a trainer is like choosing a therapist. What will it be, the classic taciturn Freudian or the diffuse and associative Jungian? Do you like to hear the intellectual concept behind an instruction, or just be told how to fix the problem? Does repetition make you feel secure, or condescended to? Some instructors have a little of that drill sergeant mentality, and if dispensed with good humor, it can actually be refreshing (it means they think you're capable of better things). But if the hectoring is either incessant or aggressive, it can demolish your drive.

I can't stress enough that this is an organic process. In some sense, you're asking your ideal instructor to be two people. One is the good parent who leaves you free to learn as an individual but keeps you within safe boundaries. The other is a mentor or a guide who leads you down exciting new paths to unperceived truths. There are some things that can be gleaned from an initial lesson, but if you feel comfortable enough to commit to an establishment, it might well take four or five lessons to get a sense of whether you and your instructor are a good fit. There are no blueprints for spotting the right instructor, but here are some key benchmarks to help you get a sense of how lessons are likely to go.

Is he/she audible? If you have to strain to hear, you won't be able to focus on your mount. If you need to, ask your instructor to speak up—if he objects or doesn't seem to improve, you might have a problem. It's not uncommon to have diminished hearing in midlife, so cheerfully acknowledge that the problem may be yours (or the fault of the ring acoustics, or—a common problem in the country—nesting birds), and *then* ask the instructor to turn up the volume.

Does the instructor put you at ease? As I've said in describing a typical lesson, if you're a first-time rider, you should be taken right through the basics from how to approach the horse to how to mount. There should be some balance of practical information or reminders if you're a returning rider—where to place your legs, how to hold the reins, and anything else that may have escaped your perfectly respectable intellect during your nonriding years. You also want contextual information—how horses move their bodies, how they respond to physical and aural signals, how to gain their trust, and so on.

As a first-time rider, you might end up on a lunge line at first. (This is a long canvas rope that attaches to the horse's bridle or a special halter and allows the horse to be controlled by the instructor holding the other end.) Don't be offended. This isn't just for safety: relieved of the burden of having to direct a horse (particularly a smart school horse who knows in a hot second who's in the driver's seat), you may be able to get the feel of the situation a lot faster. You will also be in a more dependent position, but the instructor should still speak to you as an adult. You don't want your riding level confused with your intellectual one.

Does the instructor listen to you? This seems minor, but an instructor who doesn't listen to you about small things may miss big ones, and inattention could be an indicator of fear and anxiety, boredom and impatience, or just plain incomprehension.

I remember being irked by a young teacher at the Chelsea Equestrian Center with whom I had a first lesson in many years. I had told him I had a lot of Pony Club and competition experience behind me (*way* behind me), yet he proceeded to explain the rudiments of each gait as if I were a rank beginner—wasting both his time and mine.

Is the instructor a good communicator? Teaching riding is like being a simultaneous translator at the United Nations. The instructor has to mediate a physical experience (a right-brain function) *and* convey understanding about that experience (left brain), and in a way that is both intelligible and vivid. When I was training for my horsemaster's degree at Potomac Horse Center in Maryland, we were always told to provide imagery—to link the unfamiliar things we might be saying to something familiar in the real world. For example, five-time Badminton Horse Trials champion Lucinda Green talks about having "rubber legs" to conjure up the idea of softness and elasticity, Sally Swift coined the term *soft eyes* for a kind of heightened awareness in the ring, and other instructors convey the need for a light touch with images of eggs or glass.

In general, regardless of the method they espouse, instructors seem to have two general modes—those who approach the issues by focusing on the horse, and those who approach them through the rider.

This becomes more evident as you begin to ask more of yourself and the animal. To give you a simple example, a horse-oriented instructor might say, "This horse has no impulsion, he needs to be more forward more vigorously at the trot," whereas a rider-focused instructor might tell you to "put your leg on that horse and rise more aggressively at the trot."

Neither way is right or wrong, but you will come to see whether one style or the other seems to suit you best.

However, the horse must be in the equation somewhere. Riding isn't something you do *to* a horse—it's something you do *with* a horse, and your teacher should be subtly educating you all along the way. Beware of what appear to be rote instructions, ones that do not seem to bear in the situation at hand or are presented as a laundry list without context or explanation. Teachers who do this always remind me of those weather reports where the local weatherman is announcing forecasts that have come off the weather service wire, clearly unaware that out his window the actual weather is contradicting everything he's saying.

My favorite example of this is the oft-repeated injunction to "keep your heels down." I'll be willing to wager that many of us never had any idea why we were asked to do this as children, except that it seemed vaguely associated with security. Later in life it becomes harder to persuade less flexible joints and sinews into that poster-pretty position. Forcing it, even if it is possible, produces stiffness and distortion throughout the body, when in fact the real aim is to encourage a flexible hip leading into a soft, independent lower leg. Yet many teachers, to the increasing bewilderment and frustration of their older students, continue to harp on this cosmetic part to the detriment of the whole.

Whether you want the part related to the whole consistently in your lessons becomes another thing to discover about your own temperament and learning style. Like differing schools of psychoanalysis—some aim at root causes, others deal with immediate problems—you have to decide how much general philosophical context is enough or too much. This is because riding is always evolving, proceeding from tiny, sometimes frustrating increments to a larger whole, the outlines of which may be clear to the instructor but not to you.

Does the instructor ask how it feels? Describing a motion, however well, still addresses only that problem-solving left side of the brain. The instructor needs to know that your body is also getting the point. And although the instructor can usually spot glaring errors of posture or technique, it sometimes helps her to make more definite and specific corrections if she knows exactly what's going on with your body. She may see a stiff hand, but if you tell her you're getting shooting pains up your shoulder she'll know the problem is higher up.

Do your lessons leave you with a sense of accomplishment? All riders need to leave a lesson feeling that something has been achieved. If you're a beginner adult, it is easy to feel that you're not progressing fast enough or that you're ungainly. And if you're a returning rider, your former self—a limber and fearless twelve-year-old, perhaps—can haunt you like Banquo's ghost. It is up to the instructor to make the student feel that it is the quality, not the quantity of the accomplishment that matters, and that she/he can see progress even on days when you can't feel it. And returning riders should be encouraged to link the more intuitive adult with the spunky inner child.

The really exciting moment will come when you realize that you know whether you've had a good or disappointing day because you can tell whether your horse has. A teacher who can instill both you and your mount with this sense is to be prized. It isn't done through empty praise but by correctly pacing the flow of information and accompanying exercises.

Pacing

The pacing of a lesson, like music or acting, also involves internal "beats." Both you and your horse will tire mentally and physically if asked to do the same thing over and over. Look for some variety and some balance between explanation and execution. Complete beginners take baby steps, of course, but even here there are ways to keep your mind stimulated even when your body has to bow to the realities of learning a new discipline. For example, if you're trying desperately to master the trot, your teacher might surprise you by removing your stirrups to secure your seat, or might find an interesting way to describe the problems you're having.

I worked with one man who'd never stop a lesson on a bad note, even if it meant riding longer: if you and the horse were having trouble with a movement and it was clearly too late to resolve that particular issue, he'd move you back to the last thing that you and the horse had done well.

How does your teacher deal with your questions? All teachers have a certain rhythm to their instruction, and if you query them too much, sometimes (as in a classroom or other learning environment) you can disrupt the flow of the very information you are hoping to elicit. Bear in mind, too, that the horse has to accompany you with a certain consistency, building up to each exercise in a way that seems logical to *him*. Every time you stop for a disquisition, you've potentially lost his focus and interest. Nevertheless, you're bound to have plenty of questions in the early stages when you're a beginner, and even more as you begin to work toward some of the more philosophical realms of riding. If your teacher seems impatient or disconcerted by deviation from her chosen course, this may not bode well for the future.

In some ways, our expectations about teachers have changed in the same way as our expectations about doctors. We adults of the postdoctrinal twenty-first century are no longer content to passively sop up information and obey. We crave explanation and inquiry. We want (or we should want) to be proactive partners in our education. The perfunctory, insecure, or militant teacher will eventually alienate us.

Are You Learning to Be a Hack or a Horseman?

I'm hoping that you are interested in becoming not just a rider but a horseman, which means learning a lot more than simply how to get up on and pilot the animal. A horseman knows how to approach, groom, and tack up a horse, and cares whether it's in a good frame of mind and body to do what we ask. As in touching children, the bond that comes through a tactile connection can't be achieved any other way, and is especially important for beginners. The nervousness you may feel about riding probably has very little to do with whether you can turn left or right and a lot to do with whether you feel you can ask this of something that outweighs you by a thousand pounds.

As you might imagine, the more you get to know horses, the more comfortable you are around them physically, the more confident you will be as a rider. A school—or a trainer—who is not attentive to this side of things is in a very real sense offering you only half a lesson. In most small stables, once they feel confident that you're safe, the understanding is that you'll groom and tack up your own horse, while in larger, better-staffed establishments you may well be a passenger for a longer time. The same goes for the other end of the lesson. If things have gone well, the horse will have worked as hard as you have and is deserving of a brush-down. If you're a real beginner, tacking up the horse should be done under supervision since it is easy to make dangerous mistakes without realizing it. Bridles can look as complex as jigsaw puzzles if they're unfamiliar to you, and a saddle put on incorrectly is at least a discomfort, and at most a danger, to both you and the horse.

Of course, you could have a perfectly nice time just being handed your horse once or twice a week and handing it back at the end of the lesson, and you might even learn to ride decently, but if you limit your experience to this, there is a whole world of satisfaction and intimacy that will never be open to you.

Warning Signs

Don't let a bad instructor ruin your horse experience. There are too many good teachers out there for you to settle for mediocrity or incompetence. You are paying for the lessons, and you shouldn't feel terrorized, shortchanged, or unsafe. Following are some behavior patterns to watch out for and retreat from.

Beware of teachers who treat you as if you were a large child, a socialite, or a dilettante. (I know one who still refers to over-forty women as "girls" and treats them accordingly.)

Beware of people who simply parrot the axioms of horsemanship ("heels down," "eyes up," etc.) without being able to elucidate them, clarify them, and relate them to you and your horse.

Beware of instructors whose response to every problem you have is to get on the horse themselves. An instructor of mine did this continuously until I complained, and then gave an articulate justification that it was easier for her to understand a difficulty a student was having when she could feel the problem herself. It made sense and was a perspective I had not previously taken into account. However, it's also true that an instructor who cannot convey the idea of a movement or a correction in a way that eventually allows *you* to execute it is failing you. After all, we don't need to pay to learn that the instructor rides better than we do! That presumably is why we came to her in the first place.

The Path Ahead

I know I've given you a lot to think about as you embark on the exciting business of choosing your school and instructor, and that you'll know what to expect and be able to tell false note from true.

17

Getting the Most from Your Lessons (And Knowing When You're Not Getting Enough)

The horse is a catalyst for . . . creativity because it carries us through the doors that stand between the familiar and the unfamiliar, limitations and freedom, and introduces us to experiences we might otherwise miss.

—**Mary D. Midkiff,** *She Flies without Wings*

Self-help is one of my least favorite expressions in the modern, synthetic, pop psychology lexicon, but let us assume for a moment that I have "helped" you to "help yourself" find a school and an instructor with which you think you can be comfortable. That step is, of course, not the end, but the beginning. Now you will want to know how to get the most from your work. In this chapter I'll review several key elements: choosing your lesson mode, setting goals, knowing when it's time to change (something), and the instructor's-eye view.

Just as you will be learning to communicate with an animal whose language—and the imperatives upon which it is based—is different from your own, understanding what instructors expect and perceive will also help you to get the maximum return on your investment of money, time, and physical and mental energy.

First, set some realistic goals for yourself, and be prepared to re-examine and alter them as you progress. This may not be as easy as you think—as you'll see in the chapter on what the pros think, the driven attitude of contemporary adults can sometimes get in our own way. Don't try to become an Olympian in a summer. On the other hand, don't set your sights too low. When I returned to riding, in my early forties, I at first thought I would work my way up to some gentle trail riding (suited to my advanced years!). A decade later, I'm back to hunting and competing in horse trials (albeit at a low level). So you're most likely goal oriented because, as we've seen, that's how adults work. And it is important to articulate goals, if you have them, because your teacher may have a different agenda entirely.

It will be easy in the early stages. A complete beginner needs to master basic aids, and that takes determination. Set goals, by all means, but make them flexible, since it will be too early to tell your own pace in a new discipline.

Returning riders pose the most challenge to ourselves and our instructors. No matter what we say, we have one clear, unexpressed goal: to be the rider we were twenty years ago—or better.

Once you and your teacher have worked together several times, she'll have a better sense of your abilities and, if you have chosen well, will craft lessons aimed at refining techniques, solving problems, or restoring your feel for particular movements. Opt for small steps—they lead quickly enough to big things and make you feel safer and more confident when they do. This is also important because adult riders can often be their own worst enemies.

If you have some idealized vision inside your head, this can sometimes prevent your body from actually doing a movement correctly. Once you're fixated on correcting one thing, you may throw the rest of your body out of alignment or fail to feel your horse. Sometimes the best advice may be that offered to solipsistic teens: get over yourself. As one colorful barnmate of mine puts it, "It's very simple. And riding instructors wouldn't have a job if women didn't make everything complicated" (and men, too, of course). Life is complicated. The challenge is not to let the complications from one sphere leak into another.

Nevertheless, goals are useful, and can be fashioned in relationship to both internal and external circumstances. An internal goal might be that you'd like to have real control over your seat at canter by the end of the season. An external goal might be that you'd like to appear in your first show or go on your first trail ride by the end of the season.

You'll want to re-examine them because everything about your relation to your instructor, to horses, to your own body will be constantly changing. What seemed safe and sensible when you started out may be easily surpassed. Or something theoretically simple, recovering your seat (which you remember as having been fluent and balanced) in the lope, takes more time than you originally thought it would. Then, too, depending on where you're riding, there is the issue of seasonality. If you're depending on good weather, your riding "year" is compressed.

Lessons: Alone or in Company

Along with outlining your goals, your first decision at the time you sign up for lessons is what type to go for in terms of participation levels and duration. There are three basic lesson formats: private (individual), semiprivate (two riders), and group (three and above). There are advantages and disadvantages to each, and considerations may range from your comfort level to your purse.

If you're a real beginner or are just returning to riding after a long absence, you may need—or at least prefer—the focus and safety of a private lesson. But once you have gotten a certain degree of proficiency and confidence, you may find that pleasure, as well as misery, loves company.

Private Lessons

Advantages

A private lesson is as it sounds—the instructor focuses on you and your horse. This gives the instructor a chance to really put you together limb by limb, skill by skill, aid by aid, and allows for that important repetition through which your body is learning what your brain is processing, a time for you to do this all at your own pace. This is also a good way to get a sense of your instructor's teaching style and to ask more questions than you could if you were likely to hold up a class by doing so.

Disadvantages

You are bearing the whole cost of the lesson, and costs can add up if you're riding once or twice a week. You're also the focus of all the critical observations, which can be intense and exhausting, both physically and mentally.

Semiprivate

Advantages

Sharing your lesson with one other person has many advantages. It doesn't halve the cost of the lessons, but most schools and instructors do have a reduced rate for semis. (If a private lesson is fifty dollars, for example, a semi would probably be forty dollars.) And working with a partner can be helpful. Most such lessons involve work you can do together, and then some time focused on each of you. This means not only that you get a breather (usually welcome), but that you get to see another rider and horse trying to execute the same aids and movements you are attempting yourself. You then have the opportunity to watch the instructor's commands and corrections and see how they actually look worked out on another pair. This is something you can do as an individual only with the aid of a videographer.

(If you can afford it or you have a friend who is a camera buff, having your lessons videotaped is an excellent idea. Even though many riding schools have mirrors in their indoor rings, that fleeting glimpse of yourself, especially when you're concentrating on your horse, is not comparable to watching the whole lesson, at leisure and in retrospect.)

Disadvantages

You and your partner should be at similar levels with similar goals, or one of you will always be either bored or intimidated. And looking ahead to the time when you might be planning such lessons with your own horse, the same rule applies. If one horse in a class is very experienced, or is very green, or has a personality disorder, the whole lesson tends to skew in this direction.

Group Lessons

What defines a group depends on the workings of the individual school or instructor, but the average is anywhere between three and seven adults (kids' classes tend to be bigger—but then, ponies are smaller!). Some instructors have regular group lessons at specific times (especially on the weekends, when crowd control is a serious issue) that you might want to petition to join. Others will organize lessons on a more ad hoc basis, letting you know if there are other riders looking to make up a group.

Advantages

There is a group energy that sometimes helps spur better work, and sometimes it's a relief, both physically and mentally, not to be the center of attention. Getting into a group lesson depends a little on the demand and lesson structure at the barn. The adult rider population, probably because of its multiple obligations elsewhere, is often in flux, and sometimes it is possible to secure a place in a lesson on an intermittent basis. Responsible teachers try to limit class sizes—six or seven are the most that can be scrutinized effectively—and smaller is better for less experienced riders. It's also worth asking whether anyone is looking for a partner. Casual riders are often hoping to add to a group or create a semiprivate lesson and reduce their own costs.

It may also be possible to combine lessons. Group lessons, because they require the careful circulation of a stable's school horses and the coordination of multiple schedules, are usually fixed, but between the interstices of the larger groups is where teachers have a little leeway, and most are happy to book their days fully. If you reach a point in your group lessons where you feel either that you are being surpassed or are surpassing, or if you just have some problems you want to gnaw on (position over a fence, for example), then sometimes it's good to go back to a closed system, at least temporarily.

Another strength of groups is that you can often compare notes, frustrations, and goals together. If you find yourselves vexed by the same things (your instructor isn't loud enough, seems to do the same exercise over and over again, assigns you to the same sour horse every blasted time), collectively you might have more influence over your instructor than you would have alone. And if you came to ride in part for social reasons, shared rigors make fast friends.

Disadvantages

You're getting only a slice of the pie and may feel that there isn't enough time for the instructor to get a point across when she has to convey it to half a dozen others (or even two or three others). You're on your own more, and you will need to be comfortable working with your horse independently, without a lot of constant supervision.

Your horse is a herd animal, and suddenly, he's in a small herd. You'll need to be more aware of the other horses and riders and the distance between you, be alert for attempts to run into the other horses and potential skirmishes, and be attuned to the equine group energy.

Lesson Duration: The Long and Short of It

Most lessons are either forty-five minutes or an hour long. If you're having an individual lesson, you may find that forty-five minutes is adequate. As I've said, private lessons take a lot of energy and focus. The school's lesson structure may also dictate your choice—many naturally prefer to offer forty-five-minute slots as this allows them to fit in more students in a day. Hour lessons are often scheduled for groups so that everyone has a chance to work fully, and for formal exercises like jumping or reining practice (when you get to that stage) since these require more preparation and performance time.

Clinics and master classes are usually longer, and larger groups participate. The exercises are often more demanding and progressive, and there needs to be time for the "master." These seasoned professionals also often have more lecture and anecdotal components to their teaching. Ninety minutes is the usual length of a clinic class.

Lesson Times: Morning, Noon, or Night

When you take your lesson may be something over which you have limited control—if you work and have only weekends available or are joining an established lesson at a fixed time—but if you have options, think about how you can best balance your riding with the rest of your day. Many health club members have discovered the joy of exercising in the early morning, before work or the clutter of the rest of the day, and in riding this has a particular advantage in that you know your horse will be fresh, too. On the other hand, an evening lesson, if you can leave behind the flotsam and jetsam of your private or professional life, can be replenishing. Another advantage to taking lessons in the off-peak hours is that you'll miss the crowds. While lesson groups have controlled enrollments, rings are still often shared, and if you're taking private or semiprivate lessons, you are especially likely to be sharing space.

However, if, like the vast majority of recreational riders, weekends are your free time, learn to make the most of the clamor. Think of it as a community of riders instead of another traffic jam in your life.

It's All about You

The most important factor in your lessons is not your instructor, your horse, or your surroundings—it's you. You with all your strengths and weaknesses, visions and distractions. Some of these will be unique—your ambitions, timidity, penchant for debate, courage—everything from yourself and your life that you bring to the experience. But adults share a surprising number of responses to teaching and riding, according to the instructors I've interviewed.

What to Wear

For your first course of lessons, while you're deciding whether this is the sport for you, you needn't do much more than invest in an inexpensive pair of breeches (for English) or comfortable, loose-fitting jeans (for Western) and a pair of sturdy boots—and, of course, a helmet (see chapter 22 on safety). Shirts can be anything that's comfortable—polos, tees, oxfords—as long as there is no restriction of motion. And bear in mind that you'll be working hard, so go for something a little lighter than the weather might suggest, with a sweater or sweatshirt or jacket you can discard. If you bulk up in heavy fabrics, you'll swoon. If even this much shopping seems like splurging, take heart: if you become completely disenchanted with riding (you won't), equestrian fashions are always popular, and you'll be able to walk the walk even if you don't like the ride. You might also want to look into consignment clothing. Many tack shops have a used/consignment section, as do a number of Internet sites.

Head First

A safety helmet is the key component of your schooling outfit (see chapter 22, "Rider Safety," for full details). If you are reluctant to invest in one while you're still in the trial stages, the school may have one you can borrow, but do not buy these used (they may be damaged), and do not grab your teenager's skateboarding helmet. Safety helmets are ergonomically designed to withstand impacts particular to each sport.

Notes for Women

Leave Victoria's Secret at home. Get a sports bra. And spreads in Hermès catalogs and *Town & Country* notwithstanding, real riders don't wear (much) jewelry (with the exception of Western riders in competition) and do not have their hair flowing down their backs.

Breathable fabrics are also recommended; take advantage of today's reasonably priced natural cottons and Lycra stretch. And gloves are not only de rigueur, you would really regret not wearing them. You know the scene in so many movies where the cowboy or laborer looks at the hand of the city slicker or society nob and says something like, "Women's hands," or "Sissy hands?" Well, that's you, for a while at least. The friction of leather or rubber reins on your hands can be painful, and you will not be able to learn to use your hands effectively if you are in pain from chafing and blisters. This holds true for either riding style.

All of this is to say that it's worth spending a little more money up front to get an optimal experience from your entry or re-entry into riding, but you don't have to turn yourself into a catalog model, either.

Private Trainers

A teacher becomes a trainer when his or her involvement in your riding life is not limited to a lesson or even a string of lessons, but becomes part of a comprehensive program designed to achieve certain goals for you and your horse. This need usually doesn't manifest itself until you have a horse of your own, or one you are share-boarding or leasing. If you find yourself moving in this direction, several kinds of options are available to you. Your current instructor can morph into your trainer. Sometimes this happens imperceptibly with a sharpened awareness, the building of goals into the lesson structures, a schedule of competitions toward which you are working. Or it might happen when you begin to look for an instructor who can move you to the next level and also has the time to devote to creating a focused program for you and your horse. If you are in a boarding situation that permits this, you can have a trainer come to you.

Be aware that, as with other aspects of riding, there are both rewards and perils involved in entering into a training relationship. For one thing, it may become fraught with expectations on both sides. All teachers hope you will do better because of their counsel, but trainers are particularly interested in the outcome, especially if you are competing, as then you become the visible measure of their reputations. You, in turn, having invested the additional time and money that a consistent training program takes, may wonder why you and your horse aren't transformed into redoubtable competitors overnight.

Trainers, by virtue of the powers invested in them, wind up invading a lot more of our psychic space, as we accord them the composite roles of teacher, psychologist, and general. Some people even work with more than one trainer in order to concentrate on different areas and problems. This is common in combined training, with its separate disciplines.

The advantages, of course, speak for themselves—intensified and strategic versions of the private lesson. An individual who knows you and your horse intimately, with whom each lesson can build on the struggles and achievements of the last, is the one who can craft a program designed to give you the maximum success and satisfaction in your sport.

18

The Politics of Changing Instructors

You know the feeling—you've had it before—about your job, your therapist, your life partner: jaded, used up, dreary. You used to go to your lessons full of anticipation and leave them tired but mentally energized. Now you approach them listlessly, enduring them with much irritation, and leave feeling disappointed, misunderstood, or exploited.

When You Outgrow Your Teacher

What happened? Well, the good news is that this may be a sign of progress—an approach or manner that worked for you when you were unschooled now seems stale and confining. The more sophisticated your riding (or at least your knowledge of riding) becomes, the more aware you are of the skills you want to learn and the way your mind and body absorb information. The hearty, unsubtle approach of one teacher that seemed so reassuring when you were a fledgling now seems to lack dimension. You're not getting to the core of a problem or movement. Or your teacher seems excessively wordy or intellectual without giving you any really practical way to communicate this forest of ideas to your horse.

Even if there is no actual disaffection between you and your trainer, the more inward you become in a discipline, of course, the more likely it is that you may wish to move at some point from the good generalist to the more highly evolved specialist. This is especially true if you should decide to get your own horse. At this point, you may well be in the market for a trainer, not simply a teacher, as I noted in the previous chapter.

When You're Not Ready to Change—But You Must

Several other less natural factors can contribute to tension and distance between you and an instructor:

The orientation of the barn, or your orientation, has changed. For example, you've been riding in a barn focused on the hunter/jumper circuit and come to realize you really want to pursue dressage. Eventually, lessons will come to seem less relevant, you will feel like an outsider when everyone else prepares for shows or competitions in which you have no interest, and the horses won't seem to give you the right opportunities to learn what you need to.

There's been a change of management, or quality of instruction, or horses at the barn. Unfortunately, in the financially challenging world of horse management, this happens all too often. Bottom line imperatives result in overcrowded classes, overworked instructors, a high degree of unsoundness in school horses (often sometimes compensated by the hasty purchase of dubious replacements). Sometimes a new, unsympathetic management results in a change of atmosphere, a lowering of morale. Changes of this kind can actually make you feel unsafe, which is always the most compelling reason for confrontation and a switch.

Social issues. If you think cliques, pettiness, and gossip happen only in schoolrooms or on *Desperate Housewives*, think again. Women especially—it has to be said—are prone to replicating the petty intrigues and power struggles of their adolescent years, replaying unresolved conflicts that therefore need endless iterations. If you seem suddenly isolated from outings, ignored in conversations, or condescended to, or if people seem to know more about your affairs than you remember imparting, one of your stablemates is probably suffering from a severe case of teen regression. Deal with this according to your own temperament: confront or retreat. It all might blow over as new boarders come in, the balance of power shifts, or the competitive season ends. It may also be that you're that rare and rational type who views the social life at the barn with amused detachment without becoming emotionally invested in it. However, if you are a frailer mortal like many of us, and what once felt like camaraderie now feels like factionalism, it may be easier to make a switch.

Philosophical disagreements. In the early days of your entry or re-entry into the exciting and challenging world of horses, you may be something of a blank slate onto which all methods and views may be usefully transcribed. But as you become a more educated, disciplined, and well-rounded rider, you will find yourself imperceptibly developing your own feel for what riding is all about, at which point you may begin to discover that your perfectly competent teacher is fundamentally at odds with your worldview. In the short term, you may still get something out of your lessons, but in the long term, you will feel increasingly uncomfortable. I wound up parting company with a very interesting teacher whose eccentric no-nonsense approach appealed to me at first but later turned out to be grounded in a completely reductive view of horses as beasts of burden. To her way of thinking, horses were incapable of love or loyalty, worthy only of being subdued.

Not only beliefs, but approaches to riding may eventually alienate you. For example, you might discover a strong partiality for an intellectual approach to riding but have a teacher who really just likes to drill the basics.

Once dissatisfaction really sets in and you have acknowledged it to yourself, it's far healthier to make a change civilly and unemotionally. Staying with a teacher or establishment past the point of sense of pleasure robs riding of its luster. Taking the daring step of moving on will be like giving yourself the gift of horsemanship all over again.

19

Advice from the Pros The View from the Other Side of the Arena

Linguist Deborah Tannen published the best-selling *You Just Don't Understand*, about how the different communication styles between men and women lead to misunderstandings, mutual confusion, and quarrels.

It would probably be useful to issue a similar volume for riders and riding instructors—a relationship where much mutual confusion reigns. As I was researching this book, it occurred to me that thoughtful instructors, who see dozens of riders at all levels and temperaments year in and year out, may be able to observe patterns, characteristics that adult riders have in common that help or impede their progress. I spoke with a range of teachers from different backgrounds and different kinds of teaching responsibilities. All have in common regular work, in daily classes or years of clinics, with adult riders at all levels. These are instructors with whom I have ridden and one dressage judge for whom I scribed at a show. I asked a range of questions about attitudes, common challenges related to teaching adults, and advice they felt they could give. I found their responses revealing—and surprisingly consonant. They should help you to gain perspective on yourself as a rider and on your instructor or potential instructor.

You might use some of these observations about teaching and class size as another gauge of effectiveness and compatibility when you're looking for a school or instructor. Christine Hastings is an instructor, competitor, and accredited dressage judge. Susan Reichelt is an instructor at the Southlands Foundation in Rhinebeck, New York, and a former competitor. Margaret Hutchison competes at the intermediate level in three-day eventing and coaches a wide range of private clients from her school in Chatham, New York. Linda McClaren teaches hunt seat to older riders and college students at William Woods College in Fulton, Missouri, where she is the senior riding instructor. Here are their thoughts.

1. Why do you enjoy teaching?

Hastings: It lets me use my imagination and creativity.

Reichelt: People come to this sport for many reasons other than riding, and the diversity is what appeals to me.

Hutchison: Because adults do this for fun, we want to make it fun; it gives me great pleasure to help them attain their goals.

McClaren: I like to see people develop more awareness about horses and the horse's perspective. I think more horses benefit from me being a teacher rather than just a trainer.*

2. Is teaching adults different from teaching children? If so, how?

Hastings: They have more insecurity and are harder on themselves than children. They are more frustrated with the slowness of the learning process.

Reichelt: Mostly for adults it's a social experience, it's a fitness experience, it's a therapy experience—it's not necessarily a riding experience.

---

* It should be noted that McClaren's work in a competition barn for students makes her context different from that of many trainers. She is making a distinction between schooling her students in the principles, not just over competition courses.

McClaren: Adults can think their way through problems better than children, but have a lot more physical and mental fear to work through than children do. Children are, in general, more athletic than the average adult. A child's body is more malleable in that a riding instructor can say, "Put your heels down," and most children can just do it. Adults spend their work week in high heels, or sprained their ankle in 1995, or don't spend a lot of time standing on the edge of a step stretching out their Achilles tendon, so putting their heels down is sometimes a physical challenge.

Both adults and children learn to be better people through becoming more empathic riders.

3. Do adults learn differently?

Hastings: Sometimes they want more theoretical knowledge. Often they can't produce these results, but they like to understand even if they can't perform it yet.

Reichelt: Adults are more cerebral and need to understand every detail of exactly what's going on; children just do it because they're told to do it. So adults are harder to teach. They have to think about everything.

Hutchison: Adults are more mental, so to speak. They're interested in the theory behind it; they want to know *why* we do things, *how* do we do things. Why does the horse do x-y-z? How do I make it not do x-y-z? They're much more interested in the mechanism as well as the ethereal than the kids are.

McClaren: I think everyone learns differently. Some people learn by watching others and copying; some people learn through seeing a video of themselves; some people learn by talking through their riding problems; some people learn by doing it over and over again. Visual aids help most people learn to ride ring figures and coursework. Explanation, demonstration, observation, repetition: that's how it works.

4. What kinds of problems/challenges do adult riding students face (a) if they are just learning, (b) if they are returning to riding after a long absence?

Hastings: Their bodies are sometimes less cooperative. They are more afraid of getting hurt. They tend to go with the flow less easily.

Reichelt: Well, the rider who has just come to the sport has maybe saved up her whole life, with a thought that she wanted to ride and has never been able to for whatever reason. When they do come they come with a fresh, youthful experience, just like teaching a child. Riders who have been riders, and have been off for a while, come with a lot more suspicion and hesitation, and I think they're much more nervous. They have families, they're wondering if they should be doing it, and it then occurs to them that they could be hurt, that their profession is at stake, and they bring a whole lot of other baggage. Who's going to cook dinner for my husband? Who's going to take care of the kids if I fall? All of that comes into play once they start riding again.

Hutchison: Mostly they're aware that they can get hurt. Children are a little bit oblivious, as a rule. So there is tension because they can't afford to get hurt; they're aware of the possibility of being hurt, and even though they might very much like to be up there, that affects their ability to progress very often.

If adults have ridden as children or young people, the hardest thing is they expect it to feel the same. They expect their confidence, their co-ordination, their sense of freedom, their sense of connection with the horse to be exactly what they remember, and it's nowhere close. And it's very frustrating to the adult riders who are expecting it to feel like when they were zooming through the woods as an eight-year-old on a pony. And it's like, "Why can't I do this? I used to be able to do this, and everything's going wrong!"

The new, totally rank beginner riders that start fresh actually can be easier, because they don't have memory—muscle memory, mental memory—about what it's supposed to be like.

I have some riders that have very powerful jobs—corporate executives, judges, police officers—and they can be intimidated on the back of a horse.

McClaren: Physical fear (fear of injury), mental fear (fear of making a mistake and/or looking silly), lack of fitness and flexibility are all problematic.

5. What techniques do you use to counteract such problems?

Reichelt: I try to give them so much to think about that they don't have time to think about it, so they have to *do*, rather than think. I just keep them very busy.

Hutchison: Very often I'm able to relate. If I find out what they do, and I kind of put the horse in the perspective of their job, all of a sudden, they're assertive. And it can make a difference.

McClaren: They need *safe, well-schooled horses*! Keep it fun, keep each exercise short, vary the drills often by using elements from each family of exercises (balancing, suppling, straightening, strengthening, relaxation, timing, eyes, legs, seat, hands). I try to balance character-building work with exercises that make the rider feel good about the ride.

6. Is there any distinction between genders in terms of attitudes, problems, and so on?

Hastings: Oh, yes! Men usually want to use strength to *make* it happen. Women (usually) have to figure out a way to finesse the horse.

Reichelt: There's a difference pretty much across the board.

McClaren: Men do seem to be stronger and more athletic; their bodies usually seem to just fall into the correct position, whereas women usually seem to require more reminders about how to mold their body to the horse, follow the horse, and get strong enough to control the horse. At the introductory levels, more women seem to be emotionally attached to horses and riding, and so there are more women riding at the lower levels. Women seem to have a better sense of feel, and are better able to learn to use their wits instead of their strength to communicate with horses.

7. What can the adult rider do to get the best out of his/ her lessons?

Hastings: Be honest about skill levels, goals, frustrations. Tell the instructor when they do not understand things or are apprehensive about trying something.

Reichelt: They put so much pressure on themselves. This should be a sport where they come to relax, they come to enjoy what they're doing, unless they want to go on and compete, but they put enough pressure on themselves in their home life, in their family life, in their job, and when they come here, they put more pressure on themselves to succeed at something they haven't done in a while. That's what helps: taking the pressure off themselves and just enjoying the experience of riding.

Hutchison: Be patient; be realistic. I think everyone has a sense of, "Time is running out, and nobody's getting any younger," so they're trying to get better quickly. If you can only ride a couple of days a week, try and develop a realistic perspective about where you are in your riding, what you need to accomplish, what you want to accomplish, and then try to realistically incorporate it into your lifestyle so that you're not constantly frustrated that you can't get where you want to go. Be realistic about where you are and where you want to go, then step back and say,

"Okay, I can get here, and then I can get there, and then I can get there," and be patient.

McClaren: Leave the rest of their life outside the ring! As an instructor, teaching people how to do this is important to me—and most adults already know how to do that even though they might not be aware of it. Most adults already have learned to compartmentalize their focus and concentration skills.

8. What's the most frustrating thing you experience with adults?

Hastings: They need to understand that you are *always* learning. You never know it all. Some days go better than others. Be patient with your horse and yourself. Let your horse know when he's done it right.

Reichelt: The amount of pressure that they put on themselves is tough. When they turn the experience back on the horse is the most frustrating for me: "Why isn't this horse performing the way it should?" Because it's never the horse. I wouldn't mount somebody on a horse I knew she couldn't ride—therefore, I know that it's never the horse. I know it's the rider. And when they turn that experience around, either blame it on the horse or put pressure on a teacher—get that pound of flesh from you, because they want you to make it right—well, it's not a perfect world and we can't always make it right. We put things in place so that things are right, but it's the attitude of the rider that shapes the outcome. It can be very frustrating.

Hutchison: Once I get to know students, I can tell if they've had a bad week, because they're tense, they're not listening, they're mechanical, they're not sensing the horse, and they need to just have a little unwind time.

McClaren: I enjoy teaching adults, but sometimes it does take a while to get through the history that they bring with them and make significant progress past it. I have come to the conclusion that there are a lot of do-ityourselfers out there who have never been mounted on a safe, well-schooled horse, or worse, riding teachers who do not recognize how important it is to teach the right feel on safe horses who know their job. As a result, many adult riders grow up absorbing bad habits or learning to be afraid because they've gotten hurt in the past.

9. What's the most inspiring or gratifying thing you experience with adults?

Hastings: They appreciate it when they learn something or perfect a skill.

Reichelt: By and large they're here because they want to be.

Hutchison: It's so great to see these tense adults come from Albany or New York, or whatever, and they just love it. They relax, they're smiling, they have a great time. It releases them from all the other pressures, and it just gives me a thrill to know I can help them enjoy it, give them a sense of accomplishment, and get pleasure from the animal and the countryside.

McClaren: That they are able to recognize the intricacies involved in horsemanship and are patient and disciplined enough to learn the steps. When they can put things together so that it works for them, they never forget it.

10. If someone is looking for a school or a teacher, what should she check for?

Hastings: That you like the style they teach. That they are safety minded. That they treat you with respect.

Reichelt: They should look at a facility that has a number of horses. A small facility with a small number of horses usually can't match the personality of horse and rider. They should look at the cleanliness of the facility, they should look at the way the horses are turned out. The care of the animals and the overall appearance will give them an idea of the standard a facility has, and the standards a facility is setting.

Hutchison: They should look for good planning and appropriate horses.

McClaren: You should go to the facility and see if the horses look happy. You should watch a lesson and see if the teaching style looks and sounds like it will agree with you. You should talk to some of the other clients and see what the program is about and if it will fit. For example, an individual looking for a fun place to ride once or twice per week may not be happy in a highly competitive training barn where the trainer is always on the road at shows with other clients, or vice versa.

11. What is the ideal class size?

Hastings: I teach from private to groups of seven. Private or semiprivate gains you more specific and focused attention on your needs.

Reichelt: I personally prefer large classes—five to seven is good to me. I think once a student has learned to ride, it cuts the cord without me cutting the cord. It's like driving in traffic—you really learn to drive when you drive in traffic. And it's the same thing about riding—I can't ride the horse every stride for them if the group is larger. They have to plan, they have to be considerate; they'll learn respect, they'll learn safety, and they can't learn that in a very small group.

Hutchison: It varies. I think everyone really likes their privates because it zeroes in on their particular problem and they can work on it, but all my adults are happy—maybe more times than I'm aware of—to have a group, because it takes the pressure off. You can work on your own, you can practice a little bit while I'm focusing on another rider, and it helps to watch other people. Everyone makes similar mistakes, and you can learn by watching other people's successes as well as little mistakes, and there's a lot of camaraderie that goes on.

McClaren: That depends on so many things! One can get a lot done in private or semiprivate lessons, but if one is planning to compete, one should learn to ride in a group so that the schooling area at the competition isn't scary.

12. Can the school environment remain satisfying, or should people who are really keen eventually think of getting their own horses?

Hastings: The ongoing relationship with a horse and their training is very satisfying, but it's a big commitment of time and money—at least five days a week. Leasing is a very good option.

Reichelt: That's strictly an individual decision. For some adults it's fine. A school program that augments the instructors with clinics and different disciplines usually is fulfilling enough for a person who comes to ride—at least here. But people are very vocal about how they want their needs met. And if they want to show, then they'll tell you that they want to show, that they have *these* goals, and then you try to meet those goals. And often it can't be done without their buying their own horse.

Hutchison: If you end up buying a horse, do your best to get the most appropriate horse for yourself, something you can get the most out of for your limited ride time. You need something that's well trained and can really take care of you. Getting things that need to be trained can be a really frustrating "hold back," "hold back," "hold back" situation, and I think really sometimes too many people get caught in that—"Oh, we'll learn together." Well, baloney, you don't have time for that. Get on something that can teach you.

McClaren: I think that if people are really serious about their riding and if they can afford to, leasing or buying a horse is a great idea, because that one-on-one relationship with a horse is part of what makes riding a special form of recreation. However, I think that a good school program with wonderful horses and the right instructor, who educates the clients about the limitations and advantages of riding school horses, can keep the weekend rider satisfied.

13. Do you recommend competition as a goal? If not, what might a rider be focused on?

Hastings: I love competition but it's not for everybody. Aim to make your horse more supple, balanced, responsive—to move better, to trust you more. The dressage tests are full of wonderful exercises. Try ground poles. Try cross-country walks—very relaxing for horse and rider.

Hutchison: It's not everybody who wants to go compete. A lot of what I would call recreational adult riders come to me and I ask them where they want to go with their riding, and some don't really know. And others—a good handful—enjoy the animal, enjoy being in the country, and really just aspire to feeling competent and safe to go enjoy the countryside. And there are those that kind of start out that way, and the next thing you know they've figured out that competing might be a little bit fun. So low-level competing, be it a little jumper thing or hunter pacing, gets to be a goal.

McClaren: "Riding is about the horse and rider working together toward perfection," Anne Kursinksi states succinctly in Margaret Cannell's *Winning Ways.* You can ride at home forever and always be working toward that goal of perfection, but competition is also a nice way to test what you know and find out what you need to work on. Poise under pressure is part of dealing with an animal who weighs over half a ton, is timid, and has a strong flight instinct. Riders should learn to get out of that comfortable home environment and practice it occasionally; it builds better riding skills!

14. Is it ever too late to learn?

Hastings: No. I've ridden for fifty years and I learn new things all the time.

Reichelt: No. I think the oldest person I started was sixty-five or sixty-six, and it's nerve-racking for the teacher, but if the student's game for it, I'm game for it.

McClaren: No!

You're in This Equation, Too

One final word: while you're seeking the best from your instructor, be sure you are giving your best as a student. Come on time, come focused and prepared to work, come ready to try anything, even if it makes you feel foolish (not, of course, if it makes you feel unsafe). Don't leave your questing intelligence, your discipline, or your sensitivity at the door, and don't usher in instead your frustrations, your ego, or your anger. Respond actively, not passively, and you'll leave each lesson invigorated, even if all you did was learn to turn the corner correctly.

Part III

Choosing Safety

20

Young Hearts, Older Bones

Riding is not the last bastion for the athletically uninclined.

—Denny Emerson

The very fact that you're considering riding again, that you're reading this book, is a sign that you're not letting your age define you. Aside from the spiritual lift that horses provide, there is increasing evidence (just recall the slew of books, magazines, and newspaper articles that cover this topic each year) that regular exercise helps prevent heart attacks, osteoporosis, and other age-related infirmities. Riding covers many of today's health buzzwords—it exercises tendons and joints, is anaerobic, sharpens hand-eye coordination, and requires mental alertness as well as physical dexterity. So Father William, if he'd stayed in the hunt field, would be very perky indeed.

Riding by itself is not a weight loss program (it expends about five calories per minute for an average person, according to some sources), but it does help you improve suppleness, coordination, and applied strength.

I've said it before, but it's worth saying again in this context. Horses weigh between 1,000 and 1,200 pounds on average, and you're not going to be able to manhandle them into anything. In fact, the very last thing you want any ride to become is a contest of strength between you and the animal. So when I say "strength" in this context, I'm really talking about strong, well-toned (but not exaggerated) muscles, supple, well supplied with oxygen, and efficiently supporting the skeletal system. Muscle fatigue makes you sloppy, achy, and prone to injury.

The whole aim of this book is to support the mature rider's desire to ride as tranquilly or boldly as he or she wishes. Nevertheless, it would be foolish to pretend that your young heart isn't housed in a slightly older chassis. After forty, as we know, joints and tendons are less flexible, and a lifetime of the sort of casual abuse most of us put our bodies through (for those of you who have maintained a rigorous fitness regime, I apologize) has begun to tell, resulting in myriad strains and syndromes. And the mishaps that barely set us back when we were younger—awkward landings, twisted stirrups, or falls—can do real and permanent damage to our less-resilient bodies.

Why Fit?

A fit rider (we'll see what that means) is a safer, more effective rider, and this matters greatly when pleasure is so closely linked to effectiveness, and when injury can not only halt our fun but devastate our livelihoods and our families.

Oh, no, you might be thinking if you're like me. I was attracted to riding because it's not one of those meaningless obsessive exercise regimes, and now you're telling me I ought to have one.

Well, yes, or at least you should consider one. Riding isn't an exercise program—it's not the sport to take up if all you want to do is get buff. It's a complex discipline asking the most of your mind, body, and spirit, and if you get serious about it you will find yourself exploring ways to enhance the experience.

In this respect we are a fortunate generation of riders. Fitness isn't for muscle-bound faddists anymore. It's embedded in our culture, and the means to achieve it—facilities, equipment, televised exercise programs, DVDs, books—are readily accessible to almost everyone.

Nutrition, too, is a common topic in a wide variety of media, and there is a host of professionals to turn to for customized programs. And while there is no special rider's diet, you will probably find yourself generally less tolerant of junk food and general excess, which can really take the edge off your riding.

So no, you don't have to change your lifestyle to ride, but you may find it subtly altering anyway.

What Is Fit?

In addition to making you a better and suppler rider, proper conditioning goes a long way toward preventing injury and reduces the risk of cardiovascular distress. As Sue Stanley, an associate athletic trainer for the University of Kentucky, wrote in an article for the *American Medical Equestrian Association News*, "Riding alone does not provide sufficient demands on the muscular and cardiovascular system to develop peak physical conditioning." In other words, to be fit to ride, you have to do more than just ride.

Assume for a moment that you are an average middle-aged American adult. I don't really believe in "average" people, but statistical norms and actuarial tables can sometimes be useful, if only as a point of departure. Depending on your lifestyle, you may be relatively sedentary, intermittently active, or robust. The aim is to see where your current self fits into the picture of the ideal athlete participating in your sport. Don't be downcast if you don't conform; it might only mean accepting certain limitations or setting new fitness-related goals in addition to those you are setting for the general progress of your riding.

The basic components of fitness for humans are the same as for horses: strength, flexibility, and stamina.

Strength. Strength training is designed to condition the different muscle groups so that they can do their jobs more efficiently. In riding, the aim is to be able to leverage your weight and to maintain yourself in the saddle in a variety of positions (off the horse's back for galloping, for instance) without strain. It doesn't hurt on the ground, either, since horse keeping comes with a certain amount of heavy labor.

Flexibility. Flexibility might be the most important component of all. Flexion, alignment, and the ability to isolate one's body parts to move independently of one another are key components to successful riding. Independence of movement is literally what allows us to speak to the horse with our bodies and to elicit the response we want.

Stamina. Aerobic and anaerobic fitness improve the respiratory and circulatory systems, which in turn help the flow of oxygen to the muscles. Even a vigorous flat lesson can leave you feeling winded, and stamina is absolutely essential for the more arduous disciplines such as endurance riding and eventing, where, in fact, the official rulebook states, "In the interest of the horse, the fitness and competence of the rider shall be regarded as essential."

Why Does It Matter?

The fitter you are, the more agreeable a partner for your horse— who, after all, has to carry you—you will be, and the more effective in helping him to do this you will be.

It's not just a matter of weight. Unfit bodies (of horses and riders alike) lack something called self-carriage—the ability to hold your frame together in a supple, dexterous way. You don't want to be a dead weight.

The Basics

Warmup

Every rider needs a basic limbering-up routine. These days, riding instruction places much more emphasis in open hips, mobile shoulders, and flexible joints than it used to in the old days of clench and kick. Even five or ten minutes' work on these aspects every day can make you a more supple and responsive rider, one who doesn't have to fight her body to achieve more. If this makes you feel silly or resistant (we've agreed you thought *riding* was the exercise you were committing to), the rewards are definitely worth it. And if you have ridden before, remember all the times your instructor would demonstrate a position from the ground? The more in touch you are with your body off the horse, the more likely it is that you can translate specific movements (isolating parts of the body is another frequent demand in riding lessons) to your actual riding position.

Exercise

Appendix B, "Resources," at the end of this book, lists books and other publications that include groups of exercises specifically designed for riders. They include stretches and aerobic workouts that you can do at home if you don't belong to a gym, and that you might wish to add to your workout program at your gym if you are already exercising regularly.

Even the mildest regime will be beneficial, and all authorities agree that fitness is linked to safety. Inflexible sinews and muscles are more prone to strains and breaks.

In addition to the regime suggested above and some of the cross-training programs, you might also consider a course in the Alexander technique. This long-established movement program, which emphasizes releasing and realigning the body to improve posture, stride, tension, and general health, might have been custom-made for riders. Often espoused by dancers, the Alexander technique was actually invented by a singer who had lost his voice. The technique teaches you to isolate and release tension in different parts of the body such as the neck and lower back, areas that are key loci of stress in riders. Yoga and Pilates are also good physical practices for riders. Both help you to separate and relax different parts of the body, and yoga's meditative aspect doesn't hurt for creating a more serene, engaged mind.

Sue Stanley also recommends three days a week of aerobic workouts. While any exercise regime that you are following is bound to be helpful, I urge you to refer to the resources I have cited at the end of the book, I have cited a few books relating to athletic programs created specifically with riders in mind. Several recommend the popular inflatable exercise balls, for which a range of exercises has been designed.

Weight and Nutrition

A Word about Weight

There probably isn't a baby boomer alive who hasn't been concerned at one time or another with body weight. Our culture is obsessed with thinness, and a variety of sources, both ostensibly professional and more perniciously by way of popular entertainment, urge us to achieve physical ideals that have nothing to do with physical well-being.

If you are overweight, there is no question that riding will be more of a challenge, for you and the animal. But there are plenty of riders, especially at the lower levels, who are a little on the hefty side and still experience the sport with undiminished enjoyment. What is true is that it is easier to be an effective rider when you can get physically close to the animal and are able to use your seat, legs, and back to subtly influence his way of going. So as with exercise and a good diet, weight loss may become a natural progression in pursuit if your goals, not an awful obstacle.

Nutrition

With an entire industry and significant amounts of bookstore real estate devoted to diet and nutrition, there is no need to elaborate on this topic here, nor does this volume in any way assume professional knowledge or authority in this area. I will touch briefly on the points about which there has been some consensus, but you are likely to already be as awash in theories and recommendations as anyone else of our generation. The real point, as a potential rider, is that how you feel physically can really affect your riding. Foods that make you sluggish, bilious, or hectic will have just that effect on your relationship with your horse. And you can't nurse a hangover while trying to perfect your trail class work. You may find yourself examining your diet in terms of how you feel during your rides and lessons. You may begin to think of your body not as a temple (that's old), but as an instrument being readied to play a good duet.

Diet and nutrition have been dominant issues—and drivers of commerce—for decades, and there are widely varying opinions on what constitutes a "good" diet and how foods actually affect the body. Even the U.S. government has revised its nutritional guidelines a number of times. This is not the place to rehearse the debates. However, most sources agree about several elements that are key to good nutrition for the rider:

- A high carbohydrate intake stimulates athletic performance.
- Excessive protein is not necessary (15–18 percent of your daily diet, according to some sources) and should be derived from a wide variety of sources.

■ Limit fat intake. This is a particularly volatile area in the nutritional community (good fats, bad fats, transfats, etc.), so you will want to keep abreast of rational developments. But generally speaking, fast food is not going to be your ideal equestrian fodder.

■ Most crucial of all is consistent fluid intake—lack of hydration is not only uncomfortable, but dangerous. Water is the most beneficial fluid, but I confess to being personally converted to Gatorade during a grueling jumping clinic on a very hot day, despite its virulently postnuclear colors.

21

Cross-Training

Football players take ballet classes. Biathletes meditate. Cross-country riders run. Why? Because different physical regimes enhance different parts of an athlete's body and mind. After years of territorial isolation it has gradually become apparent—through sports medicine and other research—that seemingly divergent disciplines might actually enhance one another. This is a very rewarding insight for riders, as it recognizes some apparent contradictions in the quest for good form, a safe seat, and effective, harmonious aids. The secure, deep seat is not achieved by perching or clenching, but by releasing into the saddle, opening the angle of the hip in much the same way a dancer or a martial artist does. An effective leg does not grip or pummel the animal but swings free from a released lower back and hip apex, so that it can be independently applied when needed. A good rider follows the motion of his horse with seat and hands. It's not done busily, straining with artificial motion, but imperceptibly, almost intuitively. A released back and seat receive and relay impulses from the horse's spine, almost as ballplayers might respond to a pitch or serve or dancers move around each other in an improvised exercise.

Cross-training provides more than a symbiosis of physical skills: the pace and temperament of different sports and physical acts brings depth and sometimes revelation to your central pursuit. Mary Wanless, author of *The Natural Rider* and proponent of a kinesthetic, right-brain approach to riding, was led to her revolutionary approach through exposure to other movement disciplines: "While learning dance, I found a new approach to body skills and learning which resonated with my own. It seemed that a revolution was taking place in the teaching of other sporting disciplines, and the new techniques had been born out of experiences similar to mine."

Rusty Lowe, an emergency medical technician and chair of the United States Eventing Association's Safety Committee, recommends any sport that promises a good cardiovascular workout and also those that help promote hand-eye coordination—tennis, racquetball, juggling, and calisthenics all qualify. One event rider, Darren Chiacchia, kills two birds with one stone by jogging his cross-country course. Sue Stanley recommends running, swimming, and biking. (Some useful references on specific disciplines are listed in appendix B, "Resources.")

Weight Training

As noted above, weight training isn't about developing super strength so as to outpull your horse, but about maintaining muscles and joints in peak working order. Weight training is also thought to help defer loss of bone mass and so is particularly important for women. Simply put, the exercises involved in weight training help create a functional and dynamic relationship among muscles, ligaments, and tendons—the very parts of the body that are challenged in riding. Especially when you are a beginner and are just learning how to hold your body in a new shape, this type of training can contribute to your comfort and well-being.

Yoga

Yoga is a discipline that reflects many of the same goals we aim for in our riding—the relationship of mind and body results in a calm and forward spirit. As Jara Steward has written in *Horse Illustrated*, "As an ancient form of exercise that develops correct breath, calmness, focus, and increased strength and flexibility, yoga is very applicable to the equestrian." The discipline's stretches and centered breathing exercises release unconsciously tense muscles—the cost of our stressful working lives. (There are actually several types of yoga practice, linked to spiritual quests. In the West we are most familiar with hatha yoga, and this is likely to be the type of class you will find most easily.) Yoga has been effective in keeping people fit to ride when they've had to be away from horses for months at a time—having babies, for instance. Some new mothers who practice their yoga faithfully have been able to get right back on a horse and do pretty well. This makes it especially attractive to the adult amateur rider whose demanding schedule might mean erratic access to a horse. Nor should yoga's spiritual aims be disregarded. A practice that calls for the rigorous displacement of self in pursuit of a higher consciousness is very much in keeping with riding's ultimate quest—a seamless union with your animal.

Martial Arts

The same principle that informs many martial arts—to use balance, leverage, and coordination to oppose brute strength—is of course at the heart of riding's central paradox of "controlling" an animal that outweighs us by half a ton. Tai chi and tae kwon do are especially applicable. Both are characterized as "soft" martial arts that operate by the use of leverage and control rather than pulverizing strength. The repetitious exercises associated with each help isolate and refine the use of your individual joints and muscles; independent use of the body is key to effective riding.

Pilates

This system of strengthening and stretching was created in the 1940s by a German, Joseph Pilates. After he immigrated to the United States, his system became popular in the dance community and has now established itself through a network of studios around the country. Like modern dance, the Pilates system teaches that the lower abdominal region is the source of the body's strength. Using special equipment such as a sliding bench with a harness for the hands and feet and a barrel-like shelf, practitioners are taken through a range of stretching and contracting exercises designed to both stretch and strengthen. Much emphasis is placed on being able to isolate and control individual parts of the body such as the shoulders, abdominals, and seat bones, and to operate from a strong central core. These same areas of the body play a significant role in riding, and equestrians who practice Pilates say that the increased toughness and flexibility allow them to more subtly control their horses' movements instead of winding up in a tug of war.

After the settling of a legal dispute about rights to the name and technique, Pilates is now taught in many studios around the country.

Meditation

Meditation, which began some years ago to make inroads with top competitors in a variety of disciplines, as Eastern and Western approaches to health, wellness, and nutrition began to converge in the 1980s, is also gaining ground among riders. Like yoga, meditation provides both physical relaxation and mental focus. Perhaps *Zen and the Art of Riding* will become a worthy successor to the counterculture classic on motorcycles.

A variety of meditative practices exist—including those related to yoga. (See appendix B, "Resources," for guides and useful listings.)

I am not saying that the practice of one of these disciplines is a prerequisite to riding, but that they have been determined to be complementary and potentially beneficial, especially if you wind up competing regularly. If you already belong to a gym, some of these classes may be on offer. Even if you don't belong to a gym, yoga and Pilates centers are opening up all over the country.

Ball Classes

Inflatable balls have become popular exercise tools and are especially helpful to riders. Ball exercises encourage extension and flexion of muscles and help to improve balance without insecurity or strain. Particularly useful is the fact that you can sit on the ball and replicate some of the same back and hip movements you will use in riding. You can also initiate, or repeat, the kinds of exercises your instructor might have you do in the saddle, such as torso twists and arm extensions.

Balance Boards

Rather like small seesaws, these boards rest on a central point, and the exercise involves trying to keep the board level, with one's feet to either side of the central point. This effort involves the play of back and leg muscles—calling for the same nuanced adjustments you will use to influence your horse. Some exercises are done blindfolded—this allows you to feel and sense your body without the distraction of an actual animal. Balance boards also develop mental concentration, so they usefully "exercise" both the left and right hemispheres of the brain.

One principle aim of training programs is to get the body to "think" differently, to make different connections. This is the purpose, for example, of physical therapy after an injury, but some of these techniques, like balance exercises, have developed as independent training tools.

Mounted Exercises

While the basic thrust of this chapter has been to urge you to consider a fitness regime of some kind to complement and enhance your riding, you will also discover, through reading or work with your instructor, a range of exercises designed to be performed on horseback. These include stretching you arms overhead (usually one at a time), reaching for the opposite toe with your outstretched hand, torso twists, head rotations—all aimed at lengthening your muscles and sinews so that you can sit more deeply in the center of the saddle and learn to move different parts of your body independently of one another. They also help improve your sense of balance and the subtle give and take that will keep you constantly and intuitively responding to your horse.

22

Rider Safety

According to a survey by the United States Equestrian Team Foundation, of one million estimated competing riders in 2001, fewer than .04 percent experienced injuries (there were two fatalities). So the good news is, riding is much safer than ice hockey, skiing, stock car racing, bungee jumping, or trapeze—or, for that matter, flying or crossing the road. The realistic news: you can break your neck. But you know that, just as you know that except for the terminally maladroit, only golf and knitting are really safe, and you've decided not to go that route just yet.

So riding has an element of danger, and it would be naive to pretend that that element isn't part of its appeal. In the first place, there is the breathtaking prospect of forming a creative partnership with a thousand-pound animal of surpassing beauty and mystery. (Please think of it that way—only bullies and ninnies imagine that their job is to "master" the horse.) Each year, at least some proportion of horse-related injuries takes place while riders are off their horses—in the barn or while the horse is in hand. Of these, a depressing proportion occurs to experienced horsemen. Statistically, of course, the more you handle horses, the more likely it is that you might sustain some injury, but it is also that old adage at work: familiarity has bred contempt, or at least carelessness.

As I mentioned in chapter 16, a really responsible riding establish-ment should take you through the basics as part of your training, but many, especially during the intense months from May through October, are incredibly busy, and your local guide may well, in the nicest of schools, be a distracted fourteen-year-old girl. So even if someone is available to show you how to groom and review basic safety procedures, you are ultimately responsible for your own well-being.

Prepare for a Safe Ride

Risk is okay. Recklessness is not. Therefore, I offer some crucial steps to a safe ride:

Dress Appropriately

We've already discussed the basic clothing you'll want to invest in as you begin your lessons (special traditions and requirements for particular disciplines are covered in part I) in terms of comfort and effectiveness, but here we're focusing on safety, which brings different criteria to the fore.

Apparel

We are not talking about discipline-specific dress codes here, but ba-sic barn and schooling wear. "Basic" means long trousers, schooling tights, or breeches. Why long trousers? Common sense, really. Even in the best-kept barns, there are too many protuberant objects, slivers of wood, bales of hay, and hooks waiting to graze you, not to mention in-sects and dust. I draw the line at insisting on long-sleeved shirts—in some seasons and some climates, this would be unbearable—but go for functional rather than sensational, even if your teenage daughter is stumping for the Barbie-at-the-dude-ranch look. (One catalog is now offering navel-baring breeches. Merchandisers are not to be trusted.)

There's been a lot of cross-fertilization in the sports apparel market, so in addition to jeans or breeches, you can get Lycra stretch tights in a variety of styles. These are durable and made of breathable fabric, an important consideration, especially in summer. There are no particular safety issues related to shirts, except that they be comfortable, breathable, and free of zippers, hooks, or tassels that might catch.

Jewelry

Jewelry is to be kept to the absolute minimum. Chains—if you must—should be worn under your shirt, but even then, if they are in any way heavy or contoured, you are better off without them. In the event of a fall they can easily be damaged and, more to the point, damage you. The same applies to bracelets, pendants, and brooches. A sturdy watch is acceptable. If you wear earrings, lose the hoops, drops, and bangles, which can rip free if you fall or even travel under a low-hanging branch. You don't want to be a customer for one of those New York subway torn earlobe advertisements, do you? Flat disks or small studs will complement your gear nicely. (The Western pleasure competition has inspired whole lines of jewelry that is both vivid and safe, and in any event worn only in a controlled environment for a short time. Western riding does not call for the Dolly Parton look while schooling or trail riding.) Hoops, unless very small, are also tricky and can catch on branches and equipment. Your chunky earrings could easily bruise or gouge in a fall. Bracelets and rings pose similar perils, as well as getting in the way of smooth hand and arm motion.

Gloves

Unless you've been working on the railroad all the livelong day, your hands are probably soft and unmuscled and will blister easily. If you are in pain or thinking about avoiding pain, you will hold your reins tentatively and be slow to respond naturally to your horse's head movements, which makes for an uncomfortable ride for both of you. In addition, you won't be able to respond quickly to sudden movements or acceleration.

The Helmet

According to a variety of sources, head trauma is the leading type of injury among riders. Why? Crudely put, heads are soft, and ground is hard. Even indoor rings with loose footing (sand, dirt, and recycled shredded rubber are common types) have wood, concrete, or hard-packed dirt beneath, as well as board, nails, and mirrored glass around the perimeter. And a significant number of these injuries take place while the rider is on the ground.

The out-of-doors is, of course, as perilous as it is pleasurable. Nature means rocks and gullies, stones and trees, as well as man-made perils like highways, machinery, and the jump you were trying to get over when you fell. And finally, falls happen to your horse as well. He might fall on or with you, kick out in a panic, or drag you if you're caught in the tack.

(Note: If you do have a fall, do not wear your helmet again, even if it looks undamaged. The ergonomic structure that is part of the protective design may be affected by concussion. Most helmet manufacturers, to encourage responsible use, have an exchange program. For a modest fee—and sometimes for free—you can turn in your helmet for a replacement.)

Now that I have thoroughly alarmed you, let's turn to what you should be buying.

The basic contoured riding helmet worn by both English and Western riders has been ergonomically designed for safety and approved by two organizations, the American Society for Testing Materials (ASTM) and the Safety Equipment Institute (SEI). An ASTM/SEI-approved helmet is the most vital element of your wardrobe. Junior riders are required to wear helmets anywhere they ride in public, and the rest of us would be mad not to. In English hunt-seat circles, where the cosmetically attractive but less sturdy velvet caps are often worn, and in Western show classes, variety and tradition are fighting a rear-guard action against common sense.

Manufacturers are eagerly rising to the challenge and have even started paying more attention to fashion. (Some safety helmets are depressingly prosthetic in appearance.) Styles include versions of traditional hunt caps that are built up on the inside to deflect concussion and with thicker chin straps; some look rather like World War II motorcade helmets. By far the most common are slightly elongated and slanted, a little like bicycle helmets. But do not make the mistake of using a bicycle helmet instead. Each type of safety helmet is uniquely designed to withstand the rigors of a particular sport. Helmets for jumping should have short brims. Some manufacturers include Troxel, IRH, and Charles Owen.

For schooling, Western and English riders wear the same types of helmets. It is in the show ring that the distinctions appear and where the Western broad-brimmed hat with the dimpled crown faces some challenges. There are even Western hard hats, though ironically, they were designed originally for people in the construction trades who wanted the cowboy look while being safe on the job.

Fortunately, fewer and fewer people promote the idea that riding helmetless is either glamorous or gutsy, and helmets are becoming as natural and necessary as safety belts in cars.

Vests

This is your second most important piece of safety apparel, though not universally worn. The safety vest is one of the changes that awaited me when I returned to cross-country jumping after a twenty-year hiatus. In the world I had left, helmets were worn (though with fewer safety standards), but the only other safety precaution was the wearing of either a long traditional "stock" tie (like a cravat) or a bandage around your waist—in case the horse got injured!

In the intervening years the riding community—especially those involved in horse trials—learned, through some tragic accidents and near misses, that the back and abdomen were almost as vulnerable as the head. This is especially true of eventing, where the falls are likely to be provoked by massive permanent obstacles like stone walls and logs. In response, manufacturers designed something like the military flak jacket—dense padded vests that are worn over shirts. They are undoubtedly a nuisance, bulky and hot, and they feel like straitjackets and have to be well fitted to allow freedom of movement. They are also not cheap ($150–$300), but it is far better to feel like Hannibal Lecter than to become paralyzed for life.

While eventing is the only discipline that *requires* vests, I have noticed them in use among adult amateurs at show-jumping classes and hunter paces.

Footwear

The stricture about shoes in the barn applies equally to riding. Appropriate boots will not only help secure your foot in the stirrup but relieve strain and keep you safer on the ground. Even if you change into your riding clothes at the barn, you should always have protective footwear of some kind to wear while grooming and tacking up your horse. I can attest to this from personal experience, as a Belgian draft horse stepped on my foot thirty years ago and I can still feel it. Horses have good spatial awareness and certainly don't seek to tread on people, but if you are working in close quarters, in an aisle or a stall, it can happen accidentally. Some horses fidget when they're being groomed, especially in summer, when the flies give them something to fidget about.

Hair

Women, especially, will also want to contain their hair in some fashion, even if they're not in the hunt field. Only in photographic dreamscapes, advertisements, and the pages of fantasy novels do women ride with long, flowing tresses. This is dangerous and uncomfortable, even for grooming, as you will spend much of your time *under* the horse with your head hanging down! If your solution is a baseball cap, note that this can alter your peripheral vision—be very aware of where you are standing in relation to your horse.

Competition Wear

Competition wear is distinct from apparel, though some items, such as helmets and vests, double as both. Much of this is related to your horse and might include boots to protect and support his legs, studs on the underside of his hooves for gripping in slippery terrain, a breastplate to keep the saddle from slipping, and protective boots for shipping.

Appropriate gear differs from discipline to discipline, but in general it comprises a more formalized version of the categories I have reviewed, enhanced by paraphernalia for the horse.

Place a nineteenth-century hunting print side by side with a photograph of a modern rider, and you would scarcely recognize them as belonging to the same genus. In the old prints, natty gents in frock coats and top hats fly insouciantly over huge fences in positions that strike us as almost comically suicidal. True, their perfectly tied cravats were meant to keep rain off the rider's neck and to double, in times of crisis, as a bandage—for the horse.

Today's competitive rider looks more like a hockey goalie for the Toronto Maple Leafs, armored in helmets and chest protectors, toting spare horseshoes and medical kits. (In three-day eventing, a cross-country competitor is required to wear an armband with a complete medical history secured to it.)

Take the Time to Do It Right

For every accident or injury that is caused by some spectacular feat of equestrian derring-do, there are a dozen that occur because of carelessness, inattentiveness, or overconfidence; girths not tightened and checked, tack put on incorrectly, hooks unlatched, ropes badly secured, incautious maneuvers, or haste. You may be taking up riding so that you can give your type A personality a break, but this is one area where you'll want to invite it along.

Know How to Behave around Horses: On the Ground and Mounted

Animals are touch sensitive and pick up quickly on nervous, ineffective gestures. If you're uncertain about how to do something, ask. By the same token, don't become excessively casual in your newfound affinity, crawling under the horse, approaching from the rear without a soothing word of warning. The key to understanding horses is seeing things from their perspective. Remember that they are prey animals, their brains imprinted with the memory of old battles with prehistoric foes. They do not attack people but will sometimes act aggressively out of fear. Don't be too daunted by this prospect. School horses are usually calm, and if your particular animal has issues (doesn't like his ears touched, is skittish or snappish when being girthed), the responsible school will let you know or will have it posted where it will be seen.

Empathy and Spatial Awareness

Take the time to read some of the very intelligent literature on horse psychology (see "Resources") and begin to see the world from the horse's point of view. This will help you to be aware of the times when you need to take extra care in working with your horse. Maybe a farmer is coming through with a combine harvester, for instance, or a strange vehicle is parked near the stables, or someone's mare is in heat. Imagine not only that you're in your horse's head, but that you *have* your horse's head—eyes set wide apart for maximum peripheral vision. As with any good habit, it is best to get it ingrained early on.

The Basics (Again)

This sense of confidence and calm will help you through the essential tasks and skills that make up any riding experience. Learning to do these will not only ensure the health and safety of you and your horse, but will make you—eventually—a horseman, not merely a dilettante.

Grooming

Grooming is important for safety and health reasons—horses need to be checked for cuts and bruises; untended dirt accumulates and can cause skin irritation and saddle sores; stones get lodged in the underside of the hoof, an area also prone to fungal infections if not cleaned regularly. But grooming is also an excellent way to bond with your animal so that you are already used to each other by the time you mount.

Mounting

The world famous piano teacher Nadia Boulanger once said that successful concert piano playing was all in the approach to the piano, and the same might be said of mounting. A clumsy, aggressive start will leave you and your horse flustered just as you're hoping to settle calmly into your lesson routine. And the moment between leaving the mounting block and sitting on the horse, though brief, can be risky. As with airplane travel, where statistically the most crashes happen during takeoff and landing, this not-quite-on, not-quite-off stage leaves you vulnerable if the horse shies or bolts or, in the case of my strong-willed gelding, begins to wander off in search of greener pastures or less work. (Mounting from the ground, even for the limber, is not much recommended these days. It strains your back, the horse's back, and the saddle.) I've always found car-to-horse comparisons somewhat reductive, but the two do have this in common: a gentle touch works better, and rough handling can shorten the life span of both you and it.

These are skills you will acquire as you progress. In the meantime, this book is as much about how to think as how to do, how to recognize what is safe and what makes sense.

A lot of safety issues around horses read like an entry in *The Worst-Case Scenario Survival Handbook*. You have to imagine that the silliest thing you or your horse might do (Could you fall off that stool you're standing on to reach his head? Could he put his foot down on the dangling halter/leadline/brush or in the bucket?) is the most likely one, and plan accordingly.

If this seems a confusing list of dos and don'ts now, it won't for long. As with most kinetic or sense-based knowledge, the laundry list of tasks will eventually dissolve into a seamless rite, performed with just that underlying alertness that allows you to expect the unexpected. (A barnmate of mine says that grooming, with its regular rhythms, close contact with the horse, and heady, comforting smells is her favorite part of the sport.)

This book is not the place to teach you these ropes (there are some admirable books out there about practical basics, not to mention your barnmates and teachers) but to give you a general sense of what constitutes safe, effective, pleasurable riding.

All of the above assumes that you will be grooming and tacking up your own horse, which I think is key to becoming a successful horseman. Learning to groom efficiently and safely means not only learning the correct methods and tools, but putting away your gear. You have to be sure that nothing's lying in the aisle, the horse's path, or the stall. In or out of the ring, awareness of the horses and riders around you and any other miscellaneous clutter, too, is key to making you not only a safe but a civil rider. No stable has staff enough to constantly monitor the detritus of a busy day: once you begin to participate, you ipso facto become a working member of that barn.

Among the skills you should master early on is the correct way to tie a horse. This is with something called a hitch, which provides anchorage but will also slip free if the horse pulls back in alarm. Panic ensues when animals feel they can't get away from threatening situations, which is why those clichéd images of tough men hauling plunging horses at the end of a line are so pernicious. Far from finding them brave or admirable, I always want the background story—what stupid thing did they do to get the horse in that state?

Establishing confidence and trust *around* your horse is one of the best ways to be safe *on* him. In addition to grooming and handling, be sure that you know how to lead correctly, with a calm horse walking apace at your side, not plunging ahead or falling behind. Learn, too, to run your eye and hands over your horse while grooming. This sometimes reveals the hidden cuts, bruises, or insect bites. Doing so is not just humane—an uncomfortable horse is an unsafe horse.

Road Manners

Though you may begin your equestrian experience as a solitary rider in the cocoon of a private lesson, much of the rest of your life as a horseman will be spent in groups—in lessons, on trails, at horse shows. Though horses are herd animals, they are also nervy and territorial, and learning to ride safely among others is of key importance.

As I've said, there are lots of ways in which riding and driving an automobile are not alike (no road rage, no long traffic jams, or crazed taxi drivers). But one way in which they are alike is the need to watch out for the other guy. While riding is more one on one—there is less of the constant maneuvering, and traffic patterns are not as dense—it is still important to keep an eye out for fellow riders and be aware of the rules of the road. These are, basically, that riders going to the left take the rail, and riders going to the right pass on the inside. Anyone walking or adjusting tack should stay to the inside of both tracks to avoid causing a jam. Good sense and good manners dictate most of the rest of the rules: don't pass too closely; alert people to your presence and intentions; be aware of patterns others are making (circles, crossing the diagonal) and try not to get in their way. If you depart from the larger track yourself, broadcast your intentions.

Keeping your distance (one horse's length) is sometimes one of the hardest things to do. The tempo and reach of a horse's gait is determined by size, breeding, and temperament, and a class with a pony and a thoroughbred, say, will require a lot of constant adjustment on the part of both riders.

This is where you practice your new horse-sensitive spatial awareness. Just as when you're driving a car, you need to know that even if you're a safe and courteous rider, others may not be. In the aisle, in the ring, and at the show, be constantly aware of other riders. Pedestrians can also be a hazard, as people with no horse experience can be spectacularly clueless about what constitutes dangerous or careless behavior around horses. Keeping adequate space between you and a hazard is a skill worth practicing and is part of what Sally Swift means when she refers to "soft eyes"—that constant, low-level awareness of the space and activities around you. You certainly don't want to arrive at a show unaware of the courtesies, unable to share a crowded space with others. And you don't want to make another horse and rider swerve in the practice ring or bump into you. In a group lesson, you don't want to be the one who can't pace her horse, and on a trail, you will quickly become unpopular with riders and their mounts if you are always crowding someone's butt.

Watch Out for the Other Thing

Horses are famous for being scared of inanimate objects, and considering the disasters that can befall them in the barn every day, it's no wonder. So please—learn to take your tack on and off correctly and safely, and find out, if you're not in a position to judge, whether it fits the way it's supposed to. No sentient horse is going to behave nicely in a saddle that slips or pinches, a bridle that chafes or bears down incorrectly, or a girth that scrapes or jabs. You also have to be ready to run resistance between the horse and any inanimate object that might fall, flap, or get stepped on. It's amazing how much heartbreak has resulted from nails, thumbtacks, and especially undone latches. But with girthing, don't be too spooked by the horse's sensitivity. The first thing you'll learn is that horses tend to distend their bellies when first being saddled and slowly let this air out as they are walked and exercised. You'll be told to check your girth several times during the course of a ride. The first time should be just before you mount—you'll usually find out that you can already go up a few holes. This should eventually become second nature, and you'll learn to do it right from the saddle.

Ride to Your Level: Baby Steps to Bigger Steps

As you progress with your riding and become more confident and perhaps ambitious, safety issues become more acute. You'll need to go beyond those standard precautions dictated by common sense and attention to detail. The actions you undertake to protect yourself will change as you grow as a rider, but there's one you'll come to grips with almost immediately: expressing fear or uncertainty. If your instructor asks you to try something risky and there is a thin voice inside you, saying, "No, no, no," even as your public voice is saying "Yes," learn to listen to that tremulous inner being and figure out when it's telling you something vital and when it's merely yanking your chain.

During lessons, when you're being asked to attempt new gaits, or begin jumping, or take the reins for the first time alone as a rider or driver, safety versus challenge becomes a delicate balance between you and your teacher's perception. Her eye is telling her one thing; your gut says something else.

As we've discussed, the blind insouciance of youth is rarely the lot of the adult rider. We have far too much at stake, and caution is ingrained in us. But try not to let this get in the way of genuine progress if your teacher feels that you're really ready to try something new.

The obverse is also true. It has to be said that some men coming to this sport later in life become reckless riders in their need to prove themselves robust and masterful—the *City Slickers* movie syndrome, I call it. My advice is to save the testosterone for the video games. This sort of thing can damage you and your horse, and in the end it makes you look only foolish, not brave. I know of one man who switched from driving Formula One racing cars to riding horses with no perceptible shift in attitude and technique. He must have been a more-than-adequate driver, but horses don't respond well to the bear-down-on-the-throttle approach.

And you need to urge your instructor to give you an honest assessment, even if it hurts. Without encouragement, instructors may be wary of alienating a paying client unless you make clear that you prefer honesty to flattery or evasion.

You'll need to examine this issue anew at every stage of your riding that might pose a threat. Where's your comfort level? If you feel that leaden dread creeping over your body, for goodness' sake, tell your teacher. Consider this description of fear by therapist Barbara Schulte in an August 2000 *Horse Illustrated* article by Sue Furman: It's "the part of your mind that looks into the future, envisions the negative outcome, and accepts it as real." Physiological reactions, however irrational, can make it impossible for you to coordinate properly. No matter how good you are, at that moment when you freeze up, you're an unsafe rider.

When to Go for It

Speaking of assessing your abilities accurately, when do you begin to compete? One instructor of mine tellingly commented after I'd had a disastrous practice ride for a hunter class I was determined to enter, "You should do this only when it's almost boring." A satisfying ride is never boring, of course, but the spirit of her remark is apt. You begin competing when the task required has become second nature. If it's physically ingrained in a way that allows you to approach your competition as a challenge about strategy, presentation, and public display instead of survival, you're probably ready to give it a shot.

This is always true, even if the effort is a fairly modest one. You're going into a walk-trot class, and you need to know that you can stay on at those gaits. And a show is a fine place to learn how to negotiate a course, but it's not the place to learn how to jump a fence!

A trusting relationship with your teacher or trainer is key. If he or she suggests a show before you feel ready, try to figure out whether your nerves have to do with stage fright or real physical uncertainty. If you're keen as mustard but she's dubious, think back on those past three lessons where you crashed into the jump standards or wound up on your horse's ears.

And it goes without saying, get there by practice. Don't enter a competition months in advance, allow your busy (and I know it is) schedule to eat up your lesson time, and turn up expecting to show effectively. There are excellent books and articles on show preparation. This is just fair warning in the context of safety. In riding, haste makes waste, and the waste is you!

Be a Good Match for Your Horse

In the end, the thing that is going to make you feel safest is your horse. Don't expect this sense of security to come right away, but at some point—a basal temperature, if you will, different for each person—the awkwardness and unfamiliarity should be sufficiently smoothed away. You begin to know the difference between feeling a bit uncertain about your skills and feeling unsafe on a horse.

School horses come from many sources, and while the best of them are willing partners in the learning process, some are sour and devious, and some are simply too willful for a rider without very secure skills.

If you've reached the stage, as I have on occasion, where the very sight of a horse's name opposite yours on a bulletin board creates a sinking feeling, speak up. At best, a sour (there's no such thing as a bad) horse will erode your pleasure and commitment; at worst, you're both an accident waiting to happen—but only if you fail to speak up. The best instructors and schools make arbitrary decisions for their own convenience. They may have no idea of what's troubling you. Schools often protect difficult, worn out, or old horses by continuing to use them. It may be a disguised humanitarian gesture that you're continually assigned to a tough horse, or it might be a compliment to your abilities. Find out which it is, and go from there. If it's your own horse, be realistic about whether you're going through a bad patch with him or you're having problems because you just can't manage him. Part IV deals with the acquisition of that horse and how to make an exciting—but realistic and safe—choice.

Keep Your Personal Health Concerns in Mind

Apart from overall fitness, which will help to prevent accidents and injuries by keeping your body toned and responsive, any latent or chronic health issues can have a negative impact on your abilities.

Veterinary medical technician Rusty Lowe, who is often part of the emergency response team at horse shows, believes that riding schools should have relevant medical histories and protocols for each rider. Episodes triggered by such chronic ailments as asthma, diabetes, or epilepsy require immediate response. Lifesaving minutes can be spared if the facility is prepared. Where's the barn phone? Does it work? Are you alone with a horse, with nobody around to help in the event of an emergency? In horse trials competition, as I've mentioned, competitors wear a medical arm band when jumping, so if you're knocked out by a fall, your doctor can be alerted. When it comes to situations such as asthma attacks and allergic reactions to bee stings, however, if you're unconscious, it's already far too late.

Even if you don't suffer from a chronic illness, Lowe recommends getting a thorough checkup before you begin riding. A doctor's findings can prepare you for the exacerbation of old injuries (a torn cartilage of mine blew up like a balloon the minute I started to ride again) or alert you to incipient arthritis or other conditions that might affect your strength and mobility.

This vigilance and common sense should also come into play if you do sustain an injury. Accidents do happen despite the best precautions, and if you have a fall, even if it seems mild, it is essential to check for any injuries, even if not immediately felt or perceived. These can range from strained tendons or ligaments to nerve damage or to concussive injuries that may prove fatal if not identified right away. And if you are unfortunate enough even to have a more serious injury, a slow, nurturing recovery is essential. Riders are often dangerously keen to get back in the saddle, and several safety committees are urging a recommendation that riders have a thorough exam before riding again. As a casual rider, you're not likely to have the oversight of professional committees. Your own common sense must be your guide.

Above all, be physically and mentally ready to ride. When riders make unsafe choices, Lowe says, "that's when they see me"—upside down, from the ground.

So if riding for you is everything it promises to be, your heart may occasionally wind up in your mouth. Wise, considerate, attentive practice will keep it beating in your body.

Part IV

Choosing a Horse

23

Taking the Plunge A Horse of Your Own

There may be no more thrilling moment than the one in which you realize that you want a horse of your own. Because this is such a huge decision, it is easy to miss the immensity of the forest while hunting through the trees of purchase. Bear in mind that, as in marriage, you are committing your life to a living creature, and in this case one whose happiness, well-being, food, lodging, and health becomes your utter responsibility. There's every reason to do this if you are really ready, and every reason not to if you just think having a horse would be fun. Of course, it will be fun (as well as arduous), but there are other, more cogent reasons to determine whether now is the time.

When Lessons Are Not Enough

1. You've been enjoying your lessons but feel that you've been riding too many different horses or that one horse on whom you've made a certain amount of progress isn't going to be able to push you to the next level. You feel you've reached your limits.

2. You've begun competing or would like to begin competing, and either there is no horse available for you, or horses are available only on a too-limited basis.

3. You'd like to compete but really want to go forward into competition with an animal with whom you will have a sustained partnership.

4. You've realized that you have found your discipline (dressage, driving, hunting) and it clearly calls for a better class of horse than you have access to.

5. You know (and I mean you know) that you want a deeper relationship with a horse than is possible when you are simply one of several people with access to a school horse. In some ways this is the best reason because all else will follow from that bond.

Now that you've made this momentous decision, there are still several options and scenarios to consider.

Buy, Lease, or Share

The purchase of a horse gives you the full pleasure, but also the full responsibility—in terms of time, money, and mental focus—for realizing your full potential on a horse. Be sure that you have the resources not only in terms of money, but in terms of an appropriate boarding and training environment. Assuming you're ready to commit to a training regime, consider, especially if you're planning to keep a horse at home, that you're about to acquire another child—larger, but with the same day-in, day-out demands. These include daily feeding and grooming, stable management, the disposal of manure, and a host of related responsibilities, including insurance. See "Resources" for books that can help guide this particular decision.

Wayward economies produce their own inventiveness, and the horse world is no different. Because many riders today have both limited means and limited time, an arrangement other than full ownership might be the one for you.

Leasing

In a lease arrangement, as with cars or equipment, you pay an owner or establishment for the use of an animal. This is a frequent scenario when the animal's owner is a college-bound student or has more horses than he or she can keep in work. You're still not the legal owner, and you do forfeit certain rights. Sometime you're asked to share in vet bills, or the terms of the lease stipulate that you pay all or part of a horse's board in lieu of a flat fee. You may have the full use of the horse for the duration of your lease, which runs for a specific period of time—a year, or a season. Be sure you know exactly what your legal risks and responsibilities are, as well as what fees you have agreed to cover, and secure the terms of the arrangement in writing even if—in fact, especially if—you're dealing with a friend. The clearer your arrangements are on paper, the less likely you are to wind up wrangling over them in person.

Sharing

This sometimes also involves an absentee owner, but you're more often sharing actual access to the horse with someone else who also rides it, dividing the board and other expenses. You work out a schedule that suits you both. There are many variations of this arrangement—the horse might be owned by a school, by a third party who is absent or no longer directly involved with the animal, or by the two of you. This last is not advisable. It didn't work for King Lear or the Biblical women counseled by Solomon, and creatures don't divide any better than kingdoms or babies. Any lease/share arrangement involving a horse requires an extraordinarily generous and level-headed owner, preferably one with a good sense of humor. But there are such people in the horse world.

One key element to the success of a plan like this is that you have similar, or at least compatible, plans and goals, and of course, that you work within the same general lexicon.

The advantages of sharing are partly economic, naturally. They also give you a taste of horsemanship without all of its responsibilities, and if your schedule is such that you can't really give full time and attention to your riding, this can be a perfect compromise. Leasing is also a useful way to get a sense of a horse before committing to buying it. An animal that seems appealing during lessons and in the confines of an arena may, when you begin to spend more time with it, reveal quirks or weaknesses you hadn't suspected.

Horse for Hire

As opposed to leasing a horse, you may want to look into hiring one. This is a very different kind of arrangement, much more allied to renting a car than testing an animal. Many areas have local dealers who hire horses for special events such as hunts or hunter paces, but this is usually a one-time deal, not a way to test-drive a specific animal. The horses can vary widely in quality, depending on the scruples of the dealer, and you need to be fairly secure in your abilities for this to be a sensible choice. In some ways, it's more useful as a way of sampling a new kind of equestrian experience than a particular animal. It's also expensive. As we've discussed in the chapter on hunting in part I, you can easily wind up paying a couple of hundred dollars for a little impulse that lasts exactly one day.

Dream Machines: Buying Your Own Horse

Let us assume for a moment that you have weighed your options, and you have decided to buy. This is the most comprehensive commitment you can make, and the one requiring the most steps, discussions, and hazards, so I'll go over this topic in detail. Some of these same points come into play, of course, even if you are sharing or leasing, particularly assessing the character of the horse, so take away from this section what is important to you right now.

Supporting Your Horse

Every project needs a budget, and make no mistake, a horse is a project. There are two principle elements to a budget, and again, they bear some relation to other large staples of our consumer culture such as cars, houses, and children. (Children? Yes, of course. A horse is a living creature whose usefulness and quality of life is going to be dependent on your economic stability, so anything else that significantly depends on or affects your stability becomes part of the equation.) There's the initial outlay, and then there's maintenance, which is by far the more costly of the two in the long run, unless you shelled out for an international-quality horse. In a sense, you need to approach the venture in reverse: figure out how much it will cost you to board, keep, and train your horse, and then determine what you can afford to spend on your initial purchase. Whatever the outcome of your calculations, the answer will always be more than you think.

Here again, these are subdivisions that will affect your choice: different types of board for different situations, none of which need affect you if you decide not to lease or buy. But once you do wind up with a horse on your hands—or even half a horse, as this common leasing arrangement has a lot to recommend it—there are some everyday expenses to consider. Who's going to feed the horse, and how much stabling will it need? The answer depends on your circumstances, the horse's individual needs, and what you can come up with in your area.

First, the deluxe solution: many training facilities offer something called "training board." This is a form of revenue enhancement for the barn and also a way of offering continuity to boarders who compete regularly. In training board, in addition to basic care, a staff member will ride the horse on a regular basis in your absence. If you and your horse are in an intensive training program (for high-level dressage, for example) where your goals can really be advanced by having a professional ride your animal, this might be worth the considerable extra expense. Otherwise, frankly, I'd be leery of these arrangements. Too often the "training" can consist of a few hasty circuits around the ring, something you could pay a reliable friend or acquaintance to do. If you're only a weekend rider, the need to keep your horse properly conditioned does arise, but the most expensive solution isn't always the right one.

The most common arrangement for horse care, other than keeping the animal in the backyard, is called "full board." Full board guarantees your horse a berth in a stall and full care, meaning that he is fed, watered, and mucked out. Some barns will allow variations in this that might alter the price—for instance, if you're available to feed and muck out your animal yourself. In general, however, these small businesses really want your money and find too many special circumstances deleterious to the smooth running of their operations.

Pasture board is exactly what the name implies—your horse is kept outdoors with one or more companions, usually in a pasture with some kind of shed to protect them in inclement weather. Grazing is supplemented with hay and feed when the grass grows thin, but basically this is a no-frills arrangement.

In most boarding arrangements, fees are charged monthly and usually include basic feed (grain mixtures and hay) only. Special supplements, veterinary care, and shoeing are all extra and are your direct responsibility, though the barn will usually be responsible for arranging these things to happen. When you're working out your budget, be sure to factor in that any special circumstances (corrective shoeing or veterinary needs, for example) will increase the basic cost. I have not put any actual figures against this sample budget because costs and fees vary widely from region to region, and even county to county. You will want to research the going rates in your area and then put together your own sample budget.

Horse "Line Items"

Board

Farrier

Wormer

Basic veterinary care

Training

Transport

Shows, clinics, master classes

Extras (there's always something)

24

Boarding Issues

We've talked a little about board in connection with fees, but let's examine some of these concepts in more detail. Considering a boarding facility is a little like looking for a school; you're looking under the surface for the substance.

First of all, a reality check: the only way you can have complete control over how your horse is cared for is to keep him yourself. Otherwise, you have to choose wisely, monitor carefully, and know that you have ceded a certain amount of authority to your proxies. Even if you board with friends, you'll find that they don't want you looking over their shoulder all the time, and often have definite ideas about what kinds of regimes, feed, and supplements might work well for your animal in the context of their stable management practices. As you do when you deal with doctors, be sure that you fully participate in any decision when it's first made, and then let them get on with it.

Having said that, the key is to be sure you have been obsessive in your initial investigations. Only then will you be comfortable with letting events and establishments take their course. There are a number of areas where you should be concerned.

"Good Housekeeping" Seal of Approval

No matter what kind of boarding arrangement you wind up with, it's absolutely vital that the horse be guaranteed regular turnout each day. Horses who are not able to run free and graze—the natural state of which domesticity has deprived them—become morose, neurotic, and prey to a host of disorders, from stable vices to ulcers to lameness. Too much confinement can render them useless for riding or even impair their health.

"No foot, no horse"—a horse, at least a working partner, is only as good as his feet. These should be cleaned daily, and a regular and attentive shoeing policy should be pursued. You, in turn, should learn enough about shoeing and various techniques and options to participate intelligently in these crucial discussions and decisions.

Your horse should be checked for injuries daily. Horses can easily damage themselves at play. Hurling those massive bodies around is bound to cause problems, and they're always at risk from a host of natural and man-made perils—fencing, insects, holes in the ground, and so on. Prompt discovery almost invariably makes the difference between a rapid recovery and a serious condition or lameness. If you spot something, draw it to the attention of the barn manager or responsible person in your setup. Then look for evidence that something is being done about it. At one barn the stable manager would always say, "I'll look into it," a phrase I came to recognize as her rote response to clients, promising no action whatever.

The establishment should be well maintained. The criteria you used to seek a school (see chapter 14) apply here but are suddenly of much greater importance. Evidence that stalls aren't cleaned daily, that dangerous implements are left lying about, that feed is not kept fresh and secure from vermin, are all threats to your horse's health and well-being.

The company he keeps should be safe and reliable. Horses are herd animals, and unless yours is a sociopath, he should be turned out with others, but only after a supervised acclimatization period during which the prospective pasture mates meet, greet, and do some (minor) playful damage to each other. Even if you're told your horse is a sociopath, you might try to find a pasture mate for him anyway. Stables sometimes use a single incident as the basis for an erroneous impression and wind up isolating animals who yearn for company.

As many purchase and boarding situations evolve from lessons and training, you may already be allied to a barn that has shaped your training and competitive goals. If you're not, your needs should factor into where you decide to move your horse. This is especially true if you don't have transport of your own. Barns often travel and compete collectively, so it is difficult to be, say, the only horse trials competitor in a dressage barn, or to try to make it to a range of trail rides when everyone around you is focused on the hunter circuit. Eventually, if you become seriously competitive, you may wish to invest in your own trailer.

If you board with friends or neighbors, there is less of a tribal imperative, but it is just as well, in all cases of boarding, to spell out what the terms are. You should have a clear understanding of your fees, the insurance coverage the barn has, whether you have free access to the barn or notice is required, what decision-making powers the barn has if your horse is ill or injured, and what level of treatment and expense you're committed to if something goes wrong.

Again, it's worth soliciting the opinions of people who already board at any place you are considering. Are they there out of apathy, or commitment, or contentment?

Taking the Plunge

Price Points

Now is the time to move boldly into a consideration of the actual price you might wind up paying for a horse. In case you haven't gathered by now, you don't always get what you pay for in the horse world. As the horse has moved from being a partner in farming and the military into the category of companion animal and luxury item, all the usual mechanisms of a consumer market have followed, building on some fine old traditions of double dealing and chicanery that were already firmly in place. Nevertheless, it is possible, with careful research, to get some idea of base prices in your area for a particular breed of horse. After that, you have to bring caution, intelligence, knowledge (your own or someone else's), forbearance, common sense, and focus to your decision. There's also an element of luck.

First, if you've come this far, you probably know by now what you want from your riding, and that in turn dictates something about your choice. (Next we'll consider what type of horse might be best for you.) Then you consider the realm of potential versus proven, or as equestrian parlance has it, "green" versus "made" (or something between the two). In the horse world, the value system that defines the purchase of consumer goods is inverted. In the car business, buying used vehicles involves calculating the risk of acquiring, for less money, something with attrition; new, theoretically at least, means the vehicle is undamaged and will perform better. In the horse world, "used" equals experienced. Unless the experience has soured or damaged a horse, you're going to pay more for it. Of course, the more traditional concerns do arise in terms of wear and tear and, more importantly, in bad training and vices, but on the whole you can expect to pay more for a made horse than a green one. Then the question becomes, "Made into what?"

It's hard to give average prices for horses because there are as many variables as there are animals. One way to get a feel for what's out there, at what cost, is to look in newspaper, magazine, and Internet listings.

Announcing that you are in the market for a horse is like publishing a notice that you're a rich widow in the market for a husband. Dozens of prospects will appear or will have been spotted by everyone from your teacher to your blacksmith. Listings will leap out at you as bridal magazines draw the eyes of prospective brides, and the thicker and faster they come, the more bewildering they seem. This is as private a language—as full of encoded meaning, obfuscation, concealment, and inflation—as car advertising and real estate. As a friend of mine observed after a frustrating summer of horse hunting, "They're always for sale just because 'the daughter's gone off to college.'" In other words, "Tell me another one."

Everyone has heard stories of miraculous bargains or even just good deals. I paid three thousand dollars ten years ago for the first horse I would own as an adult, and he proved himself worth several times the asking price. But realistically, if a horse is extraordinarily cheap by marketplace standards, there's usually a reason. Let's start with the understanding that the base price for a horse varies wildly, depending on where you live and what the local stock looks like. Two thousand dollars will buy you a really nice young endurance prospect in, say, Idaho, whereas it'll get you a creaky, retired polo pony in Millbrook, New York—maybe. You have to accurately take the temperature of your region. Okay, let's just say that two hundred bucks will hardly get you out of the barn, and twenty thousand should stand you in decent stead in the show ring. But what you're angling for is somewhere in between, so that at the modest end you might wind up paying three thousand to six thousand dollars, and at the high end, thirty-five thousand dollars (and they go higher, but generally only for outstanding competition prospects, priced for the very well-heeled amateur and professional markets).

You might find a nice, solid hunter for $6,500. You might be offered a lovely old school horse for free. You could pay $25,000 for an animal that's never sound enough to ride. So start by winkling information out of everybody you meet. How much did they pay for their horses, and where? (Keep in mind that some people will lie.) Myriad books and articles are devoted to this complex subject, in addition to my suggestions here. The classified ads in the *Chronicle of the Horse*, available online, are reputed to be the best source for professionals and are regarded as the industry standard. But a neighbor selling a horse without running any ads at all may save you mileage and money—provided it's the right horse.

Budget

To make a realistic assessment of your budget level, you'll have to know your needs, the going rates in your area, and what you can realistically afford to come up with in cash without emptying your portfolio, mortgaging you house, or depriving you child of his college education. this is one reason why it's important to have the board issues settled in advance.

But the purchase is only the beginning.

25

Buying Your Perfect Horse

"We know where we're going from where we've been," writes the poet May Sarton, and in your journey toward your own horse (be it your first or simply first in a long while), you are carrying with you the weight of your past, as well as expectations about the future. Where do you look? Where do you go? Who do you trust?

Getting Advice

In the musical *My Fair Lady*, an exasperated Henry Higgins sings, "Let a woman in your life, and your serenity is through." Substitute "horse" for "woman" and you have some idea of the confusion that can reign when you plunge into the equestrian community in search of a mount. Among the perils for Higgins: hordes of gossiping women eager to discuss his faults. Among the perils for you? Hordes of gossipingfriends/neighbors/teachers/experts eager to tell you where and how to get the perfect horse or possibly force it on you if you fail to see how brilliant their suggestions are.

There are a number of reasons to be wary about this flood of expertise, though of course you may want some input.

First of all, advice is not always free. A professional who offers to help you find a horse will almost certainly charge you a finder's fee if you wind up buying, usually 10 percent of the horse's total cost. If you're not clear about your parameters, you can wind up having a considerable sum demanded of you as payment for what might have been nothing more than a few phone calls. Remember, too, that everyone's taste and criteria are not your own. The horse world is filled with unperceived alliances and deals, and as in any burgeoning consumer market, there's a great deal of hype. Your riding instructor or trainer may also take a fee but has a vested interest in your well-being and ability to look good.

In my own field of horse trials, for example, Irish-bred horses are extremely popular. It's not unusual for the asking price for a horse to be $35,000 just because the seller talks with a brogue.

Friends' advice is another matter entirely, and there the problem is clutter. If you keep second-guessing yourself or borrowing other people's minds, you will never know your own. One good friend whose experience and judgment you trust may be a useful foil to your own expectations, as well as a companion on those long drives to view the latest prospect. The same is true of professionals, and in these days of video and the Internet, it is at least possible to get a critique of an animal without having to ship it or your expert around.

None of this, of course, precludes the standard procedures with a sale prospect of trying out the horse (several times if you can) and getting a thorough examination from a vet. Taking the horse for a trial period is the ideal solution, one you should press for, though not all sellers are in a position to comply.

Where to Look

There are an estimated nine million horses in the United States, but when you are looking for one, the right one, at the right price, it can sometimes seem as if there is none. Start with word of mouth and listings in local and national papers and establishments. The mechanisms for sale are (with some grandiose exceptions) similar at the high and low end, so all avenues are worth at least an initial exploration. As with real estate sales, this will accustom you to the nuances and the language of horse trading. And this slightly random approach is not as purposeless as it may seem: a horse is a part of someone's life cycle, and you may indeed encounter the right partner just because his rider has moved onto a different phase in his or her progress. There's also a certain amount of seasonality, especially for horses on the various show circuits. People are often looking to sell at the end of the season (October–November) so that they don't have to board a horse through the unproductive winter when they do not intend to keep him. And sometimes those stories about the kid going to college are actually true, so July and August are also good months to look!

A particularly good place to look and get a feel for what you want is horse shows and events. Depending on what discipline you've decided to pursue, shows are a good place to see prospective mounts in action, and many people use competitions as a way of displaying horses who are on the market. A friend was given a preview of a wonderful horse for sale just because it was in the trailer next to hers at a schooling trial.

Horse Traders

There is, alas, a reason why horse trading has a dubious (all right, rotten) reputation. The blurry contours of the American horse world, especially in the realm of the "average" horse, allow for all kinds of chicanery. Race horses and full breeds with well-organized breed societies behind them have reasonably secure methods for tracing the provenance and history of a horse. If you buy a horse with papers, at least you have some idea of what you're getting. But even that doesn't guarantee a whole lot—and certainly doesn't tell you anything about technical brilliance, temperament, or even conformation. Having papers on a horse still makes it less easy for a seller to gloss over a history of damage or bad behavior, or conversely, to invent a glowing history.

But only a small percentage of horses on the market are registered as being anything in particular. Once you venture outside registered stock, you're often in the realm of invention, or at least, evasion. As mentioned earlier, many a prospect, it seems, is on the market only because "the owner is going to college/having a baby/giving up riding." Someone may tell you the animal has been "shown in Ireland/hunted in Ireland/born in Ireland," generally an indication that the price tag is going to be on the high side. Bills of lading can be substituted; most reassuring is if the seller can produce a picture from an identifiable locale. As "sport horses" (the new term for crossbred horses designed to meet today's competitive expectations) become a more established sector of the equine population, the system of registry and review that exists in Europe is beginning to be established here through the American Sport Horse Registry. (To their credit, responsible sport horse breeders are eager for this to happen.) In the meantime, beware of the combination of plausibility and paucity (i.e., no real history of the animal, just vague claims), as that often signals a problematic history.

I mention this because dealers often keep a low profile and appear integrated in their local communities, or are established at a particular barn, or are your instructor, moonlighting. This is not your father's horse dealer—a stereotypical carny type with a yard full of dubious nags—but someone who always seems to have one or two horses for sale. If you're shopping, they'll make themselves known eventually, and you just have to be alert for the combination of persuasion and evasiveness that are common to the trade.

Breeders and Dealers

Some distinction, too, should be made between breeders and dealers, and it is often just the distinction you might expect. Many breeders, even modest ones, are genuinely interested in establishing or maintaining bloodlines, either of an existing breed or by exploring the potential of one of the many crossbreeds—an area that is still more an art than a science. (One man in my area of upstate New York stands a magnificent Shire draft horse stallion the size of a small raft. He usually mates with thoroughbred or half-thoroughbred mares. When the offspring of these trysts live up to their physical potential, they are magnificent—strong, bold heads on solid but lithe bodies, intuitive and gallant tempers. Sometimes, however, they wind up looking like the child's game in which one person draws the head of a character and the other, without reference to the first picture, attaches a body. Or they have no wind, or are by turns hectic and leaden.)

Local breeders, especially those whose progeny you've seen, are always worth a visit. Dealers, on the other hand, are just that. To them a horse is a commodity, and their job is to bring them in, spruce them up, and send them out as quickly as possible. This often involves a program of accelerated training and competition designed to make a horse appear finished but in a way that, like bad veneer, tends to chip off soon. Good children can come from bad homes, and good horses can come from bad circumstances, but this is not where you want to begin your search, especially if you don't have a trained eye.

The Internet

As with many other areas of global commerce, the Internet has become a significant conduit of horses in recent years. While some bold souls have made actual purchases on the basis of a picture, a history, and a vet check only, I would still use the Web as part of your first layer of research only—and arrange to see and ride the animal if at all possible. (Many people, in this new environment of digital commerce, will be willing to get a video to you so that you can see a horse more fully at rest and under saddle before committing to traveling; the investment of $100 when he is hoping to make $15,000 or more should not be an impediment to the seller.) While it is true that your vet check (see the section later in this chapter) and contractual language should protect you against being stuck with a horse who is unsound, that's not really the point. You're not planning to buy just a horse, but your horse, one who must evoke some intuitive response in you. By all means use the Internet to identify something in your price range, but try to make your final decision a personal one.

You've made this momentous decision because you think you know what you want from your riding. What will that tell you about what you want from a horse? The art dealer Holly Solomon, who represented Robert Rauschenberg, among other leading contemporary artists, tells an anecdote about once trying to dissuade some prospective buyers from taking an expensive painting because, having seen their house, she realized they wouldn't be happy with it. Unfortunately, horse people are not always so elaborately scrupulous, and anybody will be happy to sell you anything. So it's up to you, your common sense, and your bank account to have a clear idea of what you want. It's useless to pretend it's not an emotional decision, but if emotion isn't coupled with restraint, you can all too easily wind up with the opposite of what you want, a horse who prevents you from realizing your dreams.

Horses Are Like Clothes . . . Buy for Who You Are, Not Who You Wish You Were

If you're short, dark, and wiry, dyeing your hair blonde will not turn you into an alluring California screen goddess. (And gentlemen, if you're slender, or solidly built, the licensed team jersey isn't going to turn you into Shaquille O'Neill, or Derek Jeter, or whoever your sports idol is.) We're encouraged by advertising to buy products that represent things we would like to be, but this is a bad way to buy horses.

This is not to say that you are not looking for an animal who can help you to realize specific goals as a rider and possible competitor, but it must be a horse you can ride now. However beautiful or majestic or flashy, a horse who is too strong for you or who makes you nervous will begin to erode your pleasure and your confidence. And a horse that seems sluggish or apathetic or just resists going forward may perform willingly for someone more advanced than you are, but if you feel every lesson is going to be a long struggle just to get the motor going, it can be as discouraging as wondering whether you're going to be run away with or dumped.

Many horses, especially those in the medium price ranges with some schooling, have a range of basic skills. The "average" Western horse can jog and turn neatly; the "average" English-schooled horse can walk, trot, canter, and probably navigate low fences. And this may be just right for you at your current stage. It doesn't make a lot of sense to buy (at vast expense) a high-powered jumper just off the show circuit if you're just learning to jump. He'll be bored and impatient (states of mind that, at two-thirds of a ton, manifest themselves in unpleasant ways), and you'll be intimidated. Other kinds of athletes "scale back" more graciously—a retired endurance horse may be the perfect trail horse.

Of course, if you and your instructor believe you're ready to accelerate your training, by all means look for a talented animal who will help you to do that.

Green or Made?

Green

As we touched on in pricing, these two rough divisions apply to all types of horses. Green horses, relatively unschooled, are usually being sold on the basis of potential (though occasionally you get an older horse who just hasn't been trained). The breeder or dealer usually has some particular potential in mind (dressage horse, trail horse, jumper), but you are taking that assertion on trust and are also assuming the burden of realizing that potential yourself. The upside is that you are usually getting a horse with little wear and tear and many productive years ahead of him. The downside is that you will have to invest several years in time, patience, and money (possibly engaging the services of a trainer) before you can reap the benefits.

Green also has a variety of meanings in the parlance—everything from barely backed to "just started over fences" (a common note in sales listings).

Made

A horse with a past—as long as that past doesn't appear to include injury or abuse—is often just the right choice for an older rider. This is a horse who will know the basics, whatever that happens to mean for your particular milieu—basic English or Western gaits; low-level dressage; some show experience. This type of horse may actually have had a career already and just be ready to move on. The upside is that you will have a horse who can take you places now; the downside is that a horse with mileage may have some physical or mental issues, and not necessarily dramatic ones, like old injuries, but those that come naturally with age—arthritis, stiffness, hoof problems, skin tone—like us, really. With good care and maintenance, especially with current advances in nutrition, few of these should pose any problem.

More challenging are issues of attitude, temperament, and already ingrained training. Older horses are realized individuals. You may be able to work through stubbornness, timidity, or tension, but you are unlikely, late in his career, to fundamentally alter his makeup. Then, too, some horses have been trained, but not for the job you want them to do. My horse Jonathan Swift was trained as a show jumper, and he tends to be tense and overexcited. Since I'm also a dressage rider, I have had to work hard for several years to get him to relax and to hold his whole body differently.

I hasten to add that *made* doesn't necessarily mean a senior citizen. Horses are in their prime between nine and twelve years, just when they are often coming to the end of the first phase of their careers, and are ready to take you into a satisfying second decade. And if the seller really knows the horses and is relatively honest, he or she might be able to discuss limitations as well.

Your School or Instructor: Not Necessarily the First Stop

Why not? Because the path of least resistance is not always the right one, and you may be shrinking your horizons and narrowing your options before you need to. School horses have a punishing regime, even at well-run schools, being ridden two to three times a day by a variety of people at a variety of skill levels. This can result in a horse who is jaded and fretful or has a pattern of resistance. It is also true that school horses are frequently acquired because age or injury has taken them out of more competitive environments, so you may be looking at a compromised animal whose eventual health, if too much is asked of him, will be problematic.

Also, schools are businesses: without resorting to active chicanery, they are not averse to using their familiar contexts and established relationship with you to influence your choices, especially if they are likely to gain you as a paying boarder and get the purchase price of a horse. A teacher is only human, and it's easy to imagine a rider only in a particular frame or context, mounted at a certain level, if there is overt or even subtle pressure to do so. A good school horse can be a tremendous bargain, but the good ones are the ones they want to keep.

There are radiant exceptions to these slightly gloomy rules, certainly. One friend rescued a school horse so chronically lame from laminitis (a degenerative disease of the hoof) that there was talk of putting him down, only to find that with proper turnout and better shoeing he had five good years left as an event horse.

I would only say that if you lose your heart to a school horse, don't be tempted to skip the normal stages of examination to make your dream a reality. Both you and your horse will fare better for your knowing the full picture.

The Eye of the Beholder

When we want something badly, our minds often leap ahead from the possibility to the actuality, blithely eliding the careful steps between. So it is very tempting, but costly, to move quickly from the sight of a horse who pleases you to the image of the two of you in the show ring, over the course, or on the trail. But it is those crucial in-between steps that should really determine your decision.

Find out everything you can or that your contacts can tell you. Where was the horse bred? Who's owned him? What has he done? Any problems—physical or attitudinal? Current status? Age? This not only elicits information you need to have to make a decision, but it tells you something about the seller. If the person you're dealing with seems evasive or hyperbolic, he may be concealing or inventing something.

See the horse personally. Even if you've already seen photos or a video, it's not the same as watching the horse directly when he is before you. Awkward light and clumsy or adroit camera angles can disguise a horse's real motion, pace, or conformation.

Watch his movement. The ideal motion for a horse differs depending on his type and use, but in general you are looking for free forward motion without a sense of stiffness or the sort of head shaking or tail swishing that suggests either discomfort or a difficult personality. If you don't trust your own eye, this is where a friend or adviser might be helpful, and bear in mind that these are preliminary findings only. If you're close to a commitment to purchase, a vet will do a more thorough exam. In fact, sometimes a horse's behavior under saddle will suggest a line of inquiry—a difficult canter depart might indicate a sore back, for example.

You can also try to get some sense of conformation here: your prospective mount does not need to be worthy of Stubbs, but neither should she be strikingly disproportionate, appear cow hocked, or have narrow withers or splayed feet. These are not merely cosmetic issues but things that can eventually affect the health and use of an animal. Purebred horses should also more or less conform to their breed standards, examples of which can be found online and in myriad horse guides and encyclopedias.

Watch his performance under saddle. You are not only assessing an animal in motion, but an animal under saddle. How does he seem to respond to a rider? Of course, the real key is going to be how he responds to you. A professional rider can make a difficult animal presentable, so it is vital that you get a direct opportunity to try out a horse. Any seller who will not permit this definitely has something to conceal, and you are better off backing away.

Test-Driving

Insofar as it's possible, you need to get some idea of how a horse is likely to react to the types of circumstances she is going to encounter with you. This almost certainly means, among other things, that you need to try her both indoors and out. A docile horse in the ring could turn out to be flighty and spooky the minute you get her on the trail. (And unfortunately, sometimes they have been drugged into docility.) I once took a horse for a thirty-day trial period and had to insure her for that duration. I was leery after my first experience, and I found that the mare was fine at her own barn but at the age of ten had never been anywhere else and acted accordingly.

The Test-Drive

Other than terrain, treat this ride like any other ride: take time to warm up, in both directions. See whether you can get the horse to relax for you before you begin to take him through his paces. Since a test-ride functions as a sort of compressed introduction, the seller will probably have some pointers about how to get the best performance from the animal, and there is no reason not to take this advice. But you should also follow your instincts—if the horse seems only to respond to some style of riding that is totally alien to you (a death grip on the mouth, constant thumping with the leg), the experience of riding him is going to be like distorting your body to get a suit to fit.

More than during even the most stringent lessons, this is the time to listen to your body and the small changes in your mind. I have heard enough friends persuade themselves into feelings about a horse they thought was suitable, at least on paper, to know how acute hindsight can be if one hasn't been really physically attentive during the ride. In New Age parlance, this is a time to live in the moment if ever there was one.

If you plan to jump this horse, jump him; if you're going to do competitive trail riding, have the seller lay down some poles for you. If you just want an amiable hack, see whether someone can come out on a trail with you.

The Second Ride

If a horse is really beginning to appeal to you and the owner seems willing to work with you, you may want to arrange for a second ride. This can be useful for several reasons. It gives you a chance to mull over your responses and discuss them with the people you are soliciting for advice, and it might make it possible to work with the horse under different conditions, terrain, or weather.

When I bought my last horse, whom I intended to event, I first tried him out in a ring. This first ride certainly told me something about him, enough to pique my interest, but nothing about whether he could, or would, jump out of doors on a cross-country course. Since the sellers had only show jumped him, they were unable to supply the answer to my question, and in any event it would have been naive to accept their word for something I should really test for myself.

The sellers were willing to transfer him over to the barn where I board, where I was able to take him over several fences and arrange for one of my teachers to assess him. Don't be embarrassed to ask about special arrangements such as this, or just a second chance to try out the horse (perhaps it was freezing or raining the first day you went, and you were only able to ride indoors). Remember, the seller wants to sell, and as long as it's clear that you are sincere in your interest and are not asking for some outrageous accommodation, most will be willing to make it easy for you to make your decision—in their favor, they hope.

As I did with the mare, it's sometimes possible to take a horse on a trial basis, though since this raises complicated insurance and liability issues, people are often understandably reluctant to risk their animals in this way. A two-week or thirty-day trial, with you bearing the cost of the insurance, is a common arrangement if the seller is willing.

There is another reason for getting a more comprehensive look at a horse you are considering for purchase. You are not just buying a mount, but a companion animal with whom you will be in intimate contact and for whom you have specific ambitions. Be sure that you get to see him being tacked up (does he allow the bridle to be put over his ears?), that you handle him all over to be sure he is comfortable with touch (does he flinch or snap?), and that you can pick up his feet (does he lean or stamp?). There are eight-hundred-pound gorillas (well, make that thousand-pound gorillas) in the horse world—animals so expensive and talented for whatever reason that bad manners, viciousness, or vices are tolerated—but on the whole, you will find it exhausting, not to mention frightening and potentially dangerous, to work constantly with an aggressive horse. I am speaking, of course, of really outsized responses. Many horses get snappish or fidgety when their girths are tightened, or don't really like to have their feet picked up, or stamp when they're bored. And there are often issues about just how and where to tie them up—or whether they can even be tied up.

Under the Microscope

Now that you are getting a second look, either briefly or for an extended period, what are you keeping an eye out for?

Stable vices. These are often difficult to find out about unless you see a horse in his own stable and have some way of finding out about behavior patterns. Vices include such behaviors as cribbing (chewing on wooden surfaces such as stall doors and fences) and wind sucking (long observed in anxious horses, today it would probably be diagnosed as obsessive-compulsive disorder). The former ruins your stall doors and is hard on the digestive system. The latter can actually affect a horse's respiratory health and stamina. Kicking can also be damaging to both the animal and his immediate environment. This is a delicate area to investigate, because stable vices are usually a response to stress or boredom and then become learned behaviors. Better stable management can sometimes eradicate them. If you discover that a prospect has one of these problems, it is not a damning mark against him, but it should give you pause. You'll want to consult with the vet who does the vet check for an opinion about how serious an issue it might become.

Trailering. You've ridden a horse at his own establishment, and eventually you make your deal and he arrives on your doorstep. However, the first time you try to take him somewhere yourself, you find you've acquired a nightmare. The horse balks, backs, and plunges, and you either never get where you're going or arrive hours later, both of you sweating and trembling. This miserable scenario is enacted countless weekends all over the country, partly, it is sad to say, because of the blundering insensitivity with which people approach teaching a horse to load in a trailer. It doesn't take a horse whisperer to tell you this is a serious problem. It's depressing and dispiriting to face a major battle every time you want to take your horse to a show, clinic, or trail ride. As with stable vices, horses can often be trained, though not always easily, to load calmly, but again you have to think about how much time you have to devote to issues like this in the context of your life. And the training is for not only your own trailer—as we've seen, the opportunities for adult riders often occur because they're part of a community of riders, so it may well be someone else's morning, trailer, and show schedule your horse winds up disrupting.

Unless you know that the horse ships calmly (you've seen it consistently at shows or know from reliable sources that it has trailered a lot), you may want to ask to see him loaded; it will save a lot of frustrations in the long run. If he's somewhat balky but not hysterical, then the problem is probably manageable and just becomes one of those things you weigh in the balance. If he's seriously stressed, life may be too short for this.

A Colder Eye: The Vet Check

In gothic novels, the course of true love is imperiled at the moment during the wedding when the celebrant says, "If any man can show just cause why these two may not lawfully be joined . . ." and someone obligingly pops up to reveal that the bride is an imposter or the groom has a mad wife in the attic. The equivalent in the horse world is the vet check, an absolutely essential step when purchasing your horse, but one that may reveal uncomfortable truths about your horse's past life or possible future.

What vet, you say? Any reputable equine practice will have someone on staff who can conduct a vet test—your schooling instructor can probably offer some guidance if you haven't gotten to know any vets in your area. Whoever it is should not, of course, be part of the practice that currently treats the animal—you're looking for an objective outsider, not a source of conflict of interest.

The Process

For all that you've been able to tell from watching and riding your prospective horse, a trained eye and a few diagnostic tests can uncover much more. The purpose of the vet check is to discern things that cannot be seen by the naked, untrained eye, not to catch out the sellers (but is also protection against unscrupulous practices). If you are able to be present, you will find it educational and revealing, but if not, here are the basic stages that the vet will go through.

The vet will begin by asking you for a basic description and history of the animal. The vet's observations then become a useful benchmark against which to test the candor of the sellers if they are unknown to you. Although people have become somewhat more candid as vet checks for companion animals become more common, it's still possible to discover that the eight-year-old who's been in light work that you thought you were getting will turn out to be a twelve-year-old with considerable wear.

She will also ask what kind of work you plan to do with the horse and will factor that into her assessment. A horse may be capable of rigorous trail riding but not be a good long-term prospect for high-level jumping, for example. And that slightly straight shoulder, not usually a problem in low-level work, may cause strain and shortened strides in reining or high-level dressage.

No horse is perfect, just as no human is perfect, so the veterinarian's assessment is going to be made in relation to your goals and expectations—the next thing he will ask about. Are you planning long walks in the country, or long days in the hunt field? Do you plan to jump? Any defects, injuries, conformation issues, and potential or incipient weaknesses will be assessed in relation to your answers. An old impact injury or a suspensory ligament problem might be minor concerns if you're just planning to hack, but if you have an ambitious jumping career or high-level dressage in mind, these could be quickly exacerbated.

The physical exam. If you're picking up an elderly retiree and the former owners have been forthcoming about his problems, a simple physical examination by a vet may be sufficient. But if you're about to invest a significant sum, it's certainly worth it to have at least x-rays and possibly ultrasound tests done, as these can reveal bone and tissue damage that can be only guessed at from a physical exam.

Once the parameters have been established, the vet will then go off to meet your horse. As in your own first visit, she will ask to see the horse both at rest and in motion. She'll be checking for muscle tone, any sign of strain or stiffness in the back or legs, defects in eyesight, and whether teeth have been properly maintained. Horses' teeth must be "floated"—a comprehensive filing done with a rasp—regularly to prevent the sharp edges from irritating their mouths.

This is especially important in older horses—as their gums recede and the angle of their jaws changes, they are more prone to these problems. This in turn could interfere with the horse's ability to chew and digest food properly and cause him to drop weight (something horses do frighteningly fast) and lose condition. It's a "for want of a nail" situation.

Hooves. Be sure you have asked the vet to look closely at the hooves. Flinty, weak hooves often need to be extensively—and expensively— maintained, though sometimes better nutrition and targeted nutraceuticals will eventually (in about a year) produce a better hoof. The vet will be keeping an eye out for other signs of possible foot problems also— whether all four feet are the same shape, whether the hooves angle awkwardly to the ground, whether there's any sign of former damage to the wall or frog—the springy underside of a horse's hoof, which makes contact with the ground. "No foot, no horse" is an old horseman's adage.

A corrective shoe will be easy to spot, but many horses coming through schools or dealers will have been shod in the least expensive way and might well turn out to be in need of corrective shoes. Again, this is not an immediate indication that a horse should be rejected, but as it can add as much as $100 to your monthly bill and does indicate an area of concern, it should give you pause.

Happily, sometimes all that's needed is a change of diet and environment. As with people, poor nutrition often manifests itself in outward signs like a thin coat and weak hooves. My own horse, a jumper who came to me from one of those quick-in, quick-out dealers, went from being a scruffy teddy with flaky feet to a lustrous fellow with relatively stable hooves in only a year. (A good hoof supplement—one of the many products that will enter your life—helped.)

As you probably know from countless exercise books and articles, bodies respond to opposite forces, so part of what the vet will be testing is response time to certain flexion exercises and whether they occasion any discomfort. As the horse is jogged out, the vet will be checking for a balanced stride without any indication that the horse will clip himself in motion. Again, what she sees will depend on what life stage the horse is in. A green horse, barring accidents, should be relatively blemish free but might move with less balance and assurance than an older horse. The latter might have better cadence but hold himself more protectively in areas of the body that are stiff or painful. Overall conformation is always important to factor in, and while you and your trainer were looking with an eye to performance, your vet will be assessing vulnerability. The high head carriage may be a result of a contracted neck, which in turn may generate stiff shoulders and back. The long, elegant pasterns supporting a massive body could be in line for stress injuries. A scruffy coat may be a seasonal disadvantage (most outdoor horses look like badly cared-for plush toys in the early spring) or the sign of a vitamin deficiency. A lackluster eye can indicate fever or cataracts.

Once your vet has completed her exam and the test results have come back, she will issue a report that will combine hard fact with impressions. This is not evasion or fuzzy thinking, but that intuitive response that comes from seeing dozens of animals every year. These will then be referred back to the context of the goals you and she discussed at the outset. The result might look somewhat like this:

Description of animal examined:

Horse's name: Jonathan

Sex: Gelding

Age: 9

Color: Bay

Breed: Westphalian/TB cross

Markings: Whorls midway at crest both sides

Jonathan has been in regular work for the last year and has been jumping regularly. The radiographic finding of a small area of detached dorsal hoof wall in his right forefoot is not considered significant, but should be explored by the farrier for signs of White Line Disease. It is very shallow, but could pose a problem if allowed to progress without treatment. The quality of his hoof wall will make retaining shoes a challenge. Regular attention to shoeing to prevent loss of shoes and use of a supplement such as Nutri-tone/Farrier's Formula may improve this condition.

The radiographic findings of mild fusion of the medial aspect of the left and right middle joints is common in this age group, especially in jumping and dressage horses. There is no clinical sign of current inflammation, but if extensive jumping work is undertaken, it could become necessary in the future to inject these joints periodically. Use of nutraceuticals such as chondrointin sulfate and/or glucosamine (e.g., Coseqin) may be helpful to prevent inflammation as intensity of work increases.

In my opinion, Jonathan will be sound and suitable for your intended use. He is a friendly, handsome individual, and I wish you many happy years with him.

Signed:

So now the moment has come. You have as detailed a picture of your prospective horse as you can get, refracted through your own eyes and those of the vet and others you have brought in on the decision. The image of the two of you, together, rises up before you, and you pick up the phone.

Making the Offer

Horses are also like houses—the asking price is not necessarily the selling price, and there may be some room to maneuver. As with houses, antiques, and other market-dominated commodities, whether and how much a seller might be willing to come down on the price will depend on the current market, the area and local economy in which you and he live, and the attributes of the horse that are its strongest selling points. A high-end dealer selling the latest Irish import with impressive show credentials, in a wealthy area, is not likely to make a deal with you. He's asking $85,000, and he can probably get it.

This is, of course, unlikely to be the scenario with you and your first horse, unless you set your sights very high indeed.

A midrange dealer or private owner selling a less sensational performer might well be willing to come down a few hundred dollars, or even more. Time of year can be a factor, too, in several ways, as previously noted. Prices are sometimes lower, or can be lowered, in winter—people would love to save on board and keep during the off-season months if they're planning to part with the animal anyway. In spring, on the other hand, the expensive show season is just beginning, and trainer-sellers may be happy to deal in order to get cash in hand. The season itself can also affect the relative worth of a horse. One friend was considering a mare whom the owner, who was eventing her, was offering for $15,000. While my friend was trying to make up her mind, the horse won two horse trials, and the price went up $5,000.

Occasionally you'll come up against a daunting case of reverse psychology—someone who didn't really want to sell an animal but didn't realize it until you made your offer.

This advice is always easier to give than to follow, but know in your heart whether you are prepared to pay the full asking price, or whether the offer you've made is really where you need to stop—and be prepared to live with the outcome. You may well have had a preliminary conversation of this type before doing the vet check. It is a clear signal of intent to buy when you ask the seller to take the horse off the market until the results come in.

There are some ancillary conversations you should have at the same time. Most sales assume the free delivery of the horse to your barn, but be sure to confirm this. Does the horse have any tack, accessories, and so on that are included? (This is rare, but a private individual may well be willing to sell such items as bridles, boots, and blankets at a discount since these are often fitted to the animals.) Since new tack can set you back as much as two thousand to three thousand dollars or more, this is always a worthwhile conversation to have.

The Importance of a Written Contract

Be sure there is a written contract and that it clearly spells out the terms of the sale. This should include a clause allowing for the return of the animal during a two-week period following purchase if any condition or behavior that should have been disclosed reveals itself. Reputable sellers should agree to this since they operate in a small, gossipy world where word of dubious behavior travels quickly.

Now you're all set. And now, as an acquaintance chimed in when my horse arrived at her barn, "The money begins to flow."

26

Now That He's Yours

For all your research and preparation, there's still a difference between imagining yourself as a horse owner and actually being one. First of all, welcome to the horse economy. There's a reason why "horse poor" is a favorite T-shirt seen and sold at horse shows. Following are some of the major expenses that will concern you and that you should consider while laying the groundwork for your purchase.

Training Board

Training board is increasingly popular in areas of the country where an active competitive circuit is sustained by a certain amount of affluence and by weekend riders. This is an option fashioned for the driven baby-boom generation, as it is essentially a way of having your cake and eating it, too. Training board is offered by barns that are attached to teaching facilities. (There are still a great many straight boarding barns, often owned by people using the extra cash to support their own riding habit.) The idea, at least theoretically, is that your horse will be in work with a trainer-instructor in your absence so that your horse can progress and get fit and focused even when you can't ride (during the work week, for example). This type of program is often geared to competition, though there are good reasons to keep your horse in work regardless of whether or not you show.

If you are offered this option, it is worth asking exactly how the term is interpreted by the particular establishment. Trainers charge premium prices for this service, and I have seen barns where the so-called training consists of a hasty fifteen minutes' worth of schooling in the ring before the overbooked trainer moves on to the next horse.

To some extent it is putting the cart after the horse to consider out-lay—of both money and time—here; you should actually have reviewed all this before taking the plunge.

Read Up

Whatever your choice—palatial or modest—be sure it is within rea-sonable driving distance. Riding takes a good two to three hours out of any day even without travel time factored in, and your family is likely to sue the creature for alienation of affection if you add an hour-long drive on top of that. Board fees usually include feed and hay, but for older horses or special conditions, you need to factor in supplements for which your barn will charge you.

Vet Bills

Horses need an array of vaccines and minor procedures (worming, teeth cleaning) to keep them healthy. Also, like children, they are prone to scrapes, cuts, and bruises that sometimes need the vet's intervention to prevent them from becoming more serious. You can count on several hun-dred dollars per year toward such efforts. You may, if you're lucky, never have to face any severe problems, but be sure that you have cash in reserve just in case. You don't want to be faced with a devastating life-or-death decision or wind up liquidating your portfolio because you didn't think ahead. Acute conditions such as colic (a common intestinal disorder that accounts for over 50 percent of equine fatalities) can easily run you into the thousands if it becomes serious enough to warrant surgery. (Less extreme cases are more like bad indigestion but usually still warrant the vet.)

Transport

This is a conversation you should have early on in your search for a horse, especially if you hope to show. If you're not planning to get—and learn to drive—a horse trailer yourself (and as they list for anywhere from $4,500 to three times that much, this would be an ambitious commitment so early in your working relationship), then you'll be dependent on others. Find out whether other riders at your barn are likely to be able to take you to events. If not, you'll have to pay someone to trailer your horse, and this can not only cost serious money (fifty dollars per day or more), but during the height of the riding season these people are often heavily booked. So as you consider your board options and your budget, plan ahead, or you'll wind up as the Cinderella of your barn.

Farrier

Most horses need to be shod every four to six weeks when they are in work, and you can expect to pay around $90–$150 per session. The range is affected by the region you live in, the professional level of your farrier, and whether your horse has any special needs or problems that have to be accommodated (pads, corrective shoes, or synthetic hoof preparation to help structure weak feet are some examples). Make friends with your farrier—and pay promptly.

Tack

The food processor has been described as "the Barbie doll of the kitchen." Well, imagine the horse as the Barbie doll (or action figure of your choice) of the barn. The original unit is handsome but unadorned, and it comes with myriad accessories to help you create its "lifestyle." (There is an equestrian Barbie, by the way, but her improbable anatomy makes me question her as a role model.)

Saddle

The saddle is a key purchase: your horse's comfort and your own depend on your making a good investment. Prices range from several hundred to several thousand dollars, and where you wind up depends on your means and interests. At the low end of the market, serviceable saddles, often synthetic or not of the best leather, are available; at the high end, you are looking at sleek, supple English saddles with leather that breathes and gleams, or gloriously bedizened Western saddles, stenciled with designs and embossed with silver. And serious competitors sometimes have both schooling and show tack.

The jury's still out on synthetic tack. The most heavily marketed brand is Wintec. I find it chafing, and it doesn't age gracefully, but it is easy to clean and some riders endorse it enthusiastically (it has found favor in endurance riding, for example). And you can't beat the price, which is often as much as five hundred dollars less than its leather equivalent. At the least, if funds are an issue, you might find it a useful stopgap until you can afford something better.

Used tack, now available through both the Internet and at many tack shops, is another option, though you must be very careful that the tree—the skeletal system of the saddle—isn't twisted. I've recommended some sources at the end of the book that describe the varieties of saddles and their uses. The key point is to be sure the saddle fits—not just your pocketbook or your dreams (some saddles are really quite beautiful—the English ones lustrous and as shapely as Henry Moore sculptures, the Western ones like elaborate sedan chairs reminiscent of royal chaises), but you and your horse. Research suggests that an ill-fitting saddle can cause many of the movement and performance problems that can afflict horses.

Bridles

There are almost as many kinds of bridles as there are horses' faces. Be guided by resources and your friends and advisors. The key element of a bridle is the bit, as this is what most affects your horse's way of going. Bridles can be quite expensive—as much as three hundred to four hundred dollars—so there is certainly some temptation to economize, but I would warn against going too down-market. Cheap leather is stiff and often doesn't break in well, so it can chafe. It also frequently comes in a hideous American cheese color, the result of dubious dyeing and curing processes. (See appendix B, "Resources.")

Blankets and Pads

The other tack staples include saddle blankets and pads, the purpose of which is both decorative and protective. Sweat damages leather and rots stitching, and even the best-fitting saddle, with no intervening element, can rub sensitive skin, especially if the horse has been sweating. Colorful lightweight blankets (for Western tack) or bold geometric pads or plush, white sheepskin can help, as well as look great. Beware, however, of building up too much of a layer between the horse and the saddle. If the saddle fits well to begin with, padding can alter the way it sits on your horse, inadvertently causing more problems than it solves.

And There's More!

As I mentioned earlier, horse accessories have become a major industry of stuff. Open any catalog (and you will), and a wide array of aids (to help you perform a function) and accessories (to help you look good doing it) will pass before your eyes. Have fun, but don't dissolve your 401K. You can still get a good ride out of the basics.

His Fate in Your Hands

One way to look at these elements is as expenses. The other is as responsibilities. Board, vet, and farrier costs come under the heading "health"; tack, education, and competition under the heading "goals and training." Both are important. You want to see your new friend and partner thrive, but you also want to grow with him and realize a cluster of aspirations that have probably been rising slowly to the surface since you took up riding.

Health

One of the things that symbolize the fundamental generosity of horses is that, like legendary mythic creatures who form bonds with humans, they have given over some of their magic to dwell among us. The most acute loss is the ability to roam at will, and in practical terms, this is why the health of your horse is a delicate challenge. Most of the acute ailments that plague horses are the result of our intervention in the natural cycle and the (sometimes unreasonable) demands we put on their bodies. Intestinal disorders, leg and back injuries, damaged feet, all are held at bay only by care and vigilance.

"Resources" at the end of this book will refer you to books and other sources of comprehensive information about physical health and well-being. Here I'll just emphasize crucial concerns.

The first is that your horse gets a regular diet consistent with his age, weight, temperament, and workload. Be sure that your previous owner provides you with information about what he is getting. Even if in consultation with your barn manager you decide to change feed, this should be done gradually.

Find out, too, whether he has been getting any supplements or should be getting them. Commercial feeds contain a lot of additions designed to enhance their products, but additional mineral extracts such as glucosamine—for joint health—are becoming very popular, especially now that nutraceuticals have reached into this segment of the mammalian population as they have already saturated the human market. Other types add weight or improve skin texture and tone.

You should by now be confident that the barn of your choice is giving your horse fresh hay at least twice a day, depending on the amount of time your horse spends in his stall. This vital commodity alleviates boredom and provides the roughage we deprive the horse of when he ceases to be a pasture animal.

In addition to listing the food your horse eats and the quantity, the seller should tell you when the horse was last wormed. (Wormers are chemical substances fed orally or placed in food to interrupt the life cycle of the parasites horses pick up from being ground feeders and stable dwellers—the environments that are breeding grounds for internal parasites. Virtually all horses have worms of one kind or another, regardless of how wonderfully healthy they may look.) You'll also need to know what inoculations he has received, and when. Like dogs and small children, horses need a range of injections to protect against equine flu and other virulent diseases. And if you plan to travel anywhere with him, he'll also have to be tested yearly for equine infectious anemia. The (presumably negative) results of this test, called the Coggins, should be available at your barn and in your car, a sort of horse visa. Some states have additional requirements for travel, such as rabies certificates—find out what's expected in your area.

Your barn will establish a schedule for your horse's basic medical maintenance, though you will directly bear the cost. Worming is usually done by barn staff and will appear as an item on your board bill. While regular feed is included in your basic rate, supplements are not, and you may arrange to have the barn purchase these for you or provide them yourself. Ask whether your barn does bulk orders of any common items such as joint supplements or insect repellent. If you buy into such orders, you can save money.

Regular grooming helps keep a horse healthy and conditioned, helps you bond with him, and allows you to check him all over for cuts, bruises, and insect bites (ticks are an escalating crisis in many areas of the country; flies are a perpetual misery). Be especially aware of his legs and feet, the delicate base upon which the whole structure depends. A pulled shoe or lodged stone can cause immediate damage left untended.

A word to the wise: owning a horse does not require you to be a veterinarian, but neither should you be a passive owner. Buy at least one decent book on horse health ailments, keep abreast of articles in the horse magazines of your choice (the same care subjects are covered by most of them, regardless of the discipline they represent), and ask questions of your stable manager and/or vet if something is unclear. You will be more secure with a basic working knowledge of horse health, and you can become an active participant in the decision-making process. This is something we wish for ourselves in the face of the medical community, and we should want no less for our horses.

Goals and Training

Goals

Former president George H. W. Bush seemed to many to exemplify political fuzzy thinking when he mouthed the notorious phrase "the vision thing." Don't make the same mistake. Have clear goals, both short and long term, and view each day's work as a journey toward them. I emphasize short- and long-term goals because the easiest route to disappointment is to expect some version of your ultimate outcome each time you ride, forgetting all the stops and achievements that come between. There is a European time management system called TMI that tells its practitioners to imagine big tasks as "elephant tasks"—each day you address some sliver of the elephant until the whole is devoured. Your long-term goal—an important show, a first-level dressage test, your first big trail ride or carriage drive—is your elephant, and each day you ride you will be a hoofbeat closer.

And regardless of your ostensible concrete goal, there is for every horse owner the same underlying, ultimate goal: to create an exciting, trusting, loving partnership with your animal. A horse doesn't become yours when you buy him, but when you make him yours. Most professionals seem to think this stage takes about eighteen months. For you it might be shorter or longer, but know that in this respect the most casual touch can mean as much as the most exacting technical maneuver—an investment in the promise that wherever you're going, you'll arrive together.

Training

On most long journeys, it can help to have companions, and your teacher or trainer can be a great asset to your goals. With a new horse, it is easy to become obsessed by small details and difficulties, to become fragmented in your thinking and working. An outsider can see the whole picture, help figure out whether it is you or the animal who needs adjustment, plan a program with you, and help you hone your skills to get the best out of this new partner. If you have the time, resources, and inclination, you might want to try working with more than one instructor. The teacher who seemed a fine guide while you were learning canter departs or rein back on a reliable school horse might seem lacking in subtlety now that you're working toward more ambitious ends with your own horse. Or the high-powered trainer recommended by your competitor neighbor seems snobbish and remote when faced with your more modest goals. Somewhere out there will be the right person for you. And if your purchase of a horse means that you have had to cut back on lessons, read attentively and continue to work methodically, and with focus, on your own. Try to find an opportunity for an objective appraisal of your progress at least two or three times a season, whether it's by attending a clinic or having an experienced friend watch you.

What to Watch For

Bad Habits

If you train only with yourself, it is easy to relax into positions that feel more comfortable (because you are not holding yourself correctly) but are less effective, or to allow some imbalance in your horse to affect your own alignment. These habits can range from leaning forward in the saddle to encourage the canter (which actually unbalances the horse) to getting twisted in the saddle to anticipating fences and jumping before your horse does.

Road Blocks

You've gotten into a rut over some particular problem. Your horse consistently picks up the wrong lead on one side, or won't relax his head at the walk or jog, or balks at an obstacle during trail or jumping practice.

Sometimes it takes another's eyes—and mind—to suggest alternative approaches to get you unstuck.

Inertia

Sometimes you need to refresh your routine, find your way back to first principles, realign your mind and body. If you haven't got a regular training regime, sometimes it's easy to feel adrift and wonder why, precisely, you are doing this. Horses are good company, but disciplined riding engages the whole mind and body.

Competition

If the fever grips you, this is an additional pleasure, a keen sharpening of your sense of accomplishment and oneness with your horse, but it is also expensive and time consuming. (The average horse show or horse trial, for example, involves perhaps a total of an hour to an hour and a half in the saddle at most, combining class time and warm ups, but will take up your entire day and most of the previous evening.) The events themselves are also expensive and time consuming to run, and much of that expense, as in the consumer marketplace, is pushed onto the competitor. Small local shows still charge relatively modest fees, but larger, accredited shows—meaning that they've been sanctioned by the U.S. Equestrian Federation (the national oversight organization for recognized competitive sports and the discipline's governing body)—now have entry fees of as much as fifty dollars per class or over one hundred dollars for an event. And then you have to factor in travel costs—board for your horse and overnight accommodations for you if the distance to the event is too far to travel in one day, trailering if you don't have your own, and gasoline if you do. And with a competitive partnership, in addition to your basic lessons you'll also want to budget for special training opportunities: clinics, workshops, and lectures from distinguished professionals.

Just as an example, I estimate that I currently spend about a thousand dollars per year in competition-related expenses (including clinics and training sessions), and I'm a low-level event rider.

If you are likely to be principally a weekend rider, as many of us are, consider finding someone to ride your horse at least once during the week (if you have not opted for training board). In horsy areas there are often people eager to make a little extra money, and sometimes your instructor, if he or she is based at or comes regularly to your barn, can also be paid to do this. A regular routine of this type can keep your horse mentally and physically fit, making him a much easier ride for you.

Part V

Choosing Pleasure

27

Fun for the Whole Family

One of the catalysts for this book was an article I saw several years ago in which a woman wrote about the pleasure of watching her young daughter ride in a horse show, a pleasure tinged with nostalgic regret for her own riding days.

"What is the matter with you?" I ranted futilely at the printed manifestation of a total stranger. "There is no suggestion that you are physically impaired, so why aren't you riding *with* your daughter?"

In today's child-oriented society, it is easy to be persuaded that one's own private pleasure constitutes a sinful dereliction of duty. While I do not believe this, and indeed believe that a private pleasure can return you balanced and fulfilled to your family circle, a compromise may also offer a different degree of enrichment.

Let's imagine the *All in the Family* scenario first.

Families on Board

If you are the mother of a female 'tween, horses may already be dominant in at least one psyche other than your own. If you are both beginners, you may want to take lessons together, which would have the advantage of putting you on the same schedule. If your daughter, with the cruel candor of children, professes a desire for her own age group (as a son will almost certainly do), then you can arrange trail rides, schedule holidays, or compete together.

Instructors are willing to take on families, with the caveat that you leave the parental portion of your mind at the door of the arena. Some schools may even have parent-child programs or be able to set up something for you if you ask.

Shared Lessons

It can be a great pleasure to share this kind of quality horse time with a child as well as subtly reinforce the message that your role in the horse world is not limited to laundry and valet parking. (This sounds like a mother-daughter equation but has been known to create great bonds between fathers and daughters or sons also.) Increasingly, as more and more adult riders flood the scene, it is not only parents and children, but husbands and wives, looking for opportunities to ride together. It is especially nice when you can entice a spouse or partner into the ring with you because riding is time consuming and there is less chance of the other feeling neglected, but most importantly, because you will both "get it" at the same time: that frustrating, alluring, exciting communication with the horse that changes the way you look at the world.

Riding Camps

If the significant other (who need not, of course, be your husband or wife) is not willing or able to participate regularly, riding camps are a fun, limited-time option. And riding camps are proliferating (see "Horses on Holiday," chapter 28). While many are geared to children, some are not.

It is easier for a neophyte (if reasonably fit) to master a short course of riding sufficiently to enjoy holiday trail riding, even camping together. (This is one of those prime father-daughter experiences—men seem to like to feel simultaneously venturesome and grounded.) Perhaps there are friends you've been hoping to find a way to see more of on a regular basis, and an opera subscription is not for you. If you become a horse owner, your barnmates may also quickly become your lesson, clinic, and hackmates (and the kind souls who trailer you to same). I've seldom been in a barn recently that didn't have at least one pair, or a trio, of middle-aged women taking regular lessons together.

Corralling the Rest of Them

Let's think outside the box, or the stall, for a moment. You and your daughter, or your son/spouse/lover/girlfriend/cat are nicely settled in a rhythm of training and communication. This means, especially in summer, that you disappear for long periods of the day and come back to family members who are either bereft or cranky, depending on their age, sex, and temperament. You are not going to turn them into riders, so what can you do to invite them inside the paddock?

Find out when and for what volunteers are needed. No horse function proceeds without the myriad forces of unpaid labor, and volunteering is a not-too-arduous way to become part of the crowd. Activities range from building and parking to fence judging and catering. All skills—and no skills—are usually welcome, the only criteria being willingness, cheerfulness, and punctuality. If you're assigned to some task that requires specialized knowledge, like fence judging, there is always someone qualified to walk you through.

Groom. If you are not part of a tight-knit community of competitors, and even if you are, at the height of the season an extra pair of hands is always welcome at a show, clinic, or event. Let your family know how nice it is to have them, and not to have to both hold the horse *and* find the whip, collar stud, number, course map, and bathroom at the same time.

Ready for your close-up? Someone in your circle may be delighted to be asked to capture the moment on film or video.

Picnic. Many events offer some kind of food, but this is often of the hamburger, hotdog, or just plain grease variety. Even if you're nervous and focused on your event, you have to eat sometime—ask your family (if they're not traveling with you) to meet you at the show grounds with a picnic. You can even try incorporating a similar ritual into at least your weekend lessons, though weekends tend to get very cluttered with chores and errands and just driving from place to place.

I didn't know you could do that. Horses being the alluring things they are, if they continue to be a part of your world they may tap instincts or gifts that your family members didn't know they had, or create opportunities for them to use existing skills in newfound contexts.

One woman I know, an adult rider who started showing half-Arabs in her midforties, is married to a doctor who has become the official course doctor for their local show. Another is married to a textile designer who combined his eye for color and line with his love of building to create a cross-country course on their property. Another man, despite a horseless upbringing in suburban New Jersey, had a long-buried interest in watercolor sketching renewed by his attendance at shows in support of his wife. It's exciting when, in addition to being your own personal Formula 1 team, some family member develops an independent relationship to horses, the sport or the broader equestrian culture. You get to spend more time together, and who knows? You may even begin to see your world in a new way through their eyes.

Surrey with the fringe on top. This is an opportunity only available to drivers rather than riders, but once you have sufficiently mastered driving, you can double your pleasure by taking people for rides. And some competitive driving, especially classes requiring period costume, often calls for a second person to appear as a groom or companion of some kind. It's rather like being the friend of the restaurant critic, a role I've always wanted. Others, especially combined driving events (which require steering through obstacles), require navigators—a challenging but ultimately thrilling role that might be just right for the nonrider in your life.

With a little imagination on both sides, you'll find that horses offer a big enough world to include everyone.

28

Horses on Holiday

One of the fastest-growing sectors of the travel market, horse-related vacations offer fabulous opportunities for experiencing riding at a whole new level. In locales as homey as New England or as exotic as Egypt, India, or Kenya, with family, with friends, or alone, you can use a holiday with horses to fulfill long-cherished dreams, see America as the settlers saw it (or almost), travel like an Indian maharajah, or get expert advice from a world-class instructor.

There are almost as many types of horse holiday as there are types of rider. Below are some of the major classifications.

The dude ranch. Still the traditional choice for many vacationing Americans, the dude ranch is designed to accommodate people who'd like to get a little riding in their holidays but are not necessarily riders. They have slightly derogatory connotations—comically ignorant city folk on plugs being taken advantage of by smirking cowboys—but respectable dude ranches (the name derives from Western riders' name for outsiders, and most such places are still Western in orientation) offer pleasant, scenic—if not especially challenging—excursions. This can be a good choice if you are trying to get the whole family involved, and the sense of being out of doors and on a horse is sufficiently gratifying.

Ranch/range riding. This, a level up from the dude ranch, might also be called the paraprofessional mode. Some ranches offer outsiders (for a fee) the opportunity to participate in cattle drives. Think Billy Crystal in *City Slickers*—but don't think too hard. Unlike his character, a neurotic executive in search of himself, with no experience in the saddle or on the range, *you* have to have some demonstrable experience and be relatively fit to do this, even if your guide isn't Jack Palance. This type of package is similar to the archaeological holidays run by institutions such as the Smithsonian: working holidays in exotic locations. Or it's a sophisticated variation on Tom Sawyer's whitewashing ploy.

Trail rides. We are only just past the period when many people living could still remember traveling by horse (I know a women who honeymooned in New Hampshire's White Mountains with a horse and carriage), and for many of us a chance to re-create that period seems especially alluring. In these days most travel experiences are increasingly cramped and uncomfortable, a matter of endless queues and security checks, designed simply to get you where you are going as quickly as possible. It is acutely pleasurable, therefore, to travel in real time through landscape you can see and savor, not merely register as specks or blurs or stamps on your passport.

Trail riding holidays cater to both English and Western riders and are available both here and abroad in a wide variety of locales. They usually involve four to five hours of riding each day, with stops at local inns, or for the truly hardy, outdoor camps. A word of warning: don't do this or encourage your family to do this without some advance preparation. An unfit rider will experience excruciating discomfort during the first few days of a long ride as unused muscles seize up and begin screaming for relief. It can actually be difficult for a person thus afflicted to stay on the horse, so this is a dangerous, as well as a discomfiting, phenomenon. If you cannot fit in a lot of extra riding before your departure, at least step up your gym workouts.

Again, family members can certainly be considered for these excursions, but only if they are willing to commit to a little practice. And even if you've been riding regularly, you may want to begin to gradually build up to longer trail rides in your weekly or biweekly routines if you have access to trails. Otherwise, all your anticipated pleasure will be annihilated by physical wretchedness.

The term *trail* may be deceptive. Think as broadly and imaginatively as you like. You can be taking a pony up the side of a precipitous mountain pass in Belize (or, as I recently was, in Kelfalonia, Greece), riding along the beach in California, or experiencing the fall foliage as your great-grandparents might have seen it.

Training holidays. Your hunt seat reminds you of a Thelwell cartoon; your idea of cross-country is the distance between malls; you'd like to know firsthand why the Germans win so many dressage competitions; you don't believe polo need be confined to the pages of *Town & Country.* If any of these sound like you, you may be an ideal candidate for a training holiday. Many formerly exclusive schools and training barns are beginning to open up their facilities and top-flight trainers, on a selective basis, to amateurs. Some can be found by searching the Internet and perusing magazine articles, but the field is so disparate that it might be advantageous to work through a tour company that specializes in vetting and crafting such holidays (several are listed in the "Resources" appendix).

Hunting holidays. Foxhunting was banned in England in 2005 but is still practiced covertly throughout the country. It is no longer politic for travel agencies to offer holiday packages *promising* hunting in the United Kingdom. However, it is still possible to hunt in Ireland or France, where it is also still possible to stag hunt, a really medieval form of the sport. And in Ireland, you will experience hunting to the max. Irish hunts, horses, and fences are bigger and bolder than you are ever likely to encounter outside of the pages of *The Irish R.M.* This type of holiday is not for the insecure jumper or the fainthearted, but is absolutely intoxicating if you can stay the course.

Healing holidays. Winston Churchill is credited with the observation, "There is something about the outside of a horse that is good for the inside of a man." A number of programs have taken this idea to heart and offer opportunities to explore the horse as a conduit to personal growth, healing, or harmony.

You may also be interested in exploring some therapeutic disciplines more directly. They include "horse whispering," the communication technique practiced by a number of Western trainers and made popular by the Nicholas Evans best seller *The Horse Whisperer*; Tellington TTouch, a training approach devised by Linda Tellington-Jones; and Pat Parelli natural horsemanship. Workshops are offered year-round in all these techniques (some you can even do with your horse).

Riding camp. Sometimes rather like a training holiday, riding camps can also combine various elements of horse holidays such as trail riding and ring work for a more all-around, and sometimes more casual, experience. There are adult camps and camps combining classes for adults and children. Many fields now offer concentrated training opportunities beyond the one- or two-day clinic, and the style of each camp very much depends on the place and the context. The aim is probably to offer that pleasing combination of recreation and discipline that the word *camp* conjures up.

Just looking. Not all horse-related holidays need involve riding. When planning your trips abroad, check travel sources for famous studs and riding establishments that practice and demonstrate classical riding techniques. The Spanish Riding School of Vienna, home to the celebrated Lipizzaners (or the "dancing white horses," as they are popularly known), is the most famous of these. But Austria is not the only country to offer this pleasure; there are magnificent establishments in France, Germany, Hungary, and Spain.

Another increasingly popular form of adventure travel includes viewing wild horse herds, such as England's Dartmoor ponies and the American mustang. (Wild mustangs are endangered in the United States, falling victim to relentless development and brutal government legislation. Your interest may help to save this persecuted minority.)

Costs

Costs vary considerably, as you might imagine, and it is best to explore pricing thoroughly with the facility or tour operator. And because this is a significant investment in something like a dream, try to find out as much as you can before you make your choice. See whether the trip or facility has a website, an information packet, or press articles or referrals. And book early. Even with the current nightmare of airport security and the wariness of travelers in general, these trips fill up quickly.

Case Study

You cannot imagine a better example of adult riders enjoying a pastime to which they have come later in life than Marv and Shirley Kraatz, a Canadian couple I met while trekking in Greece. In their midfifties, with a successful business, they were first exposed to riding when their oldest grandchild started lessons. That prompted Shirley to take some lessons herself so that she could accompany her granddaughter on her rides. But she soon fell in love with both the sport and one of the school horses, whom she later bought. She then encouraged Marv to start riding also, and they began to take lessons together. From this modest beginning developed a great tradition of mutual adventure. The Kraatzes have been on a series of exciting equestrian holidays—touring the Loire Valley, the Scottish Highlands, Hungary, and Ireland.

For Shirley, these experiences were invigorating because "you're always riding a little bit beyond your comfort level." Husband and wife agree that middle age is a time to step forward, not back, even if, in Marvin's words, "you're bashful" at first. "You get to a certain age, and you haven't done this, and you haven't done that," they caution. For opportunities to seize the moment with the same zest as the Kraatzes, see the "Resources" appendix.

29

Beyond Lessons

Clinics and Events

Even if your regular lessons are satisfying and you seem to be on track with your goals, clinics and master classes add zest to the mix and can expose you to extraordinary teachers with whom you would not have an opportunity to train regularly. Clinics are to horse people what guest lectures are to personages in their fields—a way to earn extra money and gain exposure—so in any given season you might have a chance to be taught, or at least talked to, by champion reiners and rodeo riders, horse handlers and members of the United States Equestrian Team from various disciplines. Many well-known training stables use such clinics to enhance their own appeal and income and to expand their services to clients, so there may a number of opportunities in a given season for you to participate in such an event, depending on where you live.

In addition to regular instruction at riding schools, the country is now teeming with entertaining symposiums, exhibitions, workshops, lecture/demonstrations, and expos. Riding organizations and event planners work to sharpen your skills, knowledge, and riding pleasure by contracting with vendors and top-flight professionals from horse whisperers to ex-Olympians to present programs, not to mention the shopping!

The nice thing is that these clinics, once the province of serious professionals, are now geared to all levels of rider (other than rank beginners) so that even if you are a relative novice or have a really green horse you will be able to take advantage of these opportunities. (You are being taken advantage of in turn, of course. One reason there's such a plethora of clinics these days is that the pros have realized that they're cash cows.)

In addition to the good old-fashioned glamour of being instructed by or watching acclaimed horsemen, your whole sense of the discipline can be radiantly enhanced. Some years ago I was privileged to watch the legendary jumper trainer George Morris instruct a group of Olympic hopefuls—an extraordinary exercise in both common sense and showmanship.

By listening to problem-solving techniques and ideas from the masters, your own vocabulary—verbal and physical—increases. And you don't even need a horse to benefit from one of these occasions: they can be especially interesting for auditors, as you get to learn about problems and solutions applied over a range of horse and rider combinations. All you really need is sufficient familiarity with the vocabulary of your particular discipline to take in whatever is being said and imagine how you might apply it to your own needs.

Lecture/demonstrations usually last one to two hours and might be given in the context of an equestrian "event" (see below). Local equestrian businesses, such as tack shops, bookstores, and veterinary practices, also use these as outreach and marketing tools.

Clinics can last anywhere from one to three days, depending on the discipline and how the facility and guest instructor has decided to organize it. If you're lucky enough to live nearby, you can trailer over each day; otherwise, you'll probably need to board at the host facility and possibly stay overnight yourself as well. This can run into money, though it gives the clinic itself a nice "out-of-time" quality that can help you to focus.

Clinics are advertised in a number of ways, and you'll probably get to hear about some of them just by being a member of your own riding circle. Local training establishments usually keep abreast of one another's events—your barn may even have such a program in place itself. Flyers are often generated and posted in local stables and tack shops; competitive facilities, which are often venues for such events, usually have mailing lists and may well send you something directly. (If you are a member of any of the discipline or breed organizations, you may also be on a number of mailing lists. It's a good idea to check their websites; many have specific sections for education and training.)

Be sure also to thoroughly check any equestrian magazines or newsletters you get, since clinics are often advertised there as well as on the Web.

Because the training at clinics is often at a higher, more challenging level than people find at their day-to-day lessons, there may be restrictive qualifications for participation, such as competition at a specific level. This is sometimes a safety issue and sometimes just to ensure that people of a similar level can be training together. However, there are so many opportunities of the kind that you're sure to find something you can attend. And if you're really unable, either because of lack of the necessary qualifications, injuries, or finance, to bring your horse to a clinic in which you are especially interested, there is always auditing.

How to Get the Best out of a Clinic

Think of a clinic as something like a cruise, or of the best parts of going away to school. You and your horse are unknown (or at least the first time) to the clinician, so you are not, as sometimes happens in even the best of training relationships, bound by a fixed perception of you and your abilities. By the same token, the instructor is new to you or may be known to you only by reputation, and may be able to put certain principles or problems in a whole new light. I remember spending a week with the iconoclastic trainer and theorist Mary Wanless and complaining that I was having trouble controlling my mount at the trot. I thought this had something to do with pulling or bracing with my back. "Oh, no," she said, "the problem is that you aren't rising fully to the trot. If you're not in tune with all the horse's rhythm, you will never be able to influence it." Voilà, a completely new perspective in only one lesson.

Or it may be a matter of imagery. Your teacher can have tried to reinforce some point a dozen times, but it's not until someone says, "Soft eyes," or "Hold your lower back as if it were in a corset," or "Sit to the trot as if you were pushing down on a coffee pot," that your body and brain seem to respond.

And be prepared to listen. Clinicians often have a sort of prepared litany, because instead of having a fixed relationship with one person or group of people whom they see week after week, they have an established set of principles and observations that they use to create the framework of the program. The ritual plaints and challenges of your normal lessons do not belong here. Instead, come with a succinct description of your goals for the clinic and one area you'd like to focus on (in keeping with the spirit and level of the clinic, naturally).

A word to the wise: book early—demand is usually high.

Be prepared to wait. Unless you have arranged for private or semiprivate lessons (sometimes an option), clinic groups tend to be larger because of demand, and the instructor usually tries to give everyone a thorough exposure to the exercises. And because the circumstances may be more demanding, there is always the possibility of someone's horse acting up, which can hold up the rest of a class, since good instructors find it hard to leave a problem unaddressed.

Be willing to take some risks. That's what you're there for—change, illumination. If the instructor presents you with a combination you haven't tried before or asks you to pull your horse rapidly around in a circle on one rein or ride with your legs over the cantle—don't balk.

Take notes. Because you won't be back this way again, or at least your cycle of exposure is much more limited, it's worth taking notes on things that especially strike you in class.

Nevertheless, the clinic is not the place to solve all your basic horsemanship problems; attend one only if you have put in a program of regular work and have a defined goal that you feel will be advanced by serious work and a top professional.

Lecture/Demonstrations

Within the equestrian community are dozens of disciplines, related disciplines, and a range of programs and methodologies addressing training, health, nutrition, competition, and breeding, among other areas, and consequently, specialized courses and lectures are becoming plentiful. Individual lectures and demonstrations, such as Monty Roberts breaking a horse in a round pen or Robert Dover discussing the magical use of the half-halt in dressage, are often special presentations at equestrian exhibitions or conferences; but various courses on a variety of topics such as equine massage, TTouch (the holistic training method mentioned in chapter 28), and Western are cropping up also. And since it would be expensive and time consuming to take your horse to everything, these lectures offer a glimpse of a whole range of subjects and approaches that you might find useful in your own work.

Horse Exhibitions

A sort of cross between a circus fair and a trade show, these block-buster horse events—Equine Affaire and Horse Expo are two of the largest—last two to three days, are held in various places around the country (including Ohio, Kentucky, and Massachusetts), and provide total immersion in the horse experience. (See "Resources" for contact information.) Celebrated horsemen are on hand for symposia. These are displays of haute école dressage, musical Kür, jumping, reining, and driving, and the aisles are teeming with goods. In addition to major brands for saddlery and clothing, smaller firms use these fairs as a way of introducing new products. Walking down huge aisles crowded with displays, you might see magnets for use in magnetic therapy, fingerless gloves for easy mucking out, hand-carved saddle racks, grooming equipment, jewelry, and crafts—and, of course, the latest rain gear.

Fair prices are often discounted, and there's no shipping cost, so you may well make up what you spent to get there in bargains (or at least you can tell your spouse, who voted for the Bahamas, that that's why you're there!)

30

Horse Culture

A rich dark chestnut colt, fearless and adventuresome, broke out of
the bunch and came toward her with a long, springing trot. There was
a very fury of curiosity and expectation in his lifted head and flaring
nostrils. His cream-colored tail was lifted high, pluming out on both
sides of him, and with the full tossing light mane, he seemed to float
on the wind, hung with banners.

—Mary O'Hara, *My Friend Flicka*

Books

If you were a horsy girl or boy, your childhood was filled with horse books. Adventure, romance, sentiment, humor, danger, ambition—all were discovered in the company of the Black Stallion, Misty, Eclipse, Man O' War, Thelwell's ponies, and National Velvet's Pie. (*The Black Stallion* and *My Friend Flicka* probably appealed to boys as well.) In English circles, if you were studious you also read Alois Podhajsky's *My Horses, My Teachers*, memorized the Pony Club handbook, and yearned to have the form of riders in show-jumping books. If you were a horse owner you may have solemnly invested in Hayes's *Veterinary Notes for Horse Owners* and Jacobson and Hayes's *A Horse around the House*, but you probably didn't open them often, both because the soberer aspects of horsekeeping were likely to be someone else's responsibility and because except for memorizing things for Pony Club and 4-H exams, most of this knowledge was gained empirically. Horse books were an important part of the rite of passage, of the make-believe that helps lay the paving stones of the real.

Today, horse books can richly complement the whole of your life. They return you to the pleasurable fantasies of childhood, add a layer of complexity to satisfy a mature mind, enrich your store of knowledge as a rider and horse owner, and introduce you to new philosophies, breeds, places, and issues. There are books for every facility and stage of your equestrian life, books for the barn and the coffee table, books for recordkeeping and training regimes. And, because you can hardly be expected to keep track of all of them, there are horse book clubs to select and organize your library for you (see "Resources"). While new arrivals from the larger publishers will always be available at the major chain bookstores, many horse books are sold only through tack shops, at shows, or by mail order, so be sure to check your local outlets and the Internet.

Many of these books are devoted to either general care and horse owning or to specific disciplines, but there is also a rich array of horse fiction, gorgeous art books, and more recently, a significant number of books devoted to celebrating our relationship with horses—their gift of beauty and renewal, their kindness and courage. Notable among these is Melissa Holbrook Pierson's *Dark Horses and Black Beauties: Animals, Women, a Passion*, but other examples abound. From horse whisperers to competitors to writers (Pulitzer Prize–winner Jane Smiley, author of *Horse Heaven*, events and owns a small racing stable), everyone has something to give back to the animals who have replenished them. Lauren Hillenbrand's beautiful exploration of a brilliant horse and his time, *Seabiscuit: An American Legend*, also encouraged a trend in horse-related history books.

And it can be fun to be an armchair participant as well as a rider— during recuperation from minor surgery a few years ago, horse books were my solace, giving me a glimpse of the worlds I hoped to conquer as soon as I could mount again.

The Art of Horse

In addition to books, horses have contributed significantly to both classical and popular culture, classical and contemporary art. When you begin to see the world horse-centrically it will be luminous with rich detail you might not have noticed before. Throughout recorded history the works of painters, sculptors, photographers, and jewelers have abounded in horse-related imagery and detail. You may find their works in museums, galleries, shops, and catalogs.

HollyHorse

The local video store, catalog, or online equivalent can help you discover—or rediscover—a veritable kingdom of horse movies, some great and inspirational (*National Velvet*; *My Friend Flicka*; *Seabiscuit*), some just plain fun (*Horsefeathers*, *The Horse in the Grey Flannel Suit*), some kitschy (*International Velvet*), some young adult (*Spirit*).

Haynet to Internet

For a discipline that is more than 3,000 years old, equestrianism has found a perfect home in the dominant medium of the information age, the World Wide Web. Not only does every professional organization have its own site, often linked to complementary groups, but special horse sites like Equisearch are becoming the *Slate* and *Salon* of the horsy set. They offer feature articles on a wide variety of topics, profiles, interviews, new product reviews, and chat rooms. Can't get away for a long trip? Visit the Museum of the Horse website for fabulous online exhibits and a virtual tour of the history of the horse. Horse magazines, too, provide a veritable cornucopia of news and information. For example, here's the site for one of the country's premiere magazines, *The Chronicle of the Horse*: www.chronofhorse.com/. And here's the one for *Western Horseman*: www.westernhorseman.com/.

Browsing the Internet is another perfect way to involve your children. A generation used to looking at the world virtually will have no trouble entering imaginatively into your realm.

Racing

Ironically, while the racing industry has experienced declines in recent years, the glamour and recognition value of the "Sport of Kings" remains high. Jane Smiley's popular novel *Horse Heaven* and the runaway (as it were) success of Laura Hillenbrand's *Seabiscuit* have drawn the attention of millions to the thrilling but sometimes cruel sport of thoroughbred flat racing. And you don't have to get yourself to Churchill Downs (where the Kentucky Derby is run each year) to experience the agony and the ecstasy: many areas of the country have local tracks and special day-trip packages.

Quarter horse racing is even more prevalent, reflecting the general domination of the Western equestrian traditions in much of the country. Indeed, this breed is actually named for the early tradition of racing a quarter of a mile—at which distance these animals can give cougars and jaguars a run for their money.

And although less widespread, harness racing and steeplechasing are also practiced (sites can be identified through the respective sporting organizations; see "Resources"). So if you want a taste of a completely different horse world, get out your topper and parasol or peanuts and picnic basket, gather up the family, and—you're off!

Horse Fantasias

Horses have been used to tell stories since they first appeared on the cave walls of Lascaux, so it is not surprising that there should be contemporary attempts to incorporate their natural drama and beauty into theatrical contexts. They are a traditional part of the supporting casts of parades and circuses, but several years ago a group of French equestrians, led by an equestrian performance artist known as Bartabas, began to tour *Zingaro* (named for his horse), an elaborate, almost ritual show that combines the movements of haute école and the circus with metaphysical story lines for an evening that is stunning, sensuous, and bold. Performed to sinuous Eastern music, with flowing costumes and a multiracial cast as beautiful as their mounts, the show celebrates, in movements both mysterious (horse and rider lying down together) and spectacular (horses rearing majestically) the ancient bond between man and horse. The show has been very successful and has returned to the United States for several repeat engagements. It also engendered some copycat extravaganzas like *Cheval*, which tours the casino circuit.

As I mentioned earlier, a little bit of this enchantment can be glimpsed in the costume classes at Arabian shows, but if you have a chance, either here or abroad, to see one of these spectaculars, embrace it with pleasure. (See "Resources.")

31

Conclusion Your World and Welcome to It

Riding instructors talk a lot about alignment. When you set out to ride you probably didn't imagine how much it might realign you. As a new or returning rider, the sensation might be like that of discovering a hidden suite of rooms in a house you thought you knew. Beyond anything I can write here is your own instinct and internal path. With this book as a starting point, you'll make your own horse country and horse culture—enjoy the trip.

Appendix A

Putting on the Glitz Shopping

I was tempted to call this appendix "for women only." Let's admit it; most men shop the way they once hunted for food: go into the store, see a shirt, kill it, and drag it home. For women, shopping is a state of mind, a sensuous, acquisitive extension of whatever passion, discipline, or event they are focusing on. If you love something, why shouldn't it be color coordinated? (Of course, marketers have now identified a new demographic, the "metrosexual," an urbane fellow who likes his martinis dry and his tailoring impeccable, so perhaps this chapter is for him, also.)

Nowhere is it possible to satisfy this avocational shopping drive with more breadth than in the horse world, where the possibility of purchase spans the range from training aids to decorative accoutrements to just plain baubles. High end, low end, and everything in between, in shops, fair stalls, catalogs, and Internet sites, gear for both horse and rider is becoming more diverse and seductive every year.

There is a practical as well as frivolous side to exploring the many purchase options. Riding is believed by many to be a luxury market, with tack and kit priced accordingly. It is worthwhile doing some comparison shopping for staples such as jackets, shirts, and socks. As soon as the mysterious world of mail order pegs you as a rider, catalogs will begin to flood your mailbox—sumptuous ones representing artists, jewelers, blanket weavers, holistic medicines, and elegant clothing; comprehensive ones with all the basics from dozens of brands; and discounters. In between these two direct-mail realms is your local tack shop, which will probably carry a bit of both the high and low end and, of course, affords you the fun of actually going in and wandering around.

The sheer volume of goods and the fact that the population of riders is always in a state of flux has given rise to a whole consignment market as well. Your local tack shop may well sell pre-owned goods on consignment, and there are several websites devoted to used tack and apparel. If you're cost conscious, these are good places to start. A used saddle, for example (always arrange to try it out before purchase), can cost as much as six hundred dollars less than it lists new.

It's not difficult to find your way to these catalogs and sites, and once you begin to make horse-related purchases, they will find you through the intrusive magic of database marketing. Here, however, are a few exceptional sources for both necessary gear and unique (a very overworked word in the catalog world) items. Remember, too, that vendors will be thick on the ground at major shows and exhibitions. These often feature goods not yet available from other sources. People with new products often use shows as an inexpensive way to test the products on a core market, and smaller operations don't have the resources to make their way into major distribution channels. Local tack shops often have a presence at shows as well, and depending on the area, you can sometimes find items by regional artists and craftsman. My tack trunk and matching grooming box are lovely pieces of carved wood made by a man who exhibits at the Arabian East Coast Championships every year.

There follows a purely idiosyncratic list of some of the major catalogs and retailers. Once you begin to horse shop, you can develop your own list of favorites.

Art

There are, of course, hundreds of artists working with the horse as subject, and your local bookstore will guide you to some of them. Auction house websites are also useful combinations of temptation and education; look for sales involving sporting art, naturally, but you'll find these works seeded among broader categories of contemporary art as well. Here are a few other sites you may wish to check out.

Sites

ebay.com—Categories include everything from actual horses to toys and collectibles.

www.horse-art.com

www.equestrianartists.co.uk/

www.aaea.net/galleries/oppegard/default.htm

www.equidae.com/saratoga/index.html

uniquine.com

www.tfaoi.com/newsm1/n1m180.htm

Artists

Yann Arthus Bertrand (www.yannarthusbertrand.com/v2/yab_us.htm)—This French photographer has been photographing farm and domestic animals against extraordinary backdrops for over two decades; the results are works as intimate and playful as anything by Annie Lebowitz or Richard Avedon and as magnificent and voluptuous as Old Master paintings.

Rita Dee (www.ritadee.net/) creates extraordinary sculptures of horses using intertwined tree branches.

Tim Flach (www.timflach.com/) creates surreally humorous and luminous photographs of horses and other animals.

Robert Vavra (www.robertvavra.com/)—Creator of lush, dreamlike horse pictures—the closest thing to the fairy tales of your child's imagination. Vavra has authored more than thirty books, including *Horses of the Sun*, and has a CD, *Horses of the Wind*, combining horse sounds and classical music.

Publications

Horses in Art Magazine (www.equineartguild.com/~equinevision/)

Art Horse Magazine (www.arthorsemagazine.com/)

Clothes

Upmarket

Hermès (www.hermes.com/index_us.html)—Branded elegance for equestrian fashionistas since forever. Known for its signature horse-themed scarves, Hermès more recently introduced a charming range of bracelets with horse designs.

Clothes by Stella McCartney for Chloe (now collectibles)

Ralph Lauren (www.ralphlauren.com)—There's a reason it's called "Polo." Lauren has featured horse motifs and faux equestrian sensibility—both English and Western—in many of his collections and branded shops.

Alice Roi (www.aliceroi.com/collections.html)

Any Market

Ariat (www.ariat.com/)—Probably the leading equestrian apparel company, it has expanded its line of traditional riding clothes to include a range of sprightly leisure wear.

Equine couture (www.equestriancollections.com/storeitems.asp?department=Horses&bc=672&cc=horseapparel)—A purveyor of elegant, nontraditional horsewear.

Mountain Horse (www.mountainhorse.com)—This apparel manufacturer is stocked by many tack shops and now has its own catalog. Its sturdy, practical, stylish, problem-solving sportswear (vest, sports bras, etc.) is really prime stuff, particularly for cold-weather riding. And it looks great.

General Catalogs

Most catalogs carry combinations of equine and equestrian apparel, supplies, and accessories.

Back in the Saddle (www.backinthesaddle.com)—Despite the modest title, an extremely elegant catalog with unusual gift and practical items—equestrian linens and enamelware, for example.

Bit of Britain (www.bitofbritain.com/)—An upmarket catalog of everything from sheets to screensavers, morphed from an elegant shop.

BMB (www.bmbtack.com/)—Good Western wear, tchotchkes, and day clothes!

Chick's Harness & Supply (www.chicksaddlery.com)—A cozy catalog especially useful for Western gear.

Country Supply (www.countrysupply.com)—Like the *Yankee Magazine* of horse catalogs—very down-home.

Dover Saddlery (www.doversaddlery.com/)—Founded in 1975 by U.S. Equestrian Team members, this catalog and site features a large selection of reasonably priced horse and rider items, with frequent sales year-round.

The Equine Collection (www.theequinecollection.com)

Kiehl's (www.kiehls.com/_us/_en/pets/equine.aspx)—This legendary store, known for its range of health and beauty products for people, has branched out into horses!

Omaha Vaccine Company (www.omahavaccine.com)—Valuable source of many grooming and maintenance basics at lower prices than most tack stores—you'll want to remember this one if you become a horse owner.

SmartPak (www.smartpakequine.com/)—"Supplements simplified" declares the website for this innovative horse nutrition catalog (also caters to dogs) that prepackages servings of a wide range of nutritional products to simplify the lives of busy horse owners.

Stateline Tack (www.statelinetack.com)—Probably the leading midrange catalog. Good prices on basic, unglamorous gear and clothing.

Sundance (www.sundancecatalog.com/)—Features particularly beautiful jewelry, sometimes horse inspired, and other goods and apparel with Western and Southwestern motifs.

Other

Breakthrough Publications (www.booksonhorses.com/)—A comprehensive horse book source that also carries a wide range of videos.

Equestrian Edge Book Club

P.O. Box 6310

Indianapolis, IN 46206-6310

ShowEvent.com (www.showevent.com/pets/horses_equine.shtml)—An equestrian resource site that features this useful list of additional resources.

The "Resources" appendix that follows includes links to key industry and breed associations. Some have limited apparel and miscellaneous product lines.

Appendix B

Resources

Horsemanship manuals are among the oldest surviving forms of historical literature. (The earliest surviving version, by the horsemaster to a Hittite king, dates to 1345 BC.) And as horsemanship progressed from mere survival, its practitioners began to articulate principles other than "hang on and don't get killed."

Today, of course, we are in the information age—an age of media proliferation and social networking, of events, and organizations, and gurus, so an embarrassment of riches awaits you as a new rider and potential horse owner. And you will find the pursuit of new knowledge both useful and pleasurable. In addition to making you savvier about the nuts and bolts of riding, you never know when you will come upon just the book or article to untie your particular Gordian knot. If, like me, you had a good basic Pony Club education twenty or thirty years ago, you'll be astonished by the changes the horse world has undergone.

Many more breeds and disciplines are active in the field, and thanks to resources like the Internet, even the narrowest interests can be ferreted out and served. Advances in treatments, technology, and society have placed horse care almost on a par with our own, with the clinical field including everything from dramatic surgical interventions to animal communicators. So open a book, or click on a website, and read on into the sunset. In addition to published works, a host of organizations exists to promote the various breeds and disciplines and to represent special interests and causes.

For convenience, this resource list corresponds to the sections and chapters in the book.

Part I: Choosing a Path

Chapter 1: The Basics: English or Western?

United States Equestrian Foundation
4047 Iron Works Parkway
Lexington, KY 40511-8483
(859) 258-2472
www.equestrian.org and www.usef.org. The foundation is the national governing body for most of the major equestrian disciplines and has committees to oversee all aspects of training and competition.

Chapter 2: English Pleasure

American Saddlebred Horse Association
4083 Iron Works Parkway
Lexington, KY 40511
(859) 259-2742
www.asha.net

NEA Sidesaddle Association
P.O. Box 224
Thompson, CT 06277
www.sidesaddleinfo.com

International Side Saddle Organization
P.O. Box 161
Stevensville, MD 21666-0161
(918) 685-0072
www.sidesaddle.com

Chapter 3: Hunt Seat

American Hunter-Jumper Foundation, Inc.
P.O. Box 369

West Boylston, MA 01583

(508) 835-8813

www.ahjf.org

The United States Pony Clubs, Inc.

4041 Iron Works Parkway

Lexington, KY 40511

(859) 254-7669

www.ponyclub.org

Chapter 4: Hunting

Masters of Foxhounds Association of North America

P.O. Box 363

Millwood, VA 22646

(540) 955-5680 office

(540) 955-5682 fax

Office email: office@mfha.com

The oversight body for all registered foxhound packs and hunts in the country, as well as a great resource for hunting protocol, lore, and political representation. The MFA celebrated its centenary in 2007.

Wadsworth, William P. *Riding to Hounds in America: An Introduction for Foxhunters.* Berryville, VA: The Chronicle of the Horse, 1962.

The bible of American foxhunting. Rules on helmets for foxhunters have changed since this book was written, but otherwise, its instructions are still followed to the letter.

Chapter 5: Show Jumping

American Hunter-Jumper Foundation, Inc.

P.O. Box 369

West Boylston, MA 01583
(508) 835-8813
www.ahjf.org

American Grand Prix Association
1301 Sixth Ave. West, Suite 406
Bradenton, FL 34205
(800) 237-8924 or (941) 744-5465
www.stadiumjumping.com/AGA/index.cfm

Chapter 6: Dressage

United States Dressage Federation
4051 Iron Works Parkway
Lexington, KY 40511
(859) 971-2277
www.usdf.org
The federation has an adult education council.

Chapter 7: Horse Trials

United States Eventing Association
525 Old Waterford Rd., NW
Leesburg, VA 20176
(703) 779-0440
www.useventing.com

Chapter 8: Western Pleasure and Trail

American Paint Horse Association
P.O. Box 961023
Fort Worth, Texas 76161-0023
(817) 834-APHA (2742)
www.apha.com

Provides a free *Guide to Recreational Riding* (and other guides are available as free downloads) and has a self-monitoring trail riding program called Ride America.

The American Quarter Horse Association (AQHA)
P.O. Box 200
Amarillo, TX 79168
(806) 376-4811
www.aqha.com

Chapter 9: Western Kicked Up a Notch: Reining, Roping, and Barrel Racing

Barrel Horses.com
A website devoted to this sport, including show, horse, and supply information.
www.barrelhorses.com

The International Barrel Racing Association
P.O. Box 425
Valley City, OH 44280
(330) 483-9608 office
(330) 483-9708 fax
www.ibra.us

United Professional Horseman's Association
4059 Iron Works Parkway, Suite 2
Lexington, KY 40511
(859) 231-5070
www.uphaonline.com

National Reining Horse Association
3000 NW 10th Street
Oklahoma City, OK 73107

(405) 946-7400 office
(405) 946-8425 fax
www.nrha.com

Chapter 10: Endurance and Competitive Trail Riding

American Endurance Ride Conference
P.O. Box 6027
Auburn, CA 95604
(530) 823-2260 and (866) 271-AERC (2372)
www.aerc.org
www.endurance.net
An online resource for endurance riders.

Trail Blazer Magazine
www.trailblazermagazine.us
www.horsetraildirectory.com
A directory of horse trails in America.

Chapter 11: Polo

The United States Polo Association
4037 Ironworks Parkway, Suite 110
Lexington, KY 40511
(859) 219-1000 office
(859) 219-0520 fax
www.us-polo.org

Chapter 12: Out of the Saddle: Driving, In-Hand, Minis

American Miniature Horse Association
5601 S. Interstate 35 W
Alvarado, TX 76009
(817) 783-5600
www.amha.org

American Driving Society
1837 Ludden Dr., Suite 120
P.O. Box 278
Cross Plains, WI 53528
(608) 237-6468
www.americandrivingsociety.org

United States Trotting Association
750 Michigan Avenue
Columbus, OH 43215
(877) 800-USTA (8782) or (614) 224-2291
www.ustrotting.com

Fair Winds Farm
511 Upper Dummerston Rd.
Brattleboro, VT 05301
(802) 254-9067 or (802) 254-7128
www.fairwindsfarm.org
For lessons in driving draft horses.

Rural Heritage Magazine
P.O. Box 2067
Cedar Rapids, IA 52406
(319) 362-3027
www.ruralheritage.com

Small Farmer's Journal
Box 1627
Sisters, OR 97759
(800) 876-2893 or (541)549-2064
www.smallfarmersjournal.com

Part II: Choosing to Learn

American Riding Instructors Association (ARIA)
28801 Trenton Court
Bonita Springs, FL 34134-3337
(239) 948-3232
www.riding-instructor.com

United States Pony Clubs, Inc.
4041 Iron Works Parkway
Lexington, KY 40511
(859) 254-7669
www.ponyclub.org

Smith, Mike. *Getting the Most out of Riding Lessons.* North Adams, MA: Storey Publishing, 1998.

Still available from Amazon.com.

Articles

Horse & Rider, September 1999. Baby-Boomer issue—various articles.

"Getting Reconnected," *Practical Horseman*, February 1999, pp. 64–67, Guide for returning adult riders.

Phalen, Katie McLaughlin. "Beginning Adult Rider: Starting Out," *Practical Horseman,* August 2001 (and subsequent issues), pp. 48–54.

See also Equisearch.com, below, which archives articles from a wide range of horse magazines.

Part III: Choosing Safety

American Association for Horsemanship Safety
4125 Fish Creek Road
Estes Park, CO 80517
(866) 485-6800
www.horsemanshipsafety.com

The American Medical Equestrian Association

P.O. Box 130848

Birmingham, AL 35213-0848

(866) 441-AMEA (2632)

asci.uvm.edu/equine/law/amea/amea.htm

"Riding Helmet Safety Standards Explained," www.equisearch.com/horses_
riding_training/tack_apparel/english/safety100803/.

International Riding Helmets

www.irhhelmets.com

Part IV: Choosing a Horse

Meyer, Jennifer Forsberg. "No More Buyer's Remorse," *Horse & Rider*, November 2000, pp. 61–66.

Horseman's Classified LLC

16B Mill Lane

Salem, CT 06420

(860) 859-0770

www.steedread.com

Korda, Margaret, and Michael Korda. *Horse Housekeeping: Everything You Need
to Know to Keep a Horse at Home*. New York: Harper Collins, November 2005.

Breed Organizations

Appaloosa Horse Club

2720 West Pullman Road

Moscow, ID 83843

(208) 882-5578

www.appaloosa.com

Arabian Horse Association

10805 E. Bethany Drive

Aurora, CO 80014
(303) 696-4500
www.arabianhorses.org

American Morgan Horse Association
122 Bostwick Road
Shelburne, VT 05482-4417
(802) 985-4944
www.morganhorse.com

American Paint Horse Association
P.O. Box 961023
Fort Worth, TX 76161-0023
(817) 834-APHA (2742)
www.apha.com

American Quarter Horse Association
P.O. Box 200
Amarillo, TX 79168-0001
(806) 376-4811
www.aqha.com

American Saddlebred Horse Association
4083 Iron Works Parkway
Lexington, KY 40511
(859) 259-2742
www.asha.net

American Warmblood Society
2 Buffalo Run Rd.
Center Ridge, AR 72027
(501) 893-2779
www.americanwarmblood.org

The Warmblood Connection

www.warmbloodconnection.com

A commercial marketing service, not a breed club.

Irish Draught Horse Society of North America

4037 Iron Works Parkway, #160

Lexington, KY 40511

(859) 455-8090 office

(858) 761-0264 fax

www.irishdraught.com

Part V: Choosing Pleasure

Chapter 27: Fun for the Whole Family

The list of possible riding camps is too extensive to be easily featured in book form, but many can be researched online. Google and Yahoo both have directory search functions that make it easy to isolate listings, as does Horseman's Yankee Pedlar, www.pedlar.com.

Chapter 28: Horses on Holiday

The world of equestrian travel has expanded so mightily that this is of necessity a selective list of travel agencies specializing in horse holidays.

Equine Adventures: www.equineadventures.co.uk/home.html

Equitours: www.ridingtours.com

In the Saddle: www.inthesaddle.co.uk

Ridingholidays.com: www.ridingholidays.com

Unicorn Trails: www.unicorntrails.com

See also:

Dude Ranches of North America: www.duderanches.com

Horse Trail Directory: www.horsetraildirectory.com

Nationwide Overnight Stabling Directory: www.overnightstabling.com/ about.htm

North American Trail Ride Conference: www.natrc.org

Holistic Horse Riding Holidays: www.lvweb.co.uk/holistichorses/holistic ridingholidays.htm

Chapter 29: Beyond Lessons

Equine Affaire

2720 State Route 56 SW

London, OH 43140

(740) 845-0085

www.equineaffaire.com

Horse & Rider, January 2001 issue, p. 60.

List of expos and contact information.

HorseWorld Expo

Equestrian Promotions, Inc.

P.O. Box 924

Bel Air, MD 21044

(301) 916-0852

www.horseworldexpo.com

Western States Expo

www.horsexpo.com/

The Harness Museum

P.O. Box 590

240 Main Street

Goshen, NY 10924

www.harnessmuseum.com

International Museum of the Horse at the Kentucky Horse Park
4089 Iron Works Parkway
Lexington, KY 40511
(800) 678-8813 or (859) 233-4303
www.imh.org/museum

The Museum of Natural History, New York
The museum presented a historical exhibition about the horse throughout history from May 17, 2008, through January 4, 2009. Elements from the exhibit can still be viewed online at www.amnh.org/exhibitions/horse/.

John Lyons Symposiums
8714 County Road 300
Parachute, CO 81635
(970) 285-9797 or (877) 564-6596
www.johnlyons.com

Monty Roberts Join Up
www.montyroberts.com/index.html
TTouch Training
www.ttouch.com

General Interest

American Horse Council
1616 H Street NW, 7th floor
Washington, DC 20006
(202) 296-4031 phone
(202) 296-1970 fax
www.horsecouncil.org

The horse industry's lobbying arm, it also publishes a useful guide to all the major breed associations, *The Horse Industry Directory*, which can be ordered at horsecouncil.org/publications.html.

Equisearch

www.equisearch.com

Horses-etc.com

www.horses-etc.com

HorseShow Central

www.horseshowcentral.com/lc/equestrian_fairs_and_expos/15086/1

Special Needs

North American Riding for the Handicapped Association (NARHA)

P.O. Box 33150

Denver, CO 80233

(800) 369-RIDE (7433)

www.narha.org

Riders with disabilities participate in many disciplines and also enjoy competitions and events designed for their special needs. This organization will help put you in touch with a wide range of possibilities.

Professional Horseman's Association of America

P.O. Box 425

Valley City, OH 44280

(330) 483-9608 office

(330) 483-9708 fax

www.nationalpha.com/

Assists horsemen in need.

Unwanted Horse Coalition

1616 H Street, NW

7th Floor

Washington, DC 20006

(202) 296-4031

www.unwantedhorsecoalition.org

Suggested Reading

Note: Not all books are currently in print, but libraries and out-of-print book services on the Internet may help you locate the more elusive ones.

Barbier, Dominique, with Mary Daniels. *Dressage for the New Age*. New York: Prentice Hall, 1990.

Bayley, Lesley, and Caroline Davis. *The Less-Than-Perfect Rider: Overcoming Common Riding Problems*. New York: Howell House, 1994.

Bean, Heike. *Carriage Driving: A Logical Approach through Dressage Training* (updated edition/classic edition). New York: Howell Book House, 2004.

Benedik, Lisa, and Veronica Wirth. *Yoga for Equestrians*. North Pomfret: Trafalgar Square Publishing, 2001.

Budiansky, Stephen. *The Nature of Horses: Exploring Equine Evolution, Intelligence and Behavior*. New York: Free Press, 1997.

Clay, April. *Training from the Neck Up: A Practical Guide to Sports Psychology for Riders*. Available for download at http://e-library.net/Training-from-the-Neck-Up-A-Practical-Guide-to-Sport-Psychology-for-Riders__ebooks446.htm or directly from the author at http://www.bodymindmotion.com/books.htm.

Conley, Kevin. *Stud: Adventures in Breeding*. New York: Bloomsbury, 2002.

Dines, Lisa. *American Mustang Guidebook*. Minocqua WI: Willow Creek Press.

Edwards, Elwyn Hartley. *The Encyclopedia of the Horse*. New York: Dorling-Kindersley, 1994.

Gahwyler, Max. *The Competitive Edge: Improving Your Dressage Scores in the Lower Levels* (revised edition). Boonsboro, MD: Half Halt Press, 1990.

German National Equestrian Federation. *The Principles of Riding*. Boonsboro, MD: Half Halt Press, 1987. The federation has published a number of books for different riding levels.

Hayes, Daniel, et al. *Veterinary Notes for Horse Owners* (revised edition). New York: Simon & Schuster, 2002.

Hearne, Vicki. *Adam's Task: Calling Animals by Name*. New York: Harper Perennial, 1982.

Irwin, Chris, with Bob Weber. *Horses Don't Lie: What Horses Teach Us about Our Natural Capacity for Awareness, Confidence, Courage and Trust*. San Francisco: Marlowe & Co., 2001.

Jacobson, Patricia, and Marcia Hayes. *A Horse around the House* (revised edition). New York: Crown, 1999.

Loving, Nancy. *Go the Distance: The Complete Resource for Endurance Horses*. North Pomfret: Trafalgar Square Publishing, 2006.

McGuane, Thomas. *Some Horses.* New York: Lyons Press, 1999.

Midkiff, Mary D. *Fitness, Performance, and the Female Equestrian.* New York: Howell Book House, 1996.

Midkiff, Mary D. *She Flies without Wings: How Horses Touch a Woman's Soul.* New York: Delacorte Press, 2001.

Morris, George. *Hunter Seat Equitation.* New York: Doubleday, 1971.

Museler, Wilhelm. *Riding Logic.* New York: Prentice Hall, 1983.

O'Connor, Sally. *Practical Eventing* (revised edition). Boonsboro, MD: Half Halt Press, 1998.

Pierson, Melissa Holbrook. *Dark Horses and Black Beauties: Animals, Women, a Passion.* New York: Norton, 2000.

Podhajsky, Alois.*The Complete Training of the Horse and Rider.* New York: Wilshire Book Company, 1967.

Price, Steven. *The Whole Horse Catalog* (revised edition). New York: Simon & Schuster, 1998.

Rosen, Michael J. *Horse People: Writers and Artists on the Horses They Love.* New York: Artisan, 1998.

Sassoon, Siegfried. *Memoirs of a Fox-Hunting Man.* Alcester, UK: Obscure Press, 2006 (among many editions of this classic).

Smiley, Jane. *Horse Heaven.* New York: Knopf, 2000.

Somerville, E. Œ., and Martin Ross. *The Irish RM.* Middlesex: Penguin, 1984.

Swift, Sally. *Centered Riding.* North Pomfret: Trafalgar Square, 1985.

Thelwell, Norman. *A Leg at Each Corner.* New York: Dutton, 1963.

United States Dressage Federation, Inc. *Classical Training of the Horse.* Lincoln: United States Dresssage Federation, 1998.

Van Laun, Richenda, with Sylvia Loch. *Flexibility and Fitness for Riders.* Allen Photographic Guides. Tonbridge: J. A. Allen, 2001.

Walrond, Sally. *Driving Do's and Don'ts.* Threshold Picture Guides No. 37. Boonsboro, MD: Half Halt Press, 1997.

Wanless, Mary. *For the Good of the Horse.* North Pomfret: Trafalgar Square, 1997.

Wanless, Mary. *The Natural Rider: A Right-Brain Approach to Riding.* North Pomfret: Trafalgar Square, 1987.

Magazines

Chronicle of the Horse

P.O. Box 432

Mt. Morris, IL 61054
(800) 877-5467
www.chronofhorse.com/

Dressage Today
656 Quince Orchard Rd.
Gaithersburg, MD 20878-1472
(800) 877-5396
www.dressagetoday.com

Equestrian (free to members)
United States Equestrian Federation
4047 Iron Works Parkway
Lexington, KY 40511
(859) 225-6923

Equus
656 Quince Orchard Rd.
Gaithersburg, MD 20878-1472
(800) 829-5910
equus-subscription.com

Horse & Rider
P.O. Box 921
North Adams, MA 02147-0921
(800) 358-6327
horseandrider.com

Horse Illustrated
P.O. Box 6040
Mission Viejo, CA 92690
(800) 365-4421
www.horsechannel.com

Practical Horseman (English and Western editions)
P.O. Box 420235
Palm Coast, FL 32142
(800) 829-3340
www.practicalhorseman.com

Trail Blazer Magazine
4241 North Covina Circle
Prescott Valley, AZ 86314
(888) 799-0333
trailblazermagazine.us

Western Horseman
P.O. Box 7980
Colorado Springs, CO 80933
westernhorseman.com

Appendix C

Giving Something Back

To paraphrase a famous political address, ask not what your horse can do for you, but what you can do for your horse. From the sheltered perspective of our own lives, where (we hope) the horses we own or know are well cared for and treated humanely, it is hard to imagine the wilderness of stupidity, neglect, and cruelty that stands without.

Each year hundreds of cases of equine abuse appear in the papers—and sometimes in the courts. Now dozens of animal rights and welfare groups are attempting to ameliorate and combat not only the single instances of abuse, but larger systemic issues. Some of this work has given rise to heated debates about the legal status of horses and the rights of breeders and owners. Whatever position you wind up responding to, somewhere there will be an organization with a mission that speaks to you.

If you have derived pleasure from your riding and marveled at the gift of freedom and grace that horses offer us, find a way to give something in return. Donations are always welcome, but you should also research your local area, which may have programs in place with which you can become more directly involved as a volunteer or organizer. Some organizations are mentioned here, but Internet and local research will yield the names of dozens of others.

Adopt-A-Horse Ltd.
7609 W. Josephine Rd.
Lake Placid, FL 33852
(941) 382-4483

American Horse Protection Association
1000 29th St., NW, Ste. T-100
Washington, DC 20007
(202) 965-0500

Animal Legal Defense Fund
www.aldf.org/
For putting your decisive action where your mouth is.

Best Friends Animal Sanctuary
5001 Angel Canyon Road
Kanab, UT 84741-5001
(435) 644-2001
www.bestfriends.org

The Exceller Fund
www.excellerfund.org
Named after Exceller, a successful American thoroughbred who ended his life in a slaughterhouse in Sweden. The Exceller Fund is making a difference in the disastrous and sometimes deadly postprofessional lives of discarded racehorses.

Horses Haven
www.ismi.net/horseshaven/index.htm
A superb site, if you have the heart for it. Read their "Farm Journal" on the Web. You can donate used tack and blankets (cleaned and in good condition) to this charity, as well as money—well worth the effort.

Horse Lovers United Inc.
P.O. Box 2744
Salisbury, MD 21802-2744
(410) 749-3599

Mylestone Rescue
227 Still Valley Rd.

Phillisbury, NJ 08865

(508) 995-9300

www.mylestone.com

ReRun, Inc. (Adopt a Thoroughbred)

P.O. Box 113

Helmetta, NJ 08828

www.rerun.org

Thoroughbred Retirement Foundation

P.O. Box 3387

Saratoga Springs, NY 12866

(518) 226-0028 office

(518) 226-0699 fax

www.trfinc.org/contact_us.php

True Innocents Equine Rescue (T.I.E.R.)

7900 Limonite Ave., Ste. G, #278

Riverside, CA 92509

(951) 360-1464

E-mail: info@TIERRescue.org

Index